UNIVERSITY OF NORTH CAROLINA AT CHAPEL HILL
DEPARTMENT OF ROMANCE LANGUAGES

NORTH CAROLINA STUDIES
IN THE ROMANCE LANGUAGES AND LITERATURES

Founder: URBAN TIGNER HOLMES
Editor: FRANK A. DOMÍNGUEZ

Distributed by:

UNIVERSITY OF NORTH CAROLINA PRESS

CHAPEL HILL
North Carolina 27515-2288
U.S.A.

NORTH CAROLINA STUDIES IN THE
ROMANCE LANGUAGES AND LITERATURES
Number 294

MAPPING THE SOCIAL BODY
URBANISATION, THE GAZE, AND
THE NOVELS OF GALDÓS

MAPPING THE SOCIAL BODY

URBANISATION, THE GAZE, AND THE NOVELS OF GALDÓS

BY
COLLIN MCKINNEY

CHAPEL HILL

NORTH CAROLINA STUDIES IN THE ROMANCE
LANGUAGES AND LITERATURES
U.N.C. DEPARTMENT OF ROMANCE LANGUAGES
2010

Library of Congress Cataloging-in-Publication Data

McKinney, Collin S.
  Mapping the social body : urbanisation, the gaze, and the novels of Galdós / Collin McKinney.
      p. cm. – (North Carolina studies in the Romance languages and literatures; no. 294).
  English and Spanish.
  Includes bibliographical references.
  ISBN 978-0-8078-9298-5 (hardcover)
    1. Pérez Galdós, Benito, 1843-1920 – Criticism and interpretation. 2. Urbanization in literature. 3. Gaze in literature. 4. Visual perception in literature. 5. Identity (Psychology) in literature. 6. Social classes in literature. 7. Group identity in literature. 8. Gender identity in literature. 9. Literature and society – Spain – History – 19th century. I. Title.

PQ6555.Z5M39 2009
863'.5–dc22   2009046348

© 2010. Department of Romance Languages. The University of North Carolina at Chapel Hill.

ISBN 978-0-8078-9298-5

CONTENTS

	Page
INTRODUCTION	9
CHAPTER 1: MAPPING THE CITY	15
The power of maps	16
Urban cartography	17
Discourse as cartographic enterprise	26
The fear of contamination	28
The criminal element	34
CHAPTER 2: MAPPING CLASS IN *LA DESHEREDADA*	47
Madrid as spectacle	48
Isidora's quest for distinction	51
The strength of blood	61
Prostitution and flow	65
A portrait of desire	71
CHAPTER 3: MAPPING GENDER IN *TORMENTO* AND *LA DE BRINGAS*	76
Fashioning gender	77
Fallen angels	86
Models of masculinity	95
Masculinity intact	107
CHAPTER 4: MAPPING THE FAMILY IN *FORTUNATA Y JACINTA*	109
Setting roots	110
Pruning and grafting	115
Corrupt lines	124
Bearing fruit	128

	Page
CHAPTER 5: MAPPING THE BODY IN *NAZARÍN*	136
Reading with an ethnographer's eye	137
Ambiguous bodies	139
Female offender?	144
Hysteria/mysticism as feminine rebellion	148
Carnival and the undecidability of identity	153
CHAPTER 6: MAPPING THE SOUL IN *MISERICORDIA*	158
Seeing the soul	159
On the surface	162
Beyond the surface	166
Opening our eyes	172
CONCLUSION	174
BIBLIOGRAPHY	177
INDEX	187

INTRODUCTION

> I admit nothing but on the faith of the eyes.
> –Francis Bacon

A recent anthropological study by Constance Classen (2005) shows that cultures are characterised by "sense ratios". According to this theory, a culture is said to be visual, tactile, oral/aural, etc., depending on the extent to which it emphasizes one sense above the others, whether as a means of communication, through the manner in which it interacts with its environment, or in constructing a worldview. By way of example, the inhabitants of the Andes are an oral/aural society inasmuch as they are "animated by sound" (Classen 2005: 148), the Mayan culture, especially the Tzotzil of the Chiapas highlands, display a "thermal cosmology" and can therefore be considered a tactile culture (Classen 2005: 148-52), and the Ongee people of the Andaman Islands are an olfactory society using odour as "the reason for communal life" (Classen 2005: 153).

Because vision provided the basis for personal identity and dictated social relationships, there can be little doubt that nineteenth-century Madrid was a visual culture. In a century of notable scientific progress, which saw significant advances in microscopy, the invention of photography, and the continuing belief–popularised by Locke and the other sensationalists but inherited by Comte and the positivists–that knowledge comes through the senses and that vision is the most reliable of the senses, it is understandable that Spain's middle classes would turn to the so-called noblest of the senses as they tried to solve the problem of social disorder brought about by urbanisation. With this in mind it is easy to see why Wylie Sypher referred to the nineteenth century as being "among the most visual periods of Western culture, the most given to ideals of precise observation", a bias that was shared by scientists, painters and novelists alike (Sypher 1971: 74).

But vision is culture-specific, and the causes and manifestations of Madrid's preference for *lo visual* during the second half of the nineteenth century are therefore complex and unique. Madrid's well-documented population boom during the period in question proved to be a source of considerable apprehension for the rising middle class, whose social position depended in large part on a series of binaries, hierarchies and divisions that were perceived to be under threat by the disorderliness of urban growth. The solution? Enact a campaign of social mapping based on the pre-eminence of vision and the power of discourse. The result? The marginalisation, both physically and socially, of groups views as Other (non-bourgeois/male/Catholic/Spanish).

It is within this cultural and literary context of sensorial favouritism and categorising fervour that Galdós composed his novels.[1] From physiognomy to fashion, Galdós's work constantly examines the link between social relations and the categorising power of the gaze. And while his interest in the visual remained constant, his attitude toward it did not. Galdós's early novels, beginning with *La desheredada* (1881), demonstrate a faith in the categorising gaze, most notably in the form of physiognomic reliability, that gradually gives way to a deprecation of the gaze in his works of the late 1880s and the 1890s.

In an article titled "Foucault's Art of Seeing" (1988), John Rajchman identifies a prevalent idea in Foucault's work: that the "visual thinking" of a period is linked with the "psychologizing practices" Foucault associates with modernity. "The same organisation a period assigns to inner or psychological processes", he continues, "recurs in external 'public' ones such as making maps" (Rajchman 1988: 92). Cartography does indeed provide a useful analogy for various practices of exclusion examined by Foucault and used by

---

[1] Galdós is not unique in this respect. As Martin Jay points out in his examination of the gaze in French thought, visual observation was *the* guiding principle of French realism and naturalism (2003: 110-11, 173), to which Galdós's own artistic formation is clearly indebted.

Spain's middle class. Often these practices of exclusion were physical, as in the case of asylums, prisons and other correctional institutions that were erected during the period. But more often the exclusionary tactics of the middle class were social, based on the power of discourse. Inasmuch as the dominant discourses of nineteenth-century Spain caused or fortified social divisions, they functioned like a map, which, according to John Short, is not just an image on paper, but "a theory, a story, a claim, a hope, a scientific document, an emotional statement, an act of imagination, a technical document, a lie, a truth, an artefact, an image, an itinerary, a mode, an inscription and a description. A map, like a speech act or musical event, is performative" (Short 2001: 11-12).

La desheredada, *Tormento* (1884) and *La de Bringas* (1884) offer a relatively straightforward depiction of social mapping. In these novels class and gender, as well as physical and moral degeneration, are presented as qualities that can be predicted reliably through a combination of visual signs–clothing, gestures, physical features– and inhabited space. In this respect Galdós offers a conservative view of social norms, whereby those that do not meet middle-class standards of normalcy are viewed with mistrust and even hostility.

Fortunata y Jacinta (1886-87), considered by many to be the Spaniard's finest novel, is a transitional piece with respect to Galdós's exploration of social mapping. *Fortunata y Jacinta* revolves around the image of the family tree and is thus engaged in dialogue with medical discourse, which posited a link between degeneration and heredity. Indeed much of the novel supports the popular claim that physical and psychological abnormalities were the result of corrupt family lines. However, within the novel itself there is an evolution in the way the narrator, a seemingly rational if somewhat biased mediator between the reader and the text, views the desire to establish order via a categorising gaze. What begins as an acceptance and affirmation of degeneration theory eventually turns into a new, sceptical attitude toward the middle-class dream of physiognomic reliability. It signals a change in attitude that will become fully developed in Galdós's works of the 1890s.

By the time Galdós wrote *Nazarín* (1895) his attitude toward the middle class, like his attitude toward visually-based categorising practices, had changed radically from what he expressed in his novels of the early 1880s. At the outset of his career, in an essay titled "Observaciones sobre la novela contemporánea en España" (1870),

Galdós expressed great faith in the middle class as both a literary subject and as a progressive, organising force in society:

> Pero la clase media, la más olvidada por nuestros novelistas, es el gran modelo, la fuente inagotable. Ella es hoy la base del orden social: ella asume por su iniciativa y por su inteligencia la soberanía de las naciones, y en ella está el hombre del siglo XIX con sus virtudes y sus vicios, su noble e insaciable aspiración, su afán de reformas, su actividad pasmosa. (Pérez Galdós 1972: 122)

But his optimism eventually faded, and by the time he gave his famous speech to the Real Academia Española in 1897 he had already turned his attention away from the middle class–which he believed "no tiene aún existencia positiva" (Pérez Galdós 1972: 178) but was overly concerned with "monopoliza[ndo] la vida entera, sujetándola a un sin fin de reglamentos, legislando desaforadamente sobre todas las cosas, sin excluir las espirituales" (Pérez Galdós 1972: 178)–concentrating instead the marginal figures of society: beggars, the physically abnormal, nonconformists, and the like. This change in attitude is explicit in his work. Just four years before the publication of *Nazarín* Galdós penned the following words, which he placed in the mouth of Ángel Guerra, the protagonist of a novel by the same name:

> ¡Fuerte cosa que no pueda uno vivir con sus propios sentimientos, sino con los prestados, con los que quiere imponernos esta imbécil burguesía, entremetida y expedientera, que todo lo quiere gobernar: el Estado y la familia, la colectividad y las personas, y con su tutela insoportable no nos deja respirar! (Pérez Galdós 1967: V, 1233)

Clearly unhappy with the middle class's efforts to control society through discourse and other mapping techniques, Galdós took to ridiculing and undermining this categorising desire. In *Nazarín* the narrator invites the reader to engage in physiognomic typing only to reveal that the characters defy all attempts at categorisation.

This chronological progression of Galdós's works, which betrays a growing wariness with respect to the supposed objectivity of visual classifications, culminates in the publication of *Misericordia* (1897). Written during what some scholars have dubbed Galdós's "spiritual period" (Hoff 2006: 1059; Casalduero 1974), *Misericordia* offers perhaps the most drastic rejection of visual reliability. Within the narrative, the only character who appreciates Galdós's heroine, the unattractive, simple, and selfless Benina, is the blind beggar Almudena. Almudena is an amalgam of Otherness–Jewish/Arab, blind, poor, and diseased–, the antithesis of middle-class ideals and thus the unlikeliest of characters to experience the power of visionless insight.

As this study will show, to control an image–of a city, of a class, of gender, of the family, of the body–is to appropriate and normalize its reality. *Nazarín* and *Misericordia* suggest, however, that the normalised vision of society offered up by the middle class and its dominant discourses can be overcome by looking at the world with new eyes.

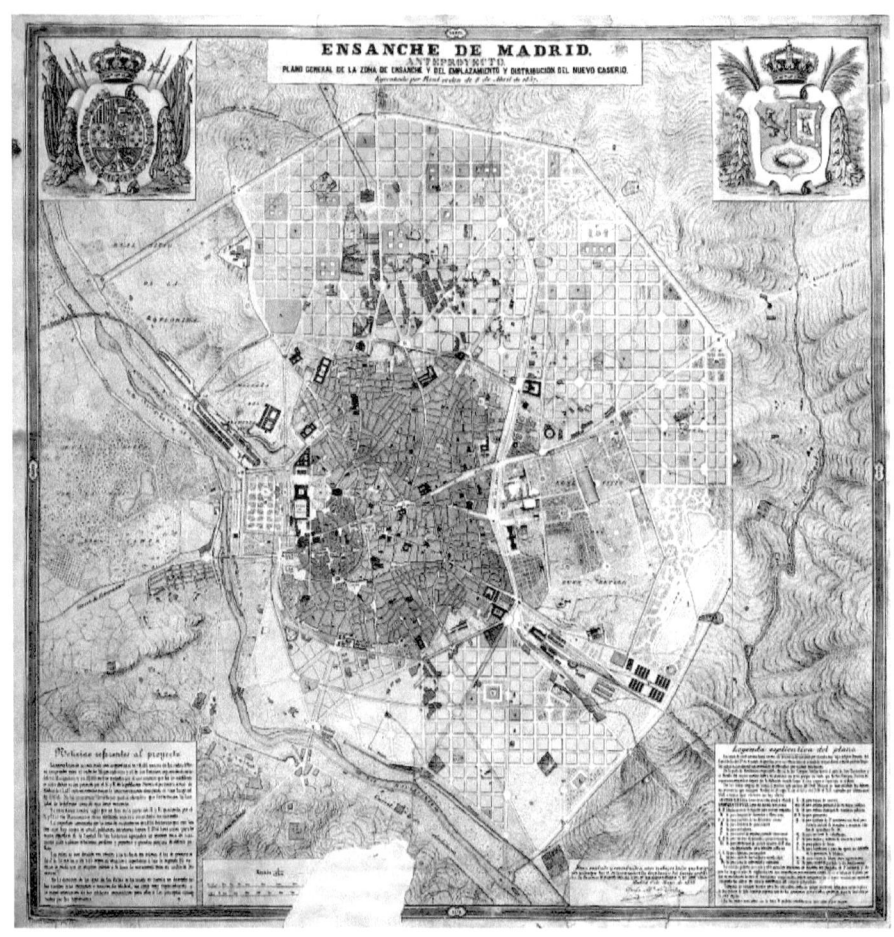

Figure 1: Carlos María del Castro's *Ensanche de Madrid* (1861).

CHAPTER 1

MAPPING THE CITY

> The cities of the nineteenth century were landscapes of the unknown.
> –Richard Sennett

CARTOGRAPHY is the science or art of map-making, and in the age of satellite imagery, aerial photography and specialized computer software, one might assume that making maps is a straightforward and objective enterprise. Such assumptions form part of what J. B. Harley calls "our cultural mythology", in which we fail to acknowledge that maps are always made for some particular purpose or set of purposes (Harley 2001: 63). Scholars of cartography know that in addition to charting geographic bodies, maps also express desires, conflicts and collective anxieties: "Maps are not neutral transmitters of universal truths, they are not bearers of neutral knowledge"–explains John Short–"Maps are social constructions, fictions if you like, narratives with a purpose, stories with an agenda" (Short 2001: 10).

What story, then, might a map of Madrid taken from the nineteenth century tell us about that particular society? As a manifestation of the link between maps and knowledge/power, Carlos María del Castro's proposed *Ensanche de Madrid* (1861; see Figure 1) reflects the attitudes of the dominant bourgeoisie toward Otherness. As is evident in his grid-like design for the city and his proposal for class-segregated neighbourhoods, Castro's plan represents middle-class anxieties related to the lower classes and the spaces they inhabit, anxieties that were echoed in the discourses on public hygiene and criminality.

The Power of Maps

Maps are never value-free but always value-laden images, participating actively in the construction of our social reality rather than passively reflecting landscapes. In his history of mapmaking J. B. Harley discusses this subjectivity when he states that "the surveyor, whether consciously or otherwise, replicates not just the 'environment' in some abstract sense but equally the territorial imperatives of a particular political system" (Harley 2001: 54). Maps name, delineate boundaries, locate people and places, in some cases they indicate a course of action. In short, maps function in/on society as a form of power-knowledge.

As a type of visual knowledge maps represent, and in many cases produce, power. Harley identifies two variants of power with respect to cartography, internal and external. The most obvious instance of external power comes in the from of patronage: the cases of dynastic Egypt, the Sultans of the Ottoman Empire, Islamic caliphs, and the Church of medieval Europe illustrate how cartography has always been the domain of those in power, a "science of princes" (Harley and Woodward 1987: 506). Often such patronage was linked with imperialism and military campaigns, as lands were usually claimed on paper before they were ever occupied. One might argue that Castro's plan of Madrid, which was commissioned by the monarchy and called for the realignment of physical borders in order that they might correspond to social boundaries, can therefore be viewed as an example of urban imperialism.

Maps also possess an internal power. Foucault's mantra that power is embedded in knowledge (Foucault 1991: 27) certainly applies to cartography. A map "structures the geography it depicts according to a set of beliefs about the way the world should be, and presents this as truth" (Cosgrove 1984: 8). The conventions of mapmaking are arbitrary, and the manner in which maps are compiled, the criteria upon which locations, geographic bodies, and other information are selected or ignored, formed into hierarchies, and laid out on the page reveals a specific worldview: "There is no scientific reason why north should be at the top [...] Cultural tradition dictates cartographical design just as it determines whether writing should be from left to right, right to left, or top to bottom" (Klinghoffer 2006: 21). While it may be going a bit far to say such conventions are completely subjective, they are certainly pervaded by ideology. Arthur Klinghoffer, in *The Power of Projections: How Maps Reflect Global Politics and History* (2006), offers several examples of ethnocentrism in cartography, including the way maps are laid out so as to situate certain regions in the privileged central position. So-called "T-O maps"–which depicted Jerusalem as the earth's central point–were common in Christian nations between the eighth and fifteenth centuries, from the late-sixteenth century onward the Chinese depicted their nation as the "middle kingdom" or "central state", and European cartographers have long placed Europe at the heart of their own maps (Klinghoffer 2006: 18-26).

Even size, colour and script size contribute to the visual prominence, and thus a privileging, of certain regions. Consider also the re-naming of places in Latin America following its colonization by the Spanish. In the eyes of the rest of the world, maps that bore Spanish nomenclature and declared Latin America the domain of the Spanish empire legitimized Spain's power in that region. In short, to control an image as the cartographer does is to appropriate a geographic reality and normalise society's understanding of that place. As a consequence of the internal and external elements of mapmaking, maps constitute a visual articulation of power.

URBAN CARTOGRAPHY

A unique feature of nineteenth-century cartography is the birth of the street map. As migrants flooded the cities in search of work and tourists arrived via the new railroad networks, there was a ready market for cheap, up-to-date street plans (Elliot 1987: 68). Rapid growth in urban centres also meant that city maps quickly became outdated, putting pressure on cartographers to constantly revise and reissue their plans (Elliot 1987: 69). This growing cartographic interest in the city was not only reflected in the number of maps produced, but also in the styles and types of maps being made. Urban growth created an impression of disorder, which in turn elevated interest in the distribution and use of urban space. Consequently, reform maps, such as Castro's proposed *Ensanche de Madrid* and Cerdà's plan for Barcelona (1861), which called for new layouts for those cities that were suffering from problems associated with urbanisation, became increasingly important in the second half of the century.

Madrid's maps, dominant discourses, and other dividing practices are products of the historical context in which they developed. Throughout the nineteenth century Spain, like much of Europe, struggled with how to secure economic progress in light of the political and moral threat posed by the condition of the working class. This "social question", as it became known, became more acute after the 1830s with the dismantling of the guilds, proletarianisation and, most significantly, the nationwide migratory movement of working-class individuals from an impoverished countryside to the nation's larger cities (Fuentes Peris 2003: 9). Unfortunately, this increase in population did not coincide with an increased level of industrialization. As a result, the city could not absorb this new work force. Thus the problems commonly associated with urbanisation –poverty, crime, epidemics, prostitution (Gilfoil 2006: 130-32)– were felt more forcefully in Madrid than in other industrialized cities such as London, Paris, and even Barcelona, where the pace of industrialization was on a par with the population boom.

As these problems came into sharper focus certain discourses gained prominence and the middle class turned to the power of dividing practices as they looked to maintain a social order that appeared to be on the brink of falling apart. The opening of the Leganés insane asylum in 1851, the passing of Madrid's first ordinance to control prostitution in 1865, the revision of the Penal Code in 1870, the inauguration of the Cárcel Modelo de Madrid in 1883, and the reinstated gathering of statistics on criminality by Royal Decree in 1884 suggest that Madrid residents lived in a climate of fear in which there was a strong desire for "el orden, la disciplina, la jerarquización, la imposición de normas, el condicionamiento de las conductas" (Álvarez-Uría 1979: 173).

This collective anxiety found an outlet in the form of urban planning. The city has long been a preferred metaphor for society. According to this tradition, the more ordered a city is, the more nearly it approaches the ideal of a utopian space. As Stanley Cohen notes: "The patterning of the city, its spatial arrangements, hierarchies, functional specifics, served as a mirror image of what the wider social reality could and should be like" (Cohen 1985: 206). Given this belief, it is no wonder Madrid's middle class feared social collapse in the latter half of the nineteenth century when urbanisation plunged the city into a state of disorder. As masses of migrant workers fled an impoverished countryside for the nation's urban centres, cities like Madrid found epidemics more devastating, crime more common and spatial disorder more prevalent. In a recent history of the Spanish capital, Santos Juliá bleakly refers to nineteenth-century Madrid as "una ciudad sucia y oscura", noting that the streets were "angostas e insalubres", the residences shabby, and the neighbourhoods lacking in police presence (Juliá 1995: 335), hardly a description one would expect of the capital of a formerly great empire.

Madrid was a dirty and dismal place in the nineteenth century but it was not the only European capital to be described as such. In 1845 social critic Victor Considérant referred to Paris as "un immense atelier de putréfaction" (Considérant 1979: 42), and in 1887 Sir Arthur Conan Doyle described London as "that great cesspool into which all the loungers and idlers of the Empire are irresistibly drained" (Conan Doyle 1960: 3). These citations reflect the unattractive realities of city-life in Europe as a consequence of industrialization and urbanisation. However, as I indicated earlier, Madrid's underdeveloped industry and growing population led to high unemployment, which in turn led to mendicancy, crime, prostitution and overcrowded, squalid housing, making its disorderliness more extreme. Foreigners and Spaniards alike shared the opinion that Madrid was an unsavoury city to live in during the nineteenth century. In his *Handbook for Travellers in Spain* (1844) Richard Ford calls Madrid a "disagreeable and unhealthy" place to reside, noting that in this "corrupted city" one can never feel safe (Ford 1966: III, 1075, 1079). Though understandably more sympathetic in their critiques, locals also expressed their dissatisfactions with the condition of Madrid. In 1851 journalist Nicolás Malo called Madrid a city without importance in the world (Juliá 1995: 335). This disenchantment escalated in the latter decades of the century, so much so that at the beginning of the twentieth century the *Enciclopedia Universal Ilustrada* offered the following retrospective estimation of the Spanish capital: "En el último tercio del siglo [diecinueve] Madrid era un pueblo grande, feo, no muy limpio, ni muy sano" (1911: XXXI, 1385).

Feeling threatened by the disorder of the city, the middle class reacted by attempting to reform the urban landscape. As early as 1846 Ramón Mesonero Romanos argued in his *Proyecto de mejoras generales de Madrid* that expanding the city beyond the existing boundaries would improve the city's gloomy state. Expansion, he explained, would facilitate communications, improve the quality of building construction, and allow "la conveniente separación, comodidad y orden de todas las clases del vecindario" (Mesonero Romanos 1967: I, 286). This call for class segregation was frequently echoed during the remaining decades of the century and is rooted in the idea that poor and working-class neighbourhoods fomented crime and the spread of disease. For example, in 1871 Fernando de la Torriente and Manuel Quintana argued in their proposal for urban reforms that separate "barrios de obreros", located "convenientemente en los extremos de la población", would satisfy both the economic and hygienic problems associated with overcrowding (Torriente and Quintana 1871: 28). Carlos María del Castro's 1861 proposal to expand Madrid, which, unlike Mesonero's plan, gained official approval by the crown, also called for separate residential neighbourhoods for the various social classes.

That many people felt that Madrid society was careening out of control is clearly visible in Castro's plan. Foucault argues that "spaces were designed to make things seeable, and seeable in a specific way" (Rajchman 1988: 103). Castro's design called for long, straight streets forming a grid (see Figure 1). The uniform divisions created by such a layout are reminiscent of the cells of a prison building, and prompted Clementina Díez de Baldeón to describe the plan as "perfectamente delimitado" and "fácilmente controlable" (Díez de Baldeón 1986: 454).[1] In other words, Castro's plan was panoptic in conception with its functional layout designed to enhance the power of those in control by segregating and organising society into class groups and then subjecting these groups to a controlling gaze. It is also a plan that highlights society's sensitivity to visual order. The gaze of late nineteenth-century Madrid was one that favoured order through the use of social and physical boundaries, and it was shaped by the discourses and dividing practices of a middle class who sought to maintain their newly established dominance.

---

[1] Around this same time similar plans were drawn up for other large cities, such as Ildefonso Cerdà's plan of Barcelona, with proponents using the same rationale to justify their proposals. Commenting on the "repetitive homogeneity" of Cerdà's design, Josep Maria Montaner notes that Barcelona, "in all its variety and disorder, was now absorbed into a coherent plan, thus becoming part of a whole" (Montaner 1997: 25). Layouts such as those proposed by Castro and Cerdà, argues Montaner, sacrifice style for functionality.

Experts define urbanisation as population growth in cities resulting from rural-urban migration (LeGates and Stout 2000: 3). According to this definition, rapid population growth from high birth rates or similar causes would not be considered urbanisation. Madrid's growth seems to be in harmony with this definition. Ángel Bahamonde and Julián Toro assert that Madrid's population rise can only be explained as a consequence of migration because birth rates during the century failed to compensate for the high number of deaths that occurred during periodic epidemics (Bahamonde and Toro 1978: 42-43). In 1800 Madrid's population stood somewhere around 175,000. The number of residents in the capital increased throughout the following decades reaching more than half a million by the century's end. From roughly 1845 onwards the rate of growth increased dramatically–with a slight downturn from 1860 to 1869, coinciding with the economic and political troubles at the end of Isabel II's reign. In the final thirty years of the century Madrid's population nearly doubled, increasing from 292,483 to 539,835 (Bahamonde and Toro 1978: 171).

Most of this growth came by way of migration as thousands of working-class individuals abandoned a weakened agrarian structure and impoverished countryside in the provinces in order to find work in Madrid where the incipient processes of industrialization had recently begun. In 1850 it was estimated that only forty percent of Madrid's population were born in the city or province (Shubert 1990: 48). By the beginning of the twentieth century that figure had fallen to just ten percent (*Enciclopedia Universal Ilustrada* 1911: XXXI.1386). The problem of congestion was exacerbated by the establishment of the railway system during the reign of Isabel II, meaning the capital was now a prominent thoroughfare. As a result of this constant flow of migrants and travellers, Madrid's local residents experienced a sense of strangeness and unfamiliarity as they witnessed innumerable new faces, fashions and behaviour.

Judging by the response in local papers, this demographic trend was viewed with trepidation. On May 14, 1853 *La Época* ran the following report: "Todos los días entran en Madrid de 1.000 a 1.500 gallegos en busca de trabajo. Estos infelices que huyen de su país y del hambre vienen por el camino pidiendo limosna y llegan en un estado realmente deplorable" (1853: 11). The number of Galicians entering Madrid according to *La Época* appears to be something of an exaggeration when compared with the overall population increase mentioned in the official statistics cited above. Bearing in mind *La Época*'s distinctly conservative stance, such an exaggeration reflects a growing concern among members of the bourgeoisie about Madrid's rising population.

As a result of unique demographic changes during the latter decades of the nineteenth century, however, the longstanding urban/rural divide took on fresh nuances. The discursive field that emerged from Madrid's new urban existence turns on an urban/rural binary full of contradictions. This urban/rural binary or country-versus-city theme is clearly reflected in the nineteenth-century novel, but is not unique to it. The *beatus ille* motif is in fact traditional to many literary modes, reaching back to the pastoral poetry of the Garcilaso de la Vega's "Églogas" (1533-36), which evoke an idealized country life full of innocence and virtue. In the twentieth century the theme would be critically explored by members of the Generation of 1898 (Sinclair 2003: 50).

Like all binaries, the urban and the rural can only be understood in light of their opposition to one another. A simplified model, according to prevailing stereotypes of the period, would set the city against the country, with the former providing a setting for sophisticated individuals to engage in social relationships that would lead to the advancement of civilization, whereas the latter would be seen as a backward place where social relationships were impossible because those living in this setting were driven by base passions and instincts. While this dichotomy between city and country is certainly not unique to the period in question, it undoubtedly became more prominent following Jean-Jacques Rousseau's publication of *The Social Contract* (1762) in the previous century and Charles Darwin's *The Origin of Species* in 1859. What was unique about Rousseau's notion of the social contract was that it established clear ideological boundaries between nature and society. As Jo Labanyi explains, the stability of society came to depend "on the maintenance of the boundary which separates the city (that which is inside society) from the country (that which is outside society)" (Labanyi 1986: 54-55). Similarly, Darwin's theory of evolution was used to argue that the city, with its modern industry developed by scientific advances, represented the apogee of human civilization while rural inhabitants languished in an earlier stage of development. But Darwin's description of nature in *The Origin of Species* differed significantly from the idealization of country life that one finds in Horace or Fray Luis de León. While Luis de León describes life in the country as "un no rompido sueño / un día puro, alegre, libre" (León 1984: 68), Darwin paints a different picture, calling nature a "tangled bank" in which evolution occurs via a process of constant conflict and hardship (Darwin 1991: 408).

It became difficult, though not impossible, to idealise the country following the publication and dissemination of Darwin's theories, but because of the problems associated with urbanisation the city was hardly considered an ideal space either. Spain's lower classes were described by contemporary hygiene campaigners as a cancer coursing through the social body (Monlau 1984: 117-18; Salarich 1984: 285), and were criticised for bringing disorder, crime and illness to the capital through their unhealthy and immoral lifestyle. Curiously, the fact that many members of the growing working class came from rural areas was not seen as the problem. In fact, the rural environment continued to enjoy something of an idealized status throughout the nineteenth century despite the connotations described above. Whereas the city harboured criminals, diseases and immorality, life in the country was considered safe, healthy and wholesome. For city-dwellers the country provided a refuge from the malaise and insalubrities of city life.

Despite the benefits of rural life, urban residents were not about to give up their existence in the city and relocate to the country–though wealthier Madrid residents did make extended trips to the country when wanting to restore their failing health. Instead, they brought the country to the city by incorporating gardens and parks into the built urban environment. Landscaped gardens existed as a sub-category of architecture long before the nineteenth century but this period marks a change in the motivation behind such spaces. Rather than viewing them merely as decorative or recreational spaces, private Edens to be enjoyed by the wealthy, gardens came to be seen as essential to the physical wellbeing of the middle and upper classes. As Castro's proposal explains:

> La alta nobleza y el rico banquero desean ardientemente espacio en donde erigir lindos o suntuosos palacios que rodeados de elegantes floridos jardines y tapizados parques les procuren la salubridad, las comodidades y el recreo que infructuosamente buscarían en las mezquinas y mal ventiladas viviendas que hoy ocupan; como la clase media aspira al goce de esas mismas venta-

jas, puestas al alcance de sus fortunas, que le están de todo punto vedadas por la estrechez de nuestro recinto. (Castro 1861: 13-14)

Of course, the working class could scarcely afford the luxury of a garden. But in conjunction with this call for more private gardens the so-called parks movement gained momentum across Europe and America. In an effort to "combat urban vice and social degeneration, particularly among the children of the urban poor" large public parks were designed, or, in cities where such parks already existed, they were opened up to the public (LeGates and Stout 2000: 314). The Retiro and the Casa de Campo parks in Madrid are prime examples of such spaces. Hybrid spaces like parks and gardens seemed to offer the best of both worlds. They were conveniently located in the heart of the city, yet they offered the regenerative power of the country.

Despite these potential benefits, conflicting connotations associated with the two realms meant such spaces were potentially problematic. Because the cultivated gardens and parks of Madrid are simultaneously inside and outside society, that is, they are a part of and yet are distinct from the city, they constitute liminal spaces where the urban/rural binary breaks down and the particularities of each sphere are thrown into a state of non-hierarchical free play. The campaign to create parks and gardens, supposedly for the physical wellbeing of the city's residents, might have contributed to the disorder of the city by providing pockets of undecidability, contained spaces where the discursively formed conventions of social behaviour might or might not have applied. I shall return to this idea in my analysis of *La de Bringas* in Chapter 3.

While many viewed the country as an idyllic refuge from the woes of urban existence, the growing interest in theories of degeneration, which gained widespread acceptance as part of the new field of criminal anthropology, highlights a contradictory aspect of the city/nature divide. Interest in African and Latin-American tribes was very high throughout Europe during the nineteenth century. Anthropological studies of tribal life, complete with illustrations, appeared in books and newspapers and Sander Gilman even describes how one African woman was displayed, in the nude, as part of a travelling show that was the entertainment at a lavish Parisian ball (Gilman 1986: 85-86). This fascination with "savages" is due in part to the struggles of Europeans in coming to terms with urban existence. While the concept of natural habitats was only one aspect of the argument that there existed "civilized" races and "savage" races, it was a significant difference. Urbanisation, in spite of all of its accompanying problems, was hailed as a product of scientific progress, and thus an important step in the advancement of civilized societies. It provided a noticeable difference between European society and "primitive" people who live in the wild countryside. Looking at society through a prism of post-Darwinian theory, the notion that certain groups thrived in their natural habitat while they degenerate when introduced into a new environment was, according to Nancy Stepan, a way of explaining racial degeneracy (Stepan 1985: 98-99).

This theory was easily superimposed onto the situation of the rural worker who relocates to the city only to fall into a state of atavism–succumbing to vice, committing crimes or falling ill. This vision of the migrant's trip down the road of degeneracy (perhaps a less romantic way of portraying Rousseau's paradigm of the noble savage who becomes corrupted by civilization) gave ammunition to those who argued that migrant workers and degenerate races were contributing to the social woes of the city. In essence, the theory of degeneracy legitimized the exclusionary techniques of the dominant classes and became a convenient way of laying claim to the city. Modern cities like Madrid were seen as the "proper place" of white middle-class Europeans, while the unfortunate foreign immigrants (and their descendants) and rural-born workers who had had little choice but to come to the city to work were simply victims of natural selection. By viewing class difference and racial difference in this same light the middle class could base their self-ascribed supremacy on current scientific theories. As a consequence the poor in large cities were increasingly likened unto primitive tribes and savages; and social Darwinism was invoked as a justification for existing social relations and as a vehicle for a belief in the inequality of race and class. This creative reworking of Darwinist ideas reflects the obvious contradictions of the rural/urban dichotomy: that the country was a source of degeneracy and regeneration, or that the city was corrupting yet the ultimate example of progress. Such contradictions illustrate the manner in which discourse can be manipulated to serve the interests of a particular group. The bourgeoisie's effort to identify proper places provides a physical example of the role of discourse and dividing practices in mapping the shifting boundaries of Madrid society.

DISCOURSE AS CARTOGRAPHIC ENTERPRISE

Whether or not Madrid society was really under threat of collapse in the late nineteenth century is perhaps less relevant than the fact that members of the middle class perceived it as such. Their tendency to visualize difference and to associate the problems of urban existence with the poor and working class was so acute that it did not stop at class differences but extended to other spheres as well, such as gender (see Chapter 3), race (see Chapter 5) and religion (see Chapter 6). In short, the gaze of nineteenth-century Madrid was one which looked favourably on anyone who embodied middle-class standards of normalcy while marginalizing those that did not. By recognizing this optic one can appreciate the boundaries of Spain's cultural map for what they really are, frontiers of fear established by bourgeois discourse.

Discourse, like a map, reflects social conflict and has the capacity to create myths that legitimate specific power relations. This is clearly illustrated by the nineteenth-century hygiene craze and the introduction of criminology in Spain, both of which constitute exclusionary tactics whereby boundaries between "normal" and "deviant" were identified and fortified in order to alleviate the misgivings of a middle-class trying to cope with urban existence. Urbanisation was perceived as a disorganising force that threatened to upset the existing social order. The middle class reacted by embarking on a campaign of social mapping through the use of discursive trends and other dividing practices that they believed would restore order.

Every culture, indeed every faction of a given culture, has a unique way of conceptualizing its particular period. Denis Cosgrove's statement that a map "structures the geography it depicts according to a set of beliefs about the way the world should be, and presents this construction as truth" (Cosgrove 1984: 8), is a direct application of Michel Foucault's theory of discourse. Commenting on the historic variability of knowledge Foucault explains that "there are different truths and different ways of speaking the truth" (Foucault 1988: 51). Foucault does not use the term discourse in its common sense as a speech or sermon but, rather, as a body of statements and practices that constitute the knowledge or "truths" of a period:

> Each society has its régime of truth, its "general politics" of truth: that is, the types of discourse which it accepts and makes function as true; the mechanisms and instances which enable one to distinguish true and false statements, the means by which value in the acquisition of truth; the status of those who are charged with saying what counts as true. (Foucault 1980: 131)

Foucault's statement indicates that discourses rise to prominence and fall according to the specific context of a period. He also points out that groups with specific ideological interests play a significant role in the establishment and dissemination of those discourses that are most relevant to them. The evolution of discursive trends typically corresponds to changes in the dominant ideology of a given society, and while one cannot reduce discourse to statements that simply mirror the interests of a particular class, it should be recognized that by functioning as a key site of power, discourse is never ideologically neutral. "[T]ruth isn't outside power, or lacking in power" because, Foucault explains, "[t]ruth is a thing of this world: it is produced only by virtue of multiple forms of constraint. And it induces regular effects of power" (Foucault 1980: 131). As this citation suggests, truth derives not from a single source but from "multiple forms of constraint", that is, from the overlap, interplay and loose unification of various discourses–a system of dispersion known as a discursive field. Because groups with dissimilar and even contradictory interests can successfully appropriate the same discourse to promote their interests, a discourse cannot be "innocent". Discourses may be cloaked in apparent objectivity (using the language of science, for example) but the flexibility of discourse, the ability to make a discourse "true" in order to promote certain interests over others, illustrates its role in the circulation of power:

> There can be no possible exercise of power without a certain economy of discourses of truth which operates through and on the basis of this association. We are subjected to the production of truth through power and we cannot exercise power except through the production of truth. (Foucault 1980: 93)

Foucault has dubbed the manifestations of this discursively-fuelled power "dividing practices" (Foucault 1982: 208). Dividing practices are those modes of normalization (either institutionalized or non-institutionalized) by which abnormal, deviant or dangerous members of the population are identified and controlled. By combining the mediation of science with spatial and/or social exclusion, definitions of "normal" and "abnormal" are established in such a way as to promote the socio-political interests of certain groups while marginalizing the members of other groups. In *The Birth of the Clinic* (1963), *Madness and Civilization* (1964), *Discipline and Punish* (1975) and *The History of Sexuality* (1976) Foucault provides examples of such dividing practices: the incarceration and surveillance of criminals, the poor and the insane, the quarantining of diseased individuals, classificatory methods in clinical medicine, and the stigmatization of "sexual deviance" in modern Europe. Of course Foucault does not stop there. These are simply examples or generalizable models that can be applied to virtually every aspect of social life. Classifying individuals, locating and analysing them in space, and regimenting their activities are all common dividing techniques that convert the body into a docile and controllable object. While the techniques known as dividing practices may vary, the ultimate goal remains the same: the objectification, categorisation and domination of the subject.

THE FEAR OF CONTAMINATION

The fear that the perceived immorality and degeneration of the lower-class neighbourhoods would spread, like a contagious disease, to the more respectable members of society who lived in relatively close proximity led to the prominence of discourses and practices that appeared to provide effective physical and social boundaries between the various classes of Madrid. In response to the threat of contamination, calls for class segregation echoed throughout the press. Díez de Baldeón states that "ríos de tinta" filled the pages of newspapers and journals as people debated what to do about the problem of working-class neighbourhoods (Díez de Baldeón 1986: 427). As the following citation by urban reformers Fernando de la Torriente and Manuel Quintana shows, the moral health or decay of city dwellers was believed to be closely associated with the spaces in which they lived, worked and socialized:

> Así como la morada arreglada con buenas luces a calles concurridas, corrige las costumbres y estimula el amor propio, hasta el

> punto de convertir al abandonado en hacendoso, del mismo modo, se verifica la metamorfosis contraria, pues el hombre que después de su faena y de regreso al hogar, tiene que cruzar callejuelas inmundas con casas de aspecto repugnante, que lanzan miasmas a la vía pública, no puede menos de llegar a habituarse y aclimatarse, en cierto modo, a esos lugares, concluyendo por adquirir costumbres de indolencia. (Torriente and Quintana 1871: 22)

This citation clearly reflects a bourgeois perspective. Words such as "convertir", "metamorfosis", "lanzar", "habituarse", "aclimatarse" and "adquirir" all emphasize the possibility of individual degeneration when faced with the communicability of working-class immorality whose mobility was seen as a problem (Shubert 1990: 52-56). Meanwhile the mention of "miasmas" invokes the discourse of public hygiene that was so prominent in the second half of the century. According to Torriente and Quintana, Castro, and others, class segregation was the best solution to the threat of contagion. The discourse on public hygiene, like the discourse on criminality, looked to map out favourable frontiers between the various social classes on the basis of potential physical and moral threat. Only by dividing society into categories like deviant/orderly, clean/dirty, moral/immoral and normal/abnormal could the ideals and way of life of the bourgeoisie be safeguarded against the threat of urban disorder.

It was not difficult for urban reformers to find a link between the lower classes and public hygiene problems. In his proposal Castro cites the increasing health problems affecting the city as justification for his proposed changes: "Las condiciones de salubridad en el interior de las habitaciones, son las que más inmediatamente contribuyen al bienestar de sus moradores" (Castro 1861: 71). The second half of the nineteenth century witnessed a flurry of activity in the sphere of public health. In a single decade, between 1851 and 1860, Spain passed 189 acts of legislation under the category "higiene pública general", substantially more than the 117 passed during the previous century and a half, from 1700 to 1850 (González 1999). Such an increase, coupled with the overwhelming quantity of magazines, newspaper articles, speeches and books on hygiene produced during this period, attests to the public's concern (Fuentes Peris 2003: 34).

The best-known hygiene campaigner in Spain during this period was Pedro Felipe Monlau, whose books *Elementos de higiene privada* (1846), *Elementos de higiene pública* (1847), *Higiene del matrimonio* (1853), *Higiene del alma* (1855) and *Higiene industrial* (1856) were reprinted numerous times by the end of the century. Galdós's personal library boasts a number of works on the subject of personal and public hygiene including *La higiene del hogar* (1878) by Dr. López de la Vega, and *Tratado de la higiene de la infancia* (1885) and *Higiene y saneamiento de las poblaciones* (1885) by Jean Batiste Fonssagrives. Each of these works contains annotations by Galdós, suggesting more than a cursory knowledge of the subject. He also possessed a copy of a speech made by his friend, Dr. Manuel de Tolosa Latour, to the Real Academia de Medicina in 1900 on "Concepto y fines de la Higiene Popular".[2]

As is the case with the discourse on criminality, the prevailing hypotheses on the subject of hygiene linked the increase in filth and disease with the growth of Madrid's lower-class population. Madrid, or at least the ideal Madrid of the bourgeoisie, was under siege and nowhere was this more apparent than in the discourse on public health and hygiene.

Problems of overcrowding and poor living conditions in large cities exacerbated the impact of epidemics, most notably cholera. Outbreaks assailed the nation in 1833-34, 1855, 1865, and again in 1885. The press gave the subject considerable attention, indicating that the topic was clearly on the minds of the general public. Galdós, for instance, dedicated no fewer than six articles to cholera between November 1884 and August 1885, the year of the last outbreak in the capital.[3] In these articles Galdós discusses a variety of issues related to the current outbreak such as the new vaccine being developed by Jaime Ferrán as well as the government's exploitation of the cholera panic as a political weapon. Other authors mentioned the conditions of working-class neighbourhoods as a contributing factor to the spread of cholera and other diseases, arguing

---

[2] See Sebastián de la Nuez Caballero (1990: 100) for a complete list of books on hygiene in Galdós's library.

[3] These articles are "Precauciones sanitarias" (17 November 1884), "Un enemigo del cólera" (13 June 1885), "La especulación del miedo" (19 June 1885), "Epidemias y crisis" (4 July 1885), "Pánico colectivo" (30 July 1885), and "El cólera y la política" (14 August 1855), all of which appear in volume VI of *Cronicón*.

that the unhealthy living conditions of the lower classes could potentially contaminate the whole of society:

> Si en las insalubres casas de los menesterosos toman con facilidad mucho mayor origen las enfermedades llamadas con razón *populares*, poco tardan luego en irradiar desde aquellos focos hasta los palacios de los príncipes, abrazando el conjunto de la población. (Méndez Álvaro 1874: 80)

Francisco Méndez Álvaro's comment reflects the general attitude of the bourgeoisie who saw the squalid state of working-class dwellings as a concern for the entire social body.

Targeting lower-class neighbourhoods was not simply a way for hygiene campaigners to lay the blame prejudicially on the most convenient scapegoat, though it should be noted that authors like Pedro Felipe Monlau and Joaquim Salarich wrote primarily for a middle-class audience.[4] With the debate on infection in full force there really was justification for believing that the lower-class neighbourhoods of Madrid provided an ideal environment for the spread of cholera and other diseases. Both leading theories of infection at the time, miasmatism and germ theory, identified these areas as contributing to the epidemic problems of the city but they did so for different reasons. According to the miasmatic theory of disease, illnesses like cholera were caused by the miasma or "bad air" of decomposing organic refuse.[5] In the latter part of the century the pre-eminence of the miasmatic theory was contested by the germ theory or contagionism, the idea that infectious diseases are caused by the spread of living microorganisms rather than polluting "effluvia". In *Membranes: Metaphors of Invasion in Nineteenth-Century Literature, Science, and Politics* (1999) Laura Otis notes that this new understanding of how disease spread was not necessarily brought about by advances in microscopy or the technical ingenuity of Louis Pasteur and Robert Koch. After all, scientists could have determined that micro-organisms cause disease using Antony van

---

[4] For a discussion of this bias in the writing of Monlau and Salarich see Jutglar (1984: 39-48).

[5] The deleterious effects of miasmas were fundamental to the hygiene campaigners' agenda and were often discussed by experts on public health. By way of example see Juan Giné y Partagás's *Curso elemental de higiene privada y pública* (1872) in which he devotes an entire chapter to the subject (1872: II, 47-59).

Leeuwenhoek's lenses as early as the 1670s. Instead, Otis argues, it was a change in ideology that "made the idea of infectious germs believable":

> The growth of industrialism and colonialism in the nineteenth century greatly increased contact between nations and cultures. If diseases were contagious, commercially crippling quarantines had to be established, so political beliefs inevitably affected people's opinions as to whether diseases spread through foul air or human contact. Anticontagionist reformers, largely liberals and radicals, fought for scientific, commercial, and individual freedom simultaneously, regarding the three as inseparable. While the middle class stood to benefit from free trade, the landed gentry and other traditionalists had nothing to fear from embargoes that favored national interests. Contagionism consequently attracted conservatives, officers and bureaucrats who thought that centralized power structures, not individual citizens or local authorities, should control policies affecting public health. (Otis 1999: 11)

Of course the transition from miasmatic theory to germ theory was hardly so absolute in reality, especially when each European nation and even particular cities within these nations were experiencing industrialization, colonialism and political change in unique ways.[6] In Spain, where industrialization came relatively late, where colonialism was in decline, and where swings in political power occurred frequently, it is more difficult to associate changes in scientific theory with Otis's scheme. Indeed, Spain was rather slow in accepting the germ theory of infection in comparison to other nations in Western Europe. The notion that poor lighting, poor circulation of air and water, and poor hygiene were to blame for epidemics continued to hold sway in Spain until the end of the century even when

---

[6] Because of the miasmatic theory's predominance in the Italian scientific community, Filippo Pacini's discovery of the bacillus that causes cholera in 1854 was ignored (thus Koch's discovery of the cholera bacillus some thirty years later is actually a *re*discovery). This example gives credence to Thomas Kuhn's theory of scientific paradigms, which is that the body of knowledge governing "normal science" during a given period excludes theories and evidence that do not fall within the parameters of this paradigm, thus explaining why Pacini's discovery would have been ignored. When a breakthrough can no longer be ignored it brings about a scientific revolution. Foucault's theory of the *episteme*, that every period organises its thought in a particular way, is, as many have noted, a reworking of Kuhn's theory.

contagionism was relatively well established (Fuentes Peris 2003: 14-22; Otis 1999: 8-36).

Spain's inability to give up its fear of "bad air" despite the breakthroughs made by Koch and Ferrán allowed the two theories of infection to coexist, albeit a hostile coexistence, for a number of years. Galdós comments on this uneasy coexistence when he explains that, "Hay un Consejo que llaman de Sanidad en el cual los contagionistas y los anticontagionistas dan una batalla cada día, tan sin fruto, que más valdría que se fueran a sus casas", thus affirming that "las causas de la infección epidémica" clearly remained "aún un misterio" as late as 1884 (Pérez Galdós 1924: VI, 74). One explanation for this presence of seemingly contradictory theories is that while the two theories differed radically on how disease was transmitted, on the level of practical hygiene they were difficult to distinguish. Both miasmatism and contagionism associated particular places with disease, albeit for different reasons. Hygienists who subscribed to the miasmatic theory identified dark, damp and poorly ventilated living spaces–in other words, those dwellings typically inhabited by the poor and working class–with decomposition and thus with the noxious emanations that supposedly caused cholera and other diseases. For proponents of germ theory such places were simply the natural habitat of the living organisms that caused disease and the overcrowding of these spaces facilitated spread of the germs from one individual to the next. In either case lower-class neighbourhoods were culpable, whether it was the spaces themselves or the overcrowding of people within those spaces.

When Castro published his plan in 1861, he believed that expanding the city and dividing residential neighbourhoods according to social class would prevent future outbreaks of disease. He identified urban growth as the primary cause of ill health in Madrid–"el aumento rápido que la población ha tenido en pocos años, sin que en igual proporción se hayan extendido las edificaciones de la villa, está siendo causa de que cada día empeoren las condiciones higiénicas y de salubridad" (Castro 1861: 14)–and his explanation of the specific causes is based on the prevailing medical theories of the day:

> Con la humedad se multiplican en el interior de las viviendas las descomposiciones cuyo efecto es el de mezclar al aire respirable ácido carbónico, hidrógeno sulfurado, amoniaco y otros todavía

> mal definidos por la química, que bajo el nombre de *efluvios* o de *miasmas* están reconocidos como deletéreos y causa de enfermedades mortíferas. (Castro 1861: 73)

Castro, like his contemporaries, did not believe that all living quarters of Madrid were giving off these toxic odours. The problem, he suggests, could be traced to the unhygienic conditions of the working-class neighbourhoods: "peligrosas e insalubres son esas habitaciones húmedas, mal ventiladas, estrechas y sucias en que se albergan por lo general los artesanos, los obreros y los proletarios" (Castro 1861: 132). However, minimizing contact with the lower class and those spaces they occupied, which would improve one's chance of avoiding infection, was virtually impossible in Madrid where members of the various social classes lived in relatively close proximity. For this reason the division of society was seen as essential to the wellbeing of the bourgeoisie.

The Criminal Element

While the discourse on criminality may appear, at first glance, far removed from the discourse of public hygiene, both represent the middle-class desire for order and boundaries that developed in a context of social anxiety. Like the intense debate surrounding contagion, interest in criminality rose sharply in the second half of the nineteenth century, as could be seen in the growth of criminal anthropology in the 1880s and 1890s, the popularity of crime narratives, and reforms to the penal system–including the construction of a new panoptic prison in Madrid and efforts to gather and record information about criminal acts.

Reporting on "el misterioso crimen de la calle de Fuencarral" in 1888, Galdós prefaces his account of the crime by remarking on the apparent increase in criminal behaviour throughout Spain in recent years: "Estamos ahora los españoles bajo la influencia de un signo trágico. Los grandes crímenes menudean" (Pérez Galdós 1924: VII, 87). Given Foucault's identification of a paradigm shift in the way society understands and deals with crime, as outlined in his study of the discourse on criminality in *Discipline and Punish*, one might wonder whether crime was actually on the rise in Spain or whether there was simply an increased sensitivity to crime as a result of greater efforts to report and record criminal behaviour. The nineteenth century introduced a new way of talking about criminality –in other words, a new discourse–which in turn reshaped the way society understood criminality. Evidence of this shift can be seen in concrete changes to the penal system, such as the creation of the Guardia Civil in 1846, the new field of statistics, which was used to compile data on the types and rates of crimes in 1846 and again in 1884, and revisions to the penal code, which occurred in 1848 and again in 1870 (Gómez Bravo 2005; Trinidad Fernández 1982). In addition to these developments, the inability (or unwillingness?) of Madrid's middle class to distinguish between actual danger and perceived danger, as well as their conflation of delinquency with the growth of the working-class population, raised the status of discourse on criminality in a way that altered people's understanding of criminality and contributed to nineteenth-century standards of normalcy and delinquency.

In order to gauge the public's general awareness of discourse on criminality in late nineteenth-century Spain we can look at the popularization of the crime narrative. In her article on crime writing in Restoration Spain, Wadda Ríos Font points out that while traditional crime narratives (in the tradition of Conan Doyle's Sherlock Holmes stories) only really appeared in Spain at the beginning of the twentieth century–Pedro Antonio de Alarcón's short story "El clavo" (1853) being a notable exception–one could still find examples of crime narrative hot off the presses in the pages of the major newspapers (Ríos-Font 2005: 337-39). Crime journalism was especially popular in the Spanish press during the second half of the century, as Galdós explains:

> En vano se buscarían en la prensa acontecimientos políticos o literarios. Los periódicos llenan las columnas con relatos del *crimen de la calle de Fuencarral*, del *crimen de Valencia*, del *crimen de Málaga*, los *reporters* y noticieros, en vez de pasarse la vida en el salón de conferencias, visitan los juzgados a todas horas, acometen a los curiales atosigándoles a preguntas, y con los datos que adquieren, construyen luego la historia más o menos fantaseada y novelesca del espantoso drama. (Pérez Galdós 1924: VII, 87)

Galdós's comment, which is somewhat self-critical considering it appears in his own journalistic retelling of "El crimen de la calle de

Fuencarral", highlights two significant points. Firstly, by suggesting that crime has surpassed politics and literature in the amount of news-coverage it gets Galdós provides an indication of just how popular these crime stories had become. Indeed, such stories were so popular that the major newspapers collected and published them in volume form for sale or as a gift to subscribers (Ríos-Font 2005: 339). Secondly, Galdós alludes to the relationship between perceived danger and actual danger. His choice of terminology implies that writing about crime in Madrid was more a matter of invention and exaggeration than objectively reporting events. Absent are terms such as *narrar, relatar, verdadero* or *objetivo* that one typically associates with journalism, and in their place appear words like "construyen", "fantaseada y novelesca" and "drama". Galdós's diction would suggest that the fear of crime in Spain during this period was the result of imagination or paranoia rather than fact.[7] Furthermore, by focusing on crimes that happen on the very city streets where readers live and work, crime journalism depicts delinquency as a constant threat lurking just around the corner.[8]

Ironically, while cases of crimes committed against the middle and upper classes captured most of the headlines, such as the widely publicized "crimen de la calle de San Vicente", in reality the majority of victims of street crimes actually came from the lower classes (Weisser 1979: 146-47).[9] Economic need usually meant that entire working-class families would go out looking for work, leaving apartments vulnerable to intruders. Similarly, while working-class individuals had less to offer an assailant, they made easier targets on the street. Unlike members of the middle and upper classes, working-class individuals lived and socialized in neighbourhoods where

---

[7] A second example of popular crime narrative discussed by Ríos-Font is the *causa célebre*, a tale of a famous crime. Whereas the articles mentioned above typically recount contemporary, local crimes, the *causa célebre* narrates crimes committed in exotic locales in the past. Ríos-Font points out that the *causa célebre*, with its depiction of crime as something remote and fictional, counterbalances the immediacy of crime journalism and thus creates discursive tension (Ríos-Font 2005: 238-39).

[8] This feeling was accentuated by the fact that crimes were generally designated by the streets where they took place. Two notable examples are the "crimen de la calle Fuencarral" and the "crimen de la calle de San Vicente".

[9] The "crimen de la calle de San Vicente" involved an unemployed medical doctor who shot Don Juan José Fernández and his wife Carolina at point blank range, injuring the former and killing the latter, in front of their home on San Vicente Street. See Ríos-Font (2005: 342) for a detailed account of the crime and ensuing trial.

the lack of police presence and the layout of the streets made for easier getaways: "The physical environment of the working-class slum provided endless avenues of concealment and escape for the criminal; dark alleys, narrow winding stairs, rooftops and garrets presented a maze of passageways that could be used for flight from the scene of a crime" (Weisser 1979: 147). The sort of physical environment described here by Weisser recalls the descriptions of Madrid made by Castro and others when discussing the link between environment and contagion. In his analysis of criminology in the nineteenth century Trinidad Fernández reiterates Weisser's observation, adding that in Spanish cities like Madrid the urban layout, especially in the poorer parts of town, made police or military manoeuvres too difficult to be effective, thereby providing pockets of delinquency:

> Los ejércitos y la artillería son poco operativos en el laberinto de calles estrechas, en cambio, las barricadas se levantan rápidamente. La policía no puede fiscalizar lo que allí ocurre y desconoce sus habitantes, refugiados en la solidaridad y en los recovecos de las casas y calles. En conjunto, los barrios populares eran focos de ilegalismo y guaridas de delincuentes. Lugares donde se escondían las clases peligrosas. (Trinidad Fernández 1991: 100)

Fernández's comments do not describe a bustling commercial capital but, rather, a city under siege.

The authorities of Madrid reacted like other European governments had done before them. Throughout the second half of the century they focused their categorising gaze upon society in an effort to create order through divisions. Foucault argues that the most effective response to "the problem of the accumulation of men" has been to observe and regulate the body:

> The economic changes of the eighteenth century [in England and France] made it necessary to ensure the circulation of effects of power through progressively finer channels, gaining access to individuals themselves, to their bodies, their gestures and all their daily actions. By such means power, even when faced with ruling a multiplicity of men, could be as efficacious as if it were being exercised over a single one. (Foucault 1980: 151-52)

As was the case with the hygiene problems, Madrid's middle class believed the solution to the crime problem would be found in a city layout that favoured a strategic reorganisation of neighbourhoods in such a way that would favour the movements of authorities while impairing the ability of delinquents hoping to hide or communicate with one another. According to an 1875 article published in *La Ilustración Española y Americana*:

> Hay también que atender a altas consideraciones de orden público y de seguridad, que imprimen no pocas veces la elección de líneas que tienen en el interior de los pueblos el carácter de estrategias, atravesando algunos barrios populares e inquietos y enlazándolos con otros más directamente para facilitar en un caso extremo las maniobras militares. (15 April 1875, 238)

Unlike the "laberinto de calles estrechas" harbouring criminals that Trinidad Fernández describes, Castro's proposed layout, with its long, wide, straight streets and open spaces, would improve the visibility and movement of authorities in the event of an uprising or in the pursuit of a fugitive. Castro's plan, an obvious panopticon structure, thus provides a vivid example of "architecture of fear", which Charlotte Spinks defines as "risk management, in which individuals assess risk and modify behaviour and urban form to eliminate fear and minimize crime" (Spinks 2001: 9). Spinks's use of the term "fear" implies that such modifications are based on a perception of danger rather than the actual risk of victimization.

Coupled with this heightened sensitivity to the relationship between urban space and crime is the new discipline of criminology. According to Trinidad Fernández's study of delinquency in Spain from the eighteenth through the twentieth centuries, the prison and the figure of the delinquent are both products of the nineteenth century (Trinidad Fernández 1991: 112-114, 203). It is during this period, he argues, that Spain changed the way it viewed punishment. Whereas prior to the second decade of the century punishment consisted of torture or labour, after 1820 the deprivation of liberty itself came to be seen as the most effective discipline. Thus, according to the *Dictamen de una Comisión especial acerca de las cárceles* (1820): "La libertad, señor, es el mayor bien que el hombre disfruta sobre la tierra, y de consiguiente la privación de ella es el daño más terrible que puede hacérsele sufrir" (cited in Trinidad Fernández 1991: 113). The modern prison design that emerged in nineteenth-century Spain grew out of the need to isolate prisoners from "normal" members of society and thus prevent physical harm and moral contamination. It also placated the bourgeoisie's desire to "fix" Madrid's mobile population of vagabonds, prostitutes and the like.

The pinnacle of Madrid's prison reform came in 1877 when construction of the Cárcel Modelo de Madrid began. As the name suggests, the Cárcel Modelo was meant to be the perfect example of disciplinary power and would serve as a model for future prisons as well as for any institution hoping to exercise power over individuals through vision and divisions. Alfonso XII's inauguration of the Cárcel Modelo was received with enthusiasm in Madrid's newspapers. *La Época* called it "un acontecimiento notable" in Spanish history and a sign of "[el] progreso evidente en la ciencia del derecho penal" (cited in Trinidad Fernández 1991: 176). T. Aranguren, the architect of the Cárcel Modelo, designed the project according to the basic principles of Jeremy Bentham's panopticon. Bentham's design, which had been published in *The Panopticon, or, the Inspection-House* in 1791 and translated into Spanish by Jacobo Villanova y Jordán in 1834, suggested the edifice be built in a radial form with a ring of cells and a central observation point.[10] Such a structure, Bentham argued, provided the divisions and controlling gaze needed to maintain order. Individuals are divided and isolated within the cells so as to prevent conspiracy (in the case of prisoners), contamination (in the case of patients) or cheating (in the case of pupils).

Panopticism is the manifestation of a desire to immobilize individuals or groups of individuals and thereby control their movements (Foucault 1991: 218). Power derived from the classification and arranging of individuals within a given space is enhanced when those individuals are kept within the field of vision. "[Disciplinary power] imposes on those whom it subjects a principle of compulsory visibility. In discipline, it is the subjects who have to be seen. Their visibility assures the hold of the power that is exercised over them. It is the fact of being constantly seen, of being able always to be seen, that maintains the disciplined individual in his subjection"

---

[10] Villanova's work, titled *Aplicación de la panóptica de Jeremías Bentham, a las cárceles y casas de corrección de España*, was not merely a translation but an application project as well. Villanova made adjustments to Bentham's blueprints in order to improve them and make them better suited to Spain's penal system.

(Foucault 1991: 187). This spatio-visual method of discipline maintains control by converting the human body into a site of knowledge/power.

Segregation and constant surveillance maximize the potential for control by allowing a few people to control a large number of inmates. Furthermore, such a system encourages peer-surveillance among the inmates and even self-surveillance because one must assume that s/he is always being watched.[11] In *Discipline and Punish* Foucault points out that panopticism need not be limited to the structure described by Bentham: "[The panopticon] must be understood as a generalizable model of functioning; a way of defining power relations in terms of the everyday life of men" (Foucault 1991: 205). Hence the panoptic model can apply to any mode of control governed by order and visibility. As the following chapters will show, the discourses on class, gender, the family and degeneracy are panoptic inasmuch as they were meant to divide and isolate certain segments of society by means of a categorising gaze.

The new field of criminology, in particular that part of it that drew on degeneration theory, which argued that criminals could be identified based upon their physical characteristics, represents an attempt to identify and classify deviancy through visual categorisation. As such it complements Castro's urban reforms, the construction of the Cárcel Modelo de Madrid, and similar panoptic projects. The pioneer of criminal anthropology in nineteenth-century Europe was the Italian positivist Cesare Lombroso, whose books and articles, including *L'uomo delinquente* (1876), *L'uomo di genio* (1889), and *La donna delinquente* (1893), can be seen as an attempt to shore up conventional social boundaries. Lombroso incorporated into these works statistical data as well as dozens of portraits of criminals, prostitutes, and individuals with physical abnormalities in order to support his theory that the criminal was "driven by an atavistic impulse to commit anti-social acts" (Lombroso-Ferrero 1972: 52). Atavism is the notion that certain individuals were evolutionary throwbacks who reverted "to the primitive type of [their] species" and who were knowable by their "atavistic stigmata", or physical traits (Lombroso 1958: 112-13).

Like Bentham's panopticon, which controlled criminals with

---

[11] In using the term "inmate" I am referring to any individual enclosed in a panoptic apparatus, and not necessarily a prisoner.

nothing more than a relentless gaze, Lombroso's theory of degeneracy was meant to gain control over deviancy by visually objectifying and distinguishing the body of the criminal from the larger social body. The key to Lombroso's project was his faith in the reliability of physiognomic principles. A general concept of physiognomy, which dates back to antiquity, needs to be distinguished from the physiognomic practices of the nineteenth century, which were not only more developed than earlier models but also more closely linked to the contemporary social context. The earliest writing on the subject of physiognomy is Aristotle's *Physiognomonica* (written in the decades around 300 BC), which compares human body parts to analogous parts of animals. Where there exists similarity, he concludes, the person will possess the same trait as the animal. Aristotle's man/beast comparisons laid the foundation for future physiognomic treatises such as Giovanni Battista Della Porta's *De humana physiognomonia* (1586). Della Porta used a series of illustrations comparing human and animal heads in order to demonstrate that "the resemblance of forms supposes a resemblance of characters" (cited in Lavater 1797: II, 99). In the following century the French artist Charles Le Brun worked out his own system of physiognomy, again focusing on the similarities between people and animals. Le Brun presented his work to the Académie de Peinture in a series of three lectures, two on facial expressions and one on physiognomy in 1668, and created a number of illustrations to support his comments. Many of these illustrations appeared the following century in the most famous study of physiognomy to date, the *Physiognomische Fragmente* (1775-1778) by Swiss theologian Johan Casper Lavater.

Unlike Aristotle, Della Porta and Le Brun, Lavater did not limit his model of physiognomy to comparisons with animals. In the opening pages of his *Physiognomische*, which was originally written in German but translated almost immediately into French and English, Lavater indicates the scope of his project:

> I comprehend under the term Physiognomy all the external signs which, in man, directly force themselves on the observer; every feature, every outline, every modification, active or passive; every attitude and position of the human body; in short, every thing that immediately contributes to the knowledge of man, whether active or passive—every thing that shows him as he really appears. (Lavater 1797: I, 11)

His broader definition of physiognomy exemplifies his ambition. In the *Physiognomische* Lavater introduces a rigour and ambition into the field of physiognomy that had been lacking. He laboured diligently to dismiss the popular opinion that physiognomy was a branch of magic or divination and sought to re-brand it as a science. He applied mathematical ratios in measuring and analysing facial features and head size and included portraits of famous individuals from history and contemporary culture such as Goethe, George Washington, Moses, and Socrates, as evidence to support his theories.

His reformations did not go unrewarded. Physiognomy became a social phenomenon and the popularity of the *Physiognomische* elevated the Swiss theologian to celebrity status. Lavaterian scholar John Graham describes the extent to which Lavater's work was disseminated in late eighteenth and early nineteenth-century Europe and America: "the book was reprinted, abridged, summarized, pirated, parodied, imitated, and reviewed so often that it is difficult to imagine how a literate person of the time could have failed to have some general knowledge of the man and his theories" (Graham 1979: 62).

To what can we attribute this immense interest about a centuries-old theory in the nineteenth century? Viewed within its historical context it becomes easier to understand why physiognomy captured the imagination of Europe in the nineteenth century and how it functioned as a dividing practice. Physiognomy's heyday begins, more or less, with the publication of Lavater's *Physiognomische Fragmente* between 1775 and 1778 and continues throughout the nineteenth century. The introduction of physiognomy in Spain began somewhat later than in other regions of Western Europe, but in both cases its popularity corresponds to the onset of urbanisation and industrialization (Wechsler 1982: 13-17). Urbanisation, as I have already pointed out, destabilized the existing social order and introduced a sense of unease into the collective psyche. In order to re-establish the social boundaries that had become blurred and unstable the middle class looked to methods that could be used to identify and differentiate individuals from a rather undifferentiated mass. Physiognomy's promise was that the social body could be re-mapped by mapping the human body.

The Spanish press had a fundamental role in popularizing physiognomy and its scientific successors on the peninsula. For over twenty years, newspapers like the *Semanario Pintoresco Español, El*

Museo de las Familias, and *El Mundo Universal* ran articles about physiognomic topics. As might be expected, the animal/human comparisons proved very popular. Man-to-animal sketches by Grandville depicting the metamorphosis of man into a frog, or a dog into a man appeared in the *Semanario Pintoresco Español* while *El Mundo Universal* ran an illustration titled "Origen de ciertas especies de animales", which showed a woman transforming into a cat (1863: 192). While these served mainly as visual amusements, a number of scholarly articles were written as well. In May of 1836 the *Semanario Pintoresco Español* printed an article examining the visage of Napoleon, who was a favourite specimen of nineteenth-century physiognomists, followed by a physiognomic study of the nose in August of the same year. The article cites Lavater in order to support the claim, "Tal nariz, tal frente, tal alma. Esta regla admite pocas excepciones" (1836: 164). The issue of the *Semanario Pintoresco Español* of 7 May 1854 included a physiognomic puzzle consisting of six faces from which the reader was expected to determine the character revealed by each face (1854: 152).

Physiognomy also surfaced in a number of full-length books as a supplementary topic or as the central subject. In 1845, Spanish translations of J. Ottin's treatises on physiognomy were published in Barcelona and two years later Antonio Rotondo's *La fisonomía, ó sea El arte de conocer a sus semejantes por las formas exteriores; extractado de las mejores obras de Lavater* (1842) was published in Madrid. Soon after, Mariano Cubí y Soler wrote his highly successful *Elementos de frenología, fisonomía y magnetismo humano* (1849). Even as late as 1865 Lavater's name continued to appear in Spain–Mariano Aguirre de Venero's physiognomic study of the eyes, *Primer sistema del lenguaje universal, fisognomónico de los ojos: Nuevo arte de conocer a los hombres* (1865), was dedicated to the Swiss physiognomist. The quantity of publications on the subject within a relatively short period of time would suggest a certain degree of physiognomic sophistication on the part of the Spanish reading public and in a growing city full of strangers like Madrid, physiognomy may have contributed to patterns of prejudice and exclusion and provided a "scientific" justification for social proscription.

Building upon Lavater's legacy, Lombroso claimed to have discovered through scientific research the unique physical characteristics of the degenerate type. Writing in the final quarter of the nineteenth century Lombroso drew upon Charles Darwin's theory of evolution, phrenological practices initiated by Franz Joseph Gall, Bénédict Morel's notion of degeneracy as set forth in *Traité des dégénérescences* (1857), the concept of moral insanity as outlined in *Physiology and Pathology of the Mind* (1867) by Henry Maudsley, as well as efforts to justify racism through science as in the case of Arthur de Gobineau's *Essai sur l'inégalité des races humaines* (1853-1855) (Pick 1989: 112-13). Borrowing numerous ideas and attitudes from these scientific forefathers, Lombroso focused on "deviant" behaviours. The scientific basis of his work as well as the conclusions he reached were nothing new, yet his ability to justify popular prejudices and stereotypes with supposedly scientific data earned him considerable notoriety and a reputation as a cutting-edge criminologist. Like penologists and physiognomists before him, Lombroso isolated members of society from one another by dividing and classifying them into opposing groups–criminal and law abiding, mad and sane, degenerate and healthy, normal and abnormal–using visual observation as his primary tool. He focused his attention on marginal members of the social body in order to demonstrate that these types could be identified and evaluated by analysing such physical characteristics as head size, facial symmetry and body shape.

In *Faces of Degeneration* (1989), Daniel Pick convincingly argues that Lombroso's work was inextricably connected to the social and political milieu of late nineteenth-century Europe (Pick 1989: 109), which explains why it spread to areas outside of Italy. Lombroso's theories touched virtually every part of Europe and America, and the Iberian peninsula is no exception. As Luis Maristany's *El gabinete del doctor Lombroso: Delincuencia y fin de siglo en España* (1973) as well as his follow-up article "Lombroso y España: Nuevas consideraciones" (1983), Lily Litvak's article "La sociología criminal y su influencia en los escritores españoles de fin de siglo" (1974), *Lombroso y la escuela positivista italiana* (1975) by Mariano Peset and José Luis Peset, and "The Theory of Degeneration in Spain (1886-1920)" by Ricardo Campos Martín and Rafael Huertas all demonstrate, degeneration theory arrived somewhat late in Spain, but it took hold of both the professional and popular imagination of Spaniards.[12]

---

[12] See Gilman (1985), Pick (1989), Harrowitz (1994) and Horn (2003) for recent studies with information on Lombroso's reception in countries other than Spain.

In retracing the impact of Cesare Lombroso's school of thought in Spain, Luis Maristany identifies 1895–the same year Galdós wrote *Nazarín*–as the pinnacle of Lombroso's popularity on the peninsula (Maristany 1983: 362). It was not until Dr. Rafael Salillas's 1888 conference presentation at the Ateneo de Madrid, titled "La antropología en el derecho penal", that Lombroso's criminal anthropology finally infiltrated the work of Spanish penologists and anthropologists; however, by the following decade knowledge of Lombroso had reached the mainstream public. The Sociedad Antropológica Española, the *Revista de Antropología*, and the Museo Antropológico–founded in 1865, 1874 and 1875 respectively–provided an established forum for the circulation of Lombroso's ideas in the late-1880s and beyond, and translations of Lombroso's books as well as those of the other Italian positivists began to appear in anthologies such as *Antropología y psiquiatría* (1893) and *La escuela de criminología positivista* (1894) (Maristany 1983: 366-73). In the year prior to the publication of *Nazarín*, Emilia Pardo Bazán wrote a series of articles titled "La nueva cuestión palpitante" (1894) describing, evaluating, and often refuting the theories of Lombroso as well as those of Max Nordau. In one such article Pardo Bazán describes the extent to which Lombroso's work had been disseminated: "El nombre de César Lombroso va siendo bastante conocido en España. Se le lee algo, se le cita más, se le empieza a traducir, y aunque no se le tradujese, las versiones francesas de sus obras le habían puesto ya al alcance de todos" (Pardo Bazán 1973: 1159). Maristany attributes this interest to the growth of the anarchist movement in Spain, the converging of the penal system with medical trends, public interest in crimes and a literary fascination with decadence (Maristany 1983: 362).

Given the preoccupations outlined above, it would hardly be an overstatement to say that a fear of darkened spaces, disorder and social Otherness haunted urban Madrid. It was an environment in which working-class slums provided "a mental landscape within which the middle class could recognize and articulate their own anxieties about urban existence" (Jones 1976: 151). Madrid was not only geographically mapped, as in the case of Castro's proposed expansion, but socially mapped also as discursive lines separating the middle and lower classes became more impenetrable. Through the discourses on public hygiene and criminality, the poor and working classes were pushed further to the periphery of Madrid society.

In the process of converting working-class migrants into social scapegoats, the discourses born out of a fear of urbanisation placed city-life and country-life in contradictory juxtaposition. The rural environment was idealized as a locus free of crime, disease and other urban problems, yet those who are blamed for these things came from this ideal place. The result–that there was no place left that can be idealized–was understandably troubling for Spaniards. As I plan to show in subsequent chapters, the tension between city and country also carries with it implications related to gender relations and ethnographic stereotyping. It is not uncommon to find such contradictions within a given discursive field. Such incongruities demonstrate the adaptability of discourse as a way of promoting a specific social strategy, in this case the primacy of bourgeois values.

CHAPTER 2

MAPPING CLASS IN *LA DESHEREDADA*

> ¡Dama por la figura, por la elegancia, por el vestido!... por el pensamiento y por las acciones, ¿qué era?... La sentencia es difícil.
> –Benito Pérez Galdós, *La desheredada*

IN the opening chapter of Galdós's 1881 novel *La desheredada* Isidora, the novel's protagonist, encounters a map of Spain hanging on the wall of an office in Madrid's municipal lunatic asylum, Leganés. The passage presents the reader with an early example of Isidora's tendency to be seduced by visual appearances: "¡Qué bonito era el mapa de España, todo lleno de rayas divisorias y compartimientos, de columnas de números que subían creciendo, de rengloncitos estadísticos que bajaban achicándose, de círculos y banderolas señalando pueblos, ciudades y villas!" (Pérez Galdós 2000a: 87). At first glance the passage seems fairly trivial. Her reaction, "¡Qué bonito!", implies a rather naïve attraction to visual form. But the subsequent description of the map, which emphasizes the delimiting impetus of cartography, suggests the image has a more significant meaning. The map's "rayas divisorias y compartimientos" recall the segregative nature of Castro's plan, whose own dividing lines were meant to keep society divided by class. Similarly, the columns of numbers "que subían" and the rows of statistics "que bajaban" both suggest the importance of relational values as well as the possibility of progress or regression. The map embodies the phenomena of social mobility and categorisation that characterise Madrid at the time. However, the fact that the map is located in an insane asylum reinforces the discussion in the previous chapter about contamination, chaos and the need for order. It also implies that charting the movements and classificatory trends of society can be not only complex, but wrought with illusions and contradictions.

The events described in *La desheredada* take place between 1872 and 1875, during a period when Madrid's middle class is still coming to grips with its newfound prominence. Suffering from a sense of unease, the middle class is characterised by a preoccupation with social distinction, that is, a simultaneous desire to join the ranks of the elite and a desire to draw away from the lower classes through material display. In this chapter I examine this phenomenon by focussing on the protagonist of *La desheredada*, Isidora Rufete, a young woman who believes that she is the illegitimate granddaughter of the Marquesa de Aransis. After arriving in Madrid from the country Isidora sets about trying to secure the life to which she feels entitled, all the while attempting to distance herself from her actual origins. At the heart of the story is the dilemma of determining social status in a society where such a thing is subject to the ebb-and-flow of consumer capitalism. The reader is frequently made to contemplate whether an individual's true identity is constructed by that individual or something determined by nature. Isidora's persona, especially her desire to distinguish herself from the *pueblo*, is best understood when viewed against the socio-economic dynamic that contributed to the middle class's hypersensitivity to the gaze, a hypersensitivity created by the popular concepts of distinction and *cursilería*. What eventually emerges from this examination is an alternative to the theories of natural nobility and constructed social identities, that Isidora's behaviour results from biological degeneracy. And while the images associated with prostitution, especially those that depict flow and excess, certainly suggest that Isidora's social pretensions are merely the quixotic fantasies of a degenerate woman, her ability to make an impression on even the most reliable judges of character implies that this conclusion is somehow inadequate.

Madrid as Spectacle

"Tan bullicioso, tan movible", that is how the narrator describes "aquel Madrid" that serves as the setting of *La desheredada* (Pérez Galdós 2000a: 170). With the spread of urbanisation, industrialization and consumer capitalism, everything (and everyone) in Madrid was in circulation. Economic conditions in the nineteenth century provided a greater degree of social mobility in Spain's major cities than had previously been experienced, and with this mobility came a greater sensitivity to one's visual identity. As the cumulative wealth of the middle class increased and that of the nobility decreased, formerly rigid class boundaries became permeable to a throng of social aspirants. These would-be social climbers sought inclusion in the arenas from which they had earlier been excluded and they marked their ascendancy by purchasing and displaying signs of wealth. American socio-economist Thorstein Veblen's definitive study of modern affluence, *The Theory of the Leisure Class* (1899), explains how social pretenders emulated the behaviour and fashion trends of the social tier directly above them:[1]

> In modern civilized communities the lines of demarcation between social classes have grown vague and transient, and wherever this happens the norm of reputability imposed by the upper class extends its coercive influence with but slight hindrance down through the social structure to the lowest strata. The result is that the members of each stratum accept as their ideal of decency the scheme of life in vogue in the next higher stratum, and bend their energies to live up to that ideal [...] at least in appearance. (Veblen 1990: 35)

Veblen's insistence on the primacy of appearance, as well as his frequent use of the adjective "conspicuous" to describe the spending patterns and behaviour of members of the leisure class and those hopeful of joining its ranks, highlights a visual dimension of social mobility. Only when viewed by others do the signs of social standing have any real value. Commenting specifically on Spain in the latter half of the nineteenth century, Stephanie Sieburth explains how Spanish society became hypersensitive to being seen: "The gaze of the Other is all-important. [...] Since wealth now counts as

---

[1] Thorstein Veblen was an American economist and sociologist writing at the end of the nineteenth and the beginning of the twentieth century. Veblen himself does not specify a cultural context for his work and though some of the ideas expressed in *Theory of the Leisure Class* are specifically derived from American society at the end of the nineteenth century, most of it is relevant to modern affluence in general (Calbraith 1973: xvi). For applications of Veblen's theories in the context of Spanish culture, see Jagoe (1994: 21) and Aldaraca (1991: 112-13).

much as title, and since wealth is a recent phenomenon, even for many of the upper bourgeoisie, the sense of having no identity other than one's representation in public is acute" (Sieburth 1994: 37). Scientific trends caused this sensitivity to visible identities to be more pronounced. The popularity of physiognomy, discussed in the previous chapter, transcended the sphere of the scientific community and became a subject of intense interest for virtually all members of the social body. Such phenomena prepared Madrid's residents to assess one another based on the most superficial of signs.

The type of social mimicry described by Veblen in the passage above encompasses everything from activities to possessions. If the members of the upper class frequented the theatre, so too would the upper middle class and, whenever possible, those below them. If the wealthy travelled about the city in private carriages, others, who perhaps could not afford to buy their own carriages, would rent them in order to be seen parading down the same streets. And when members of the upper classes adopted new styles of clothing, the other classes were sure to follow suit. Such instances of social mimicry are clearly depicted in *La desheredada* (Pérez Galdós 2000a: 133-35, 138, 188) as well as in Galdós's other novels of the same period such as *Tormento* and *La de Bringas*.

As the most readily available feature of one's visible identity, fashion became a significant medium for expressing and evaluating social status.[2] In his book *Fashioning the Bourgeoisie* (1994), Philippe Perrot explains the role of clothing in mapping out class boundaries:

> Sign or symbol, clothing affirms and reveals cleavages, hierarchies, and solidarities according to a code guaranteed and perpetuated by society and its institutions. The nineteenth-century bourgeoisie worked out an elaborate system of appearance, which reveals the importance it attached to clothing's signifying role as opposed to its functional role. This concern extended even to the most disadvantaged segments of the middle class who needed to distance themselves from the workers precisely because they were themselves so close to working-class. (Perrot 1994: 8)

---

[2] Historians and critics have long since recognised the importance of clothing as a "social discourse" that communicates status. By way of example see Georg Simmel's *The Philosophy of Fashion* (1905) and Diana Crane's *Fashion and its Social Agendas* (2000).

Perrot highlights two important aspects of the language of fashion. First is that while such judgements of taste may not cause class divisions, they certainly legitimate them. Secondly, Perrot contends that it was not enough for the bourgeoisie to adopt the styles of those above them. Social mobility is as much about getting away as it is about getting to and therefore the need of the middle classes to distance themselves from the lower levels of society is as intense as the desire to penetrate the upper ranks. Here Perrot seems to be echoing the words of German sociologist Georg Simmel, who argued that everyone, especially those residing in large cities, is caught between a contradictory desire to be included on the one hand, and to stand out on the other. "Fashion", he argued, "is nothing more than a particular instance among the many forms of life by the aid of which we seek to combine in a unified act the tendency towards social equalization with the desire for individual differentiation and variation" (Simmel 1997: 189). Neither Simmel nor Perrot are commenting directly on the fashion trends of Spain, which came mainly from foreign models, especially the French, but their conclusions are certainly applicable to nineteenth-century Spanish culture in which, according to Galdós's narrator, "es ley que todas las clases de la sociedad [...] vistan de la misma manera [...] hay un verdadero delirio en los pequeños por imitar el modo de presentarse de los grandes" (Pérez Galdós 2000a: 188). Fashion magazines, such as *El Correo de la Moda*, *La Moda de Madrid*, *Día de Moda* and *La Última Moda*, many of which contained illustrations of fashionably-clad women borrowed from magazines published in Paris, inundated Madrid during the second half of the century so that members of every class had knowledge of the latest styles, though not necessarily the means to follow them. The rising middle class was thus equipped to project their social aspirations through their visual identities.

Isidora's Quest for Distinction

In *La deheredada* Isidora exhibits an unwaivering desire for distinction. Whether in pointing out that she already possesses this highly desirable attribute, or in suggesting she will surely obtain it, the regularity with which the text refers to distinction indicates that the concept is of central importance.³ The term *distinction* is not particularly unusual in itself, but its use in the novel connotes more than the standard definitions contained in María Moliner's *Diccionario de uso del español*. Moliner defines *distinción* as: "Acción y efecto de distinguir"; and *distinguirse* as: "Hacerse notar por alguna cualidad o por tenerla en mayor grado que otros u otras cosas" (Moliner 1998: I, 1022). These basic definitions imply that one can just as easily distinguish oneself for something negative as one can for something positive, and also that distinction can be achieved in any realm. However, even a casual examination reveals that in *La desheredada* the term *distinción* is used in a fundamentally positive way and is limited to the social sphere.

Evidence that the word *distinción* had already achieved a specialized meaning by the 1880s can be seen in tracts by social commentators, such as Rosario de Acuña's condemnation of conspicuous consumption entitled *El lujo en los pueblos rurales* (1882). In this short book the word *distinción* appears in italics, suggesting it is being used in an unusual or specific way. Whereas the term *distinción* is depicted as something desirable in *La desheredada*, in social commentaries like that of Acuña *distinción* is clearly something to be shunned. In fact, the term is used in *El lujo en los pueblos rurales* to connote pretentiousness and other negative aspects of luxurious spending. As an example of the narrator's positive use of the term in *La desheredada*, by contrast, one can turn to the description of Isidora during her interview with the Marquesa: "La hermosura de la joven, su distinción innegable, su modo de vestir, sencillo y honesto, hicieron en la noble dama profunda impresión" (Pérez Galdós 2000a: 268). By placing the quality of distinction on the same level as beauty and attractive dress the text communicates the desirability of distinction. Furthermore, that someone as prominent as the Marquesa would experience a "profunda impresión" as a consequence of Isidora's indisputable distinction suggests that distinction is related to a high level of social achievement or status. This is confirmed a short time later when Isidora's uncle encourages her to realize the potential of her noble lineage and "[hacer] lo

---

³ Galdós's interest in the idea of distinction extends beyond issues of class, to the arena of religion for instance. See Kathy Bacon's *Negotiating Sainthood: Distinction, Cursilería and Saintliness in Spanish Novels* (2007) for a discussion of religiosity and distinction in the novels of Galdós and other nineteenth-century Spanish writers.

posible por distinguirte de los demás" (Pérez Galdós 2000a: 283). Whereas the Marquesa's opinion is unclear as to the origin of Isidora's distinction–the term is sandwiched in between the concept of beauty, which is naturally occurring, and fashion taste, which is learned–the advice offerred by Isidora's uncle clearly suggests that distinction is something one must work at.

Pierre Bourdieu's classic study *Distinction: A Social Critique of the Judgement of Taste* (1979) provides further insights into the idea of distinction, taking into account its many nuances and social implications. According to Bourdieu, distinction is a marker of class, a type of "cultural nobility" (Bourdieu 2003: 2-3), and like any marker it must be perceptible to have meaning. What makes Bourdieu's work pioneering is that he goes beyond the realm of quantitative signs of distinction and questions the qualitative basis of those signs. One's education and judgements of taste become symbolic capital and are just as important in determining status, if not more so, than the actual wealth one possesses. In identifying the role played by symbolic capital in achieving distinction, Bourdieu implies that it is not simply down to what an individual has, but also how they choose it and use it. This ability to use symbolic capital effectively is what Bourdieu calls habitus. Habitus is a key term in Bourdieu's work that he defines as a "scheme of perception", or the capacity for making judgments of taste (Bourdieu 2003: 100-02), and it is subject to the influences of environment, class, and even the tastes of other classes. While Bourdieu clearly shows that habitus results from a process of social conditioning, the link between class structure and actual behaviour is subtle enough that the latter is often mistaken for an inherent characteristic of the former.

Bourdieu argues that everyone, whether they realise it or not, is engaged in a continuous quest for distinction, a quest he refers to as a "classification struggle":

> What is at stake in the struggles about the meaning of the social world is power over the classificatory schemes and systems which are the basis of the representations of the groups and therefore of their mobilization and demobilization. (Bourdieu 2003: 479)

Here Bourdieu's comment about the garnering of power through the attainment and exercise of cultural capital recalls Foucault's theory of the role of discourse in the distribution and implementation of power. For Bourdieu, the expression of taste becomes a jockeying for social position and power. In this sense judgements of taste are both reflective and constitutive (reproductive) of the social hierarchy: "Taste classifies, and it classifies the classifier. Social subjects, classified by their classifications, distinguish themselves by the distinctions they make" (Bourdieu 2003: 6). This fortification of class distinctions by the distinctions one makes in daily life is nothing short of a retranslation of the hierarchy of classes. Within the social dynamic of self-perpetuating class boundaries described by Bourdieu the frontiers between classes are therefore mobile, shifting with trends in taste. Like the physical boundaries of the city, which were re-mapped following urbanisation, so too were symbolic social boundaries re-mapped in a way that would allow those with economic capital to purchase symbolic capital and thus attain social distinction. Clothing, jewels and carriages became the walls, gardens and parks separating the various classes from one another while the discourses of fashion and taste laid down the lines.

But the quest for distinction is not without its stumbling blocks, and perhaps no symbolic barrier was as effective in undermining this quest as *cursilería*. According to Moliner, *cursi* "se dice de lo que, pretendiendo ser elegante, refinado o exquisito, resulta afectado, remilgado o ridículo" (Moliner 1998: I, 847). The term *cursi* and its variants are a constant frustration to translators, who invariably conjure up words such as "kitsch", "affected", "pretentious" or "vulgar" without entirely capturing the meaning of the word. But this lack of a suitable equivalent evinces the fact that *cursilería* is a unique product of the economic and social factors of nineteenth-century Spanish culture that were discussed above. According to Noël Valis, these English translations of *cursi* "merely point to its symptoms, not to its underlying condition, cause or context" (Valis 2002: 3). It is, after all, only in a society with permeable class boundaries that "el querer y no poder", as popular imagination defines *cursilería*, is even fathomable. In a statement that recalls Veblen's and Simmel's previously mentioned comments about social mimicry, the narrator of *La desheredada* puts it as follows: "la cursilería [...] es un modo social propio de todas las clases, y que nace del prurito de competencia con la clase inmediatamente superior" (Pérez Galdós 2000a: 224). The terms *cursi* and *cursilería* are invariably pejorative, and given the extreme anxiety surrounding the legitimacy of social standing and the role of others in validating that standing through an appraising gaze, branding another as *cursi* was as much about legitimizing one's own social standing as it was about destroying theirs: "the epithet of inadequacy and undesirable transformation becomes a barrier between subject and other, a defensive screen that barely covers [the accuser's] own cursilería" (Valis 2002: 43). Depending on whether one is labelling or being labelled, *cursi* serves as a way of mapping barriers between legitimate and illegitimate by excluding those who are *cursi*.

Isidora's pursuit of nobility traverses this exceedingly thin road between distinction and *cursilería*. *La desheredada* contains several allusions that suggest Isidora may be of noble birth, yet ultimately this possibility is undone by examples of her *cursilería*. Early on in the novel Isidora still subscribes to a now defunct social mythology in which outward appearance accurately reflects social status. Notable examples of Isidora's obsession with visual indicators of distinction appear in the fourth chapter when she and Augusto Miquis visit the Museo del Prado, the Parque del Buen Retiro and the Paseo de la Castellana. Their day out begins at the Prado, and it is here that Isidora first formulates an idea that will become something of a maxim for the young Manchega: that members of differing social classes should not occupy the same social spaces. She asks Miquis if the Prado is a place where members of "el pueblo" are permitted to enter and much to her dismay she learns that they are (Pérez Galdós 2000a: 117). The question reveals her belief that "los del pueblo" should be excluded from areas where those of greater distinction socialize. By voicing her concern about "los del pueblo," which even in its phrasing accentuates the idea of otherness, Isidora demonstrates the differentiating urge in her bid for distinction.

When the action moves to the Retiro it becomes apparent that this belief is borne of anxiety as well as pride. In the park Isidora suppresses her initial impulse to run about, which she describes as a "candoroso salvajismo," and makes a mental note to bring gloves and a parasol during her next visit. Her strong desire to imitate those "damas y caballeros" walking about the park "con guantes, sombrilla, bastón" (Pérez Galdós 2000a: 118) is matched only by her dislike of anything associated with "el pueblo." After a short time looking at the animals in the Casa de Fieras Isidora again articulates her conviction that social space and social status are somehow connected: "Esto es espectáculo para el pueblo –dijo con desdén–. Vámonos de aquí" (Pérez Galdós 2000a: 125). She clearly does not consider herself to be part of "el pueblo". But in addition to highlighting her inflated sense of self-importance, Isidora's comment serves as an allusion to the state of Madrid in the post-revolutionary period. Like other significant properties, the ownership of the Prado and the Retiro passed from the Crown to public hands following the revolution of 1868. Given the setting of this passage, early in 1872, such locations would have still borne a certain sense of transitional ambiguity; they now belonged to the people and yet they had, for centuries, been the playgrounds of the aristocracy. Within this type of transitional space, where members of various classes intermingle, yet the space itself is associated with the aristocracy, the impulse to distinguish oneself is possibly more intense. Isidora's belief that she belongs to that noble class inspires her to search out exclusive spaces, which allow for a physical separation between herself and those from whom she already feels socially distinct.[4] She once again reiterates her disdain for "el contacto del pueblo" when, upon leaving the Casa de Fieras, they stop to have lunch: "¡Qué ordinario es esto! –exclamó, sin poderse contener–. Vaya, que me traes a unos sitios [...] Esto no es para mí" (Pérez Galdós 2000a: 127). Isidora constantly eschews situations and people whom she perceives to be "vulgar" or "ordinario" (Pérez Galdós 2000a: 141), and clings to those who have some connection with the ordered and closed world of the *ancien régime*. This is clearly illustrated when she receives her first letter from Joaquín Pez, whose title of *El marqués viudo de Saldeoro* immediately inspires a "desdén muy vivo" toward Miquis, whom she suddenly sees as "tan ordinario" (Pérez Galdós 2000a: 140-41).

Isidora is brutally obvious in her quest for distinction, and consequently her fear of acting like, looking like or being near "los del pueblo" appears exaggerated. Her anxiety demonstrates how distinction is not so much a quality as it is a relational property:

> Each class condition is defined, simultaneously, by its intrinsic properties and by the relational properties which it derives from its position in the system of class conditions, which is also a sys-

---

[4] Later that same day when Miquis invites her to attend the theatre her first reaction is to ask whether the Teatro Real is a place where "personas decentes" congregate (Pérez Galdós 2000a: 138).

tem of differences, differential positions, i.e., by everything which distinguishes it from what it is not and especially from everything it is opposed to; social identity is defined and asserted through difference. (Bourdieu 2003: 170-72)

For individuals to achieve distinction they must not only assimilate the practices and appearances of the social elites, they must distance themselves in every way from those below them. As Isidora shows, this is a style of comportment verging on caricature because of its immediacy of reaction and exaggeration.

This desire is arguably most acute among members of the petite bourgeoisie, like Isidora, who find themselves precariously perched near the edge of a social boundary, liable to slip into the nearby depths of the lower class unless they can gain a more sure footing within the middle class. That she believes herself to belong to a noble family only intensifies her discomfort of being so close to the lower class. She compensates by seeking out luxurious objects. She gazes longingly at everything on display in the shop windows and even indulges on a few personal items. So powerful is her desire to possess the symbols of status that it is described as a need rather than a want: "necesitaba comprar algo, poca cosa..." (Pérez Galdós 2000a: 173). Isidora gets caught up in this desire to spend partly because of the sense of agency it gives, something we see more clearly with Rosalía in *La de Bringas* (Pérez Galdós 2001a: 236). But it is also the case that such items make Isidora feel that she belongs to the upper classes. As she strolls by the objects for sale she comes across some elegant fabrics and jewels. The description of these objects, focalised through Isidora, is significant in that they are not practical items that a lower middle-class woman might need but articles of adornment, including fine fabrics for clothing:

> ¡Cuántas invenciones del capricho, cuántas pompas reales o superfluidades llamativas! Aquí, las soberbias telas, tan variadas y ricas que la naturaleza misma no ofreciera mayor riqueza y variedad; allí, las joyas que resplandecen, asombradas de su propio mérito. (Pérez Galdós 2000a: 172)

A prime example of goods meant for a leisure class, this passage emphasizes both their impracticality and their visual quality. Words like "capricho", "superfluidades" and "soberbias" leave little doubt as to what social strata these fabrics and jewels are intended for, while the word "mérito" conveys a sense of legitimacy, as if such objects were inherently worthy of appreciation. Absent is any mention of the texture or even the smell of the fabrics; we are simply made to contemplate their visual impact, described as "pompas", "llamativas" and "asombr[osas]". These fabrics are clearly not destined to become clothes for cooking or cleaning, but robes whose sole purpose is to communicate status. Georg Simmel, writing on the subject of adornment, notes that luxurious fabrics and jewels are the most common materials used for this purpose:

> [Adornment] is a synthesis of the individual's having and being; it thus transforms mere possession into the sensuous and emphatic perceivability of the individual himself. This is not true of ordinary dress which, neither in respect of having nor of being, strikes one as an individual particularity; only the fancy dress, and above all, jewels, which gather the personality's value and significance of radiation as if in a focal point, allow the mere *having* of the person to become a visible quality of its *being*. (Simmel 1997: 207)

As Isidora examines the materials she experiences a sort of false memory syndrome: "Más que como objetos enteramente nuevos para ella, los veía como si fueran recobrados después de un largo destierro" (Pérez Galdós 2000a: 173). Isidora here raises questions about the origin of tastes. The passage suggests that taste is inherent, something one is born with and therefore not something that one can feign or even acquire with wealth, an idea Isidora states explicitly in a later episode: "El buen gusto nace con la persona" (Pérez Galdós 2000a: 216).

Isidora's mysterious feeling of familiarity in the presence of such costly objects of adornment is one of many instances where the text implies that she may actually be the Marquesa de Aransis's granddaughter, as she claims to be. Other allusions include the papers she possesses, the uncertainty of Joaquín about the validity of her story, or the fact that the Marquesa's daughter did give birth to a boy and a girl roughly the same ages as Isidora and Mariano. For much of Part I the text leaves the reader in doubt as to the facts of Isidora's parentage. Not until the chapter titled "Anagnórisis" is there a strong, though not necessarily definitive, indication that Isidora's claim is baseless.

However, lurking behind the idea that Isidora's fondness for luxury is innate is an alternative explanation that taste is not inherent but learned, a possibility in line with Bourdieu's notion of habitus. The fact that Isidora often corrects her inclinations to mirror those of Madrid's elite–as occurs in the Retiro when she stifles her desire to run about after seeing proper ladies and gentlemen behaving circumspectly as they stroll through the park (Pérez Galdós 2000a: 118)–would suggest that her behaviour and tastes are being established through imitation and not naturally occuring, nor even through the conditioning process of habitus that Bourdieu describes. This interpretation is supported by a letter she receives from her uncle who tells her to "observar lo que hacen los demás para aprenderlo y hacerlo tú misma" (Pérez Galdós 2000a: 282). If the reader accepts as legitimate Isidora's vague sense of nostalgia for elegant objects as an innate judgment of taste they may be more inclined to believe in her professed nobility. However, the narrator's consistently critical view of Isidora never really permits the reader to do so. The likelier interpretation is that taste is obtained through experience, a theory that leaves Isidora's impression seeming not only unsubstantiated but ridiculous, the mere musings of a deluded *cursi*.

Indeed, Isidora's belief that she is inherently inclined to make judgments of taste on a par with the elite of Madrid is undermined by various instances of *cursilería*. This is clearly shown early on in the narrative when she and Miquis stand and watch the spectacle of people riding or walking up and down the Castellana. The spectacle sends Isidora into a state of pseudo-mystical ecstasy (Pérez Galdós 2000a: 134), but only provokes a bemused attack from Miquis who delivers a classic denunciation of Madrid's social aspirants:

> Como cada cual tiene ganas rabiosas de alcanzar una posición superior, principia por aparentarla. Las improvisaciones estimulan el apetito. Lo que no se tiene se pide, y no hay un solo número uno que no quiere elevarse a la categoría de dos. El dos se quiere hacer pasar por tres; el tres hace creer que es cuatro; el cuatro dice: "Si yo soy cinco", y así sucesivamente. (Pérez Galdós 2000a: 137)

Miquis's stinging criticism of those parading down the Paseo de la Castellana is succinct, if not particularly unusual; the spectacle of

carriages, men on horseback and pedestrians parading past one another on the Castellana was frequently fodder for newspaper caricaturists and *costumbrista* authors. It is significant that this viewpoint is expressed by Miquis, a medical student/doctor. As a man steeped in the certitudes of science Miquis is a logical anchor point in the narrative, someone who will be swayed only by facts and not by false appearances. By placing this criticism of visual pretence in the mouth of a privileged focaliser Galdós reveals the text's underlying bias against social aspiration (one that will be stated in no uncertain terms in the novel's final chapter titled "Moraleja"), and in so doing situates the reader in a position where they are less likely to sympathize with Isidora.[5] Whereas Miquis sees "lo que todo el mundo veía" when he looks at the masses on the Castellana, Isidora, wanting to believe the spectacle before her, "veía algo más de lo que vemos todos" (Pérez Galdós 2000a: 133). Miquis identifies them as "cursi" and their appearances as mere "trampas, fanatismo, ignorancia, presunción" (Pérez Galdós 2000a: 135). Isidora, on the other hand, accepts the spectacle at face value and accuses Miquis of being "ordinario [...] grosero, salvaje, pedante" (Pérez Galdós 2000a: 135). Her inability to recognize *cursilería* is itself an indication of her *cursilería*. She wants to rise, but does not observe it as a general phenomenon for to do so would be recognizing that she is like everyone else. While the narrator stops short of actually calling Isidora a *cursi*, there are numerous examples of her bad taste and pretentiousness so that her *cursilería* is easily recognizable.[6] As proof of her bad taste, the text describes her inability to distinguish between actual elegance and objects of inferior quality: "Nada veía que no fuera para ella precioso, seductor, magnífico o por cualquier

---

[5] A similar thing occurs with the narrator. Although the narrator's social status is not made explicitly clear as it is in the case of *La de Bringas* or *Fortunata y Jacinta*, the fact that he uses Miquis as an intermediary when obtaining information about Isidora, and his use of a disparaging tone when describing members of the lower class (see, for instance, the description of Melchor Relimpio's servant (Pérez Galdós 2000a: 364), allude to a somewhat elevated position. Furthermore, the reliability of the narrator is not really called into question as occurs with other Galdosian narrators.

[6] Joaquín does refer to Isidora as a "cursilona" (Pérez Galdós 2000a: 237) in a scene that has echoes in a later Galdós novel, *La de Bringas*, when Rosalía learns that her social mentor, Milagros, once referred to Rosalía as "una cursi": "Rosalía se quedó petrificada. Aquella frase la hería en lo más vivo de su alma. Puñalada igual no había recibido nunca" (Pérez Galdós 2001a: 292). For both Isidora and Rosalía being called *cursi* is the harshest possible insult because their entire existence is revolved around an illusion of social distinction.

concepto interesante, y hasta un carro de muertos que encontró al salir de la casa, más que por fúnebre, le chocó por suntuoso" (Pérez Galdós 2000a: 170). In keeping with Bourdieu's previously cited comment about the classifying power of taste, Isidora's inability to distinguish is precisely that which distinguishes her as *cursi*.

THE STRENGTH OF BLOOD

La desheredada contains a number of passages stating that Isidora's character–everything from her taste in clothes to her penchant for philanthropy–is directly linked to her genealogy. Such a proposition is especially timely when one takes into account the medical theories being put forward at the time with regard to heredity. The two and a half decades preceding the publication of *La desheredada* were decisive years in the formulation of degeneration theory, witnessing the publication of Bénédict Morel's *Traité des dégénérescences physiques, intellectuelles et morales de l'espèce humaine et des causes qui produisent ces variétés maladives* (1857), Henry Maudsley's *Physiology and Pathology of Mind* (1867) and *Body and Mind* (1870) and Cesare Lombroso's *L'uomo delinquente* (1876). Daniel Pick defines the degenerate–as outlined in Morel's work–as "a given individual whose physiognomic contours could be traced out and distinguished from the healthy" (Pick 1989: 9). Morel was heavily influenced by Lavater's theory of physiognomy and subscribed to the same connection between exterior form and inner nature (Carlson 1985: 127). According to Morel, the degenerate displayed signs and symptoms of his or her degeneracy, which included a vast range of physical abnormalities that Morel called physical stigmata. As interest in psychopathological disorders intensified, so too did the nosological accuracy with which it was thought that physical signs of degeneracy could be identified. Some of the more common stigmata included facial tics, epilepsy, migraines, visual problems, impotence and eating disorders, which in turn prefigured or coincided with psychic disorders such as idiocy, insanity, eccentricity and moral delinquency (Carlson 1985: 127-28). Morel posited a critical link between degeneracy and heredity, arguing that degeneracy could be passed from parent to child. Furthermore, his concept of heredity was progressive, meaning that not only was a bad trait transmitted to offspring but also that with each passing generation the evil influence became greater. Morel's general theory was further developed, and in some instances modified, by the likes of Maudsley, Francis Galton, and Lombroso.

As the previous chapter's discussion about urbanisation and the problems surrounding lower-class neighbourhoods indicated, environment was also considered a contributing factor to degeneracy. While some experts may have remained entirely committed to only biological or environmental explanations, most recognized that a combination of theories provided the most convincing (and convenient) explanation for deviancy and thus argued that the deviant behaviour of a born degenerate would be uncovered, accentuated or intensified by living in squalid urban centres (Rivière Gómez 1994: 39). This combination of emphases gave the dominant classes, who were responsible for the dissemination of degeneration theory, greater power by justifying dividing practices based on both biological and environmental factors.

In *La desheredada* Galdós refuses to privilege one position over the other, especially in Part I of the novel, floating both biology and social conditioning as viable explanations for Isidora's trajectory. This positional ambiguity enhances the ambiguity surrounding her true identity, leaving the reader wondering and more sensitive to possible clues about the matter. One such clue comes in the initial chapter in the form of a physical description. The character described is Tomás Rufete who may or may not be her biological father. In the following description of Rufete we see many indicators that suggest degeneracy:

> [El padre de Isidora] es uno de esos hombres que han llegado a perder la normalidad de la fisonomía, y con ella, la inscripción aproximada de la edad. ¿Hállase en el punto central de la vida, o en miserable decrepitud? La movilidad de sus facciones y el llamear de sus ojos, ¿anuncian exaltado ingenio, o desconsoladora imbecilidad? No es fácil decirlo. (Pérez Galdós 2000a: 68)

By formulating the description as a series of questions, the narrator invites the reader to assess Rufete in the same way the asylum doctor reads the patient's corporeal clues before doubling his medication: "lee brevemente en su extraviada fisonomía, en sus negras pupilas, en el caído labio" (Pérez Galdós 2000a: 69). The double reference to "fisonomía" in these citations is significant as the term would have stood out given the veritable physiognomic craze of the nineteenth century. By constructing the description of Rufete as a series of two-pronged questions, each of which alludes to contradictory interpretations, the passage raises the issue of whether an objective assessment is possible, a doubt that is reiterated by the narrator's conclusion that "no es fácil decirlo".

But if the tone in the above passage communicates a certain degree of ambiguity concerning the reliability of reading appearances, the narrator immediately shifts to a more clinical gaze as he continues the description:

> Tiene la cabeza casi totalmente exhausta de pelo, la barba escasa, entrecana y afeitada a trozos, como un prado a medio segar. El labio superior demasiado largo y colgante, parece haber crecido y ablandádose recientemente, y no cesa de agitarse con nerviosos temblores, que dan a su boca cierta semejanza con el hocico gracioso del conejo royendo berzas. Es pálido su rostro, la piel papirácea, las piernas flacas, la estatura corta, ligeramente corva la espalda. (Pérez Galdós 2000a: 68)

The tone here is noticeably different. Gone are the questions and in their place are apparently straightforward details. The paucity of verbs in the first couple of lines diminishes the narrative quality of the passage and instead gives it a pictorial feel, as if it were a specimen under the microscope of a scrutinizing doctor who simply observes and names objects without specifying any relation between them. The subject's baldness, his sparse beard, enlarged and trembling upper lip and decrepit stature are classic signs of degeneracy, and even the comparison to a rabbit, while seemingly innocent, is a common trope of physiognomic and degeneration theory texts which use such analogies in order to highlight a degenerate's bestial nature. Added to this is the fact that the person being described is a patient in Leganés, the insane asylum outside Madrid. Through a combination of setting, physical abnormality and perspective, Galdós gives the reader every reason to believe Rufete's degeneracy is not a matter of conjecture, but an objective fact confirmed by the narrator's clinical gaze.

Tomás Rufete is not the only one whose degeneracy is communicated in such an obvious manner. Isidora's younger brother, Mariano is similarly described as exhibiting the behaviour and bearing the characteristic stigmata of the degenerate type. Predisposed to violence (Pérez Galdós 2000a: 160, 473), vagrancy (2000a: 258, 370), anti-social behaviour (Pérez Galdós 2000a: 470), physical decadence (Pérez Galdós 2000a: 437, 453, 469), and criminal conduct (Pérez Galdós 2000a: 440), Mariano, described as "bruto" (Pérez Galdós 2000a: 251, 256) and "salvaje" (Pérez Galdós 2000a: 250, 261), possesses every quality of the atavistic, degenerate type. What is more, the narrator suggests that Mariano is this way "por naturaleza" (Pérez Galdós 2000a: 370) rather than being a victim of circumstance. Such references to his brutal temperament being innate abound and support the view that criminals are born as such. As J. M. Escuder wrote in 1881, the same year Galdós published *La desheredada*: "hay hombres que nacen criminales como los lobos nacen lobos" (Escuder 1881: 34).

Given the emphasis on heredity by degeneration theorists, and the core theme of inheritance in the novel, the reader will inevitably connect the genealogical dots. Eventually the filial link between Mariano and Tomás Rufete becomes all too clear, as Mariano's descent into madness recalls Henry Maudsley's statement that insanity comes from "where his parent got it–from the insane strain of the family stock: the strain which, as the old saying was, runs in the blood" (Maudsley 1979: 47). It is perhaps an understatement to say that this conclusion raises serious doubts about Isidora's claim that she and Mariano are not the actual offspring of Rufete. Because degeneration was believed to be inherited the logical inference is that Rufete is, in fact, the actual father of Mariano and, accordingly, of Isidora. Her own inability to accept reality and the fact that she gives birth to a degenerate son with macrocephaly make this conclusion all the more credible.

Like the proponents of degeneration theory, Isidora and her uncle believe that a person's blood somehow communicates one's true identity. Isidora tries to persuade the Marquesa de Aransis that she is her granddaughter by arguing that, "La voz de la sangre me ha llamado hace tiempo" (Pérez Galdós 2000a: 265), while Isidora's uncle makes a similar assertion as to the power of blood: "Yo tengo gran fe", he writes in a letter to his niece, "en la fuerza de la sangre" (Pérez Galdós 2000a: 281). Both statements are meant as affirmations that Isidora's supposed nobility is somehow contained within her blood, something passed on from generation to generation, an idea echoed by Isidora on a number of occasions when she argues that her tastes, looks and sentiments are down to her noble lineage.

But both Isidora and her uncle are clearly situated on the fringe of reality as shown by a number of transparent associations between them and Don Quijote. Raised by her uncle in La Mancha, Isidora is prone to self-destructive fantasies and her uncle's surname is Quijano-Quijada, a clear reference to Don Quijote whose surname is said to be either Quijano or Quijada. As a result of their undeniable quixotism, their views about Isidora's noble blood, and about anything else, are undermined. But statements made in favour of the theory of degeneration, which similarly argues that the strength of blood is a telling sign of one's true character, are placed in the mouths of more authoritative figures like Miquis and the narrator. As a result, the reader may be more inclined to see degeneracy as something inherited while aristocratic tendencies would be viewed as something acquired through experience, a particularly apt rationalization given the socio-economic context in which social mobility was increasingly a matter of wealth and not birth. Both Isidora and her uncle believe that nobility is carried in the blood, yet they fail to see, or perhaps intentionally ignore, what this "gran fe en la fuerza de la sangre" includes: the prospect that her inability to rise is the result of an undesirable hereditary pedigree. Isidora's blood may be calling to her, but what it says is not what she wants to hear.

PROSTITUTION AND FLOW

In *La desheredada* ubiquitous images, both literal and metaphoric, of flow and drainage, validate the judgment that Isidora's inherited degeneracy will ultimately sabotage her quest for distinction. Labanyi argues that such imagery provides an economic context by "conveying the fluidity and fluctuations of the market-place, as distinctions break down and goods flow in an unceasing stream" (Labanyi 2000: 110). This may be true, but the images of flow and drainage, which do indeed suggest a break down of distinctions, also relate to the socio-medical discourse of the time period. On the one hand, urban planners like Castro agreed that the continuous circulation of fluids, such as sewage and water, had a direct bearing on the collective health of the community, just as medical experts argued that the circulation of bodily fluids was vital to each individual's physical wellbeing and even the wellbeing of the social body. As shown in the previous chapter, the miasmatic theory of disease was still widely accepted and stagnant water, thought to be a potent source of noxious miasmas, was described by hygienist López de la Vega (in a text Galdós possessed in his personal library) as "el primero y más mortal enemigo de la salud pública" (López de la Vega 1878: 20). By contrast, the circulation of water was considered salubrious (Fuentes Peris 2003: 37-38).

Doctors and hygienists applied similar principles to the human body, insisting that the unimpeded flow of blood and even seminal fluid was healthy while blockages only led to trouble. Physicians promoted certain foods, taking emetics or subjecting the body to leeches and bloodletting to ensure the healthy circulation of blood. Abstinence, according to seventeenth-century medical expert Giovanni Sinibaldi, produced "spermatic fevers" while regular sexual intercourse was an effective cure for a number of ailments (Comfort 1967: 24). Similarly, many eighteenth-century physicians were of the opinion that "coition lightens the body and removes many ills of the mind, [...] semen too long hoarded turns to poison and produces giddiness and clouding of the sight" (Comfort 1967: 70). Inheriting this tradition, hygienists in the nineteenth century argued that avoiding abstinence was just as important to a healthy body as avoiding the depleting effects of excessive sex. Even as late as 1902, Spanish doctors claimed that using prostitutes was "preferible a la abstinencia completa" (Bayo 1902: 42).

While the circulation of seminal fluid is ostensibly an issue of personal health, the established medical discourse suggested the issue also had implications for the welfare of society. Any impediment to the healthy flow of seminal fluid, it seemed, could potentially lead to an excess of male desire that would place women in danger. Society was in need of an outlet, a way of draining away this excess of male desire, and prostitution was considered the most viable solution. Parent-Duchâtelet, whose work *De la prostitution dans la ville de Paris* (1836) was partially translated into Spanish in 1880, the year before the publication of *La desheredada*, was not only a major proponent of state-regulated prostitution but was also a leading expert of the municipal sewage system.[7] He viewed this

---

[7] Rivière Gómez singles out the works of the Frenchman as having a considerable impact on Spanish writers working on the social implications of prostitution (Rivière Gómez 1994: 39).

dual interest as part of the same project, as both were concerned with channeling deleterious elements away from the healthy social body. Prostitution, he argued, was a necessary evil given the social climate of urban life: "Prostitutes are inevitable, where men live together in large concentrations, as drains and refuse dumps [...] they contribute to the maintenance of social order and harmony" (cited in Corbin 1990: 4). His argument was based on the notion that prostitution functions as a "seminal drain," siphoning away excess male desire in the way that sewers drain away hazardous waste. Otherwise "the man who has desires will pervert your daughters and servant girls", Parent-Duchâtelet warned, "he will sow discord in the home" (cited in Corbin 1990: 4). Parent-Duchâtelet was not alone in his reasoning. Ciro Bayo, quoting William Lecky, states that prostitution is both "el más alto grado del vicio" and "la égida de la virtud" (Bayo 1902: 42). "Sin ella", he continues, "muchas familias [...] veríanse en riesgo de mancillarse. Esa institución vil y depravada, satisface las pasiones que, de otra manera, llenarían la sociedad de deshonra y vilipendio" (Bayo 1902: 42). Ironically, Isidora's claim to nobility is built upon a breakdown of this safety valve, which protects "respectable" women from seduction, rape, unwanted pregnancy and venereal disease (assuming that prostitution was regulated and not clandestine). As the illegitimate offspring of the Marquesa's daughter, Isidora would have been the byproduct of excess desire that overflowed because it was not properly diverted.

Another common image associated with prostitution and flow is that of parasitism. In her study of prostitution in nineteenth-century Madrid, Aurora Rivière Gómez describes attitudes toward prostitutes as being comparable to the attitudes toward other "seres inferiores en la escala evolutiva", such as criminals and beggars—"eran [...] distintas manifestaciones de un único fenómeno: el parasitismo" (1994: 44). As far as host/parasite interactions go, Madrid's relationship with prostitution was "una especie de relación simbiótica" (Rivière Gómez 1994: 45). This distinction between types of parasites, those that simply deplete nourishment versus those that drain away dangerous excess, is incongruously embodied in the novel in the form of the leech. Used in medicine for bloodletting and restoring a healthy equilibrium to the body's circulation, leeches would have served as an ideal example of parasitism as a healthy corrective. In the novel, however, the references to leeches connote the very opposite of symbiosis, and what is more they have nothing to do with prostitution. Instead, the allusions to leeches refer to members of the upper classes who live comfortably at the expense of the working class.[8] Such references spew forth from the mouth of the socialist Juan Bou who incessantly condemns the "sanguijuelas del país, que chupan la sangre del obrero" (Pérez Galdós 2000a: 329). This imagery of parasitic drainage becomes all the more ironic when one considers the previously discussed notion that prostitution protected these upper and middle class leeches by maintaining a corrective flow of seminal fluid/male desire.

Prostitutes may have been tolerated as necessary, but they were still viewed with contempt. Rivière Gómez's earlier comment about prostitutes being seen as "seres inferiores" reflects a common belief at the time that prostitutes constituted a degenerate class of women: "la mujer prostituta era [...] una enferma, una anormal, la víctima de una constitución orgánica *degenerada*" (Rivière Gómez 1994: 43). This attitude that the prostitute represents the epitome of female degeneracy gained merit following the publication of Cesare Lombroso's "Imbecilidad moral en la mujer ladrona y prostituta" (1881) and later in *La donna delinquente* (1892) and *La mujer criminal, la prostituta y la mujer normal* (1893). Given the fact that Galdós makes a strong case for the degeneracy argument by pointing out the Rufete family's physical, mental and moral decadence from the very beginning of the novel, it is difficult not to agree with Isidora when she explains her decision to become a prostitute as "mi destino" (Pérez Galdós 2000a: 5000). Such a statement recalls Isidora's and her uncle's misplaced but not mistaken faith in "la fuerza de la sangre".

Prostitution was not the only female illness discussed by social critics of the nineteenth century and depicted in *La desheredada*. When Isidora is referred to figuratively as an "enferma" by Miquis and by the narrator (Pérez Galdós 2000a: 388, 398, 494), it is a reference to both her prostitution as well as her love of *lujo*. *Lujo*, which economist Antonio María Segovia described in 1869 as "el gasto superfluo e improductivo, sostenido por mera ostentación, o

---

[8] The one exception to this would be Isidora's aunt, Encarnación, whose nickname is *Sanguijuelera* because she sells leeches in her shop. Her thrift and good work ethic imply an economic dynamic that is based on healthy flow (Labanyi 2000: 119).

desproporcionado a los recursos de quien le costea" (cited in Aldaraca 1991: 100), is ostensibly a figurative illness, but this language of disease is so constant in anti-*lujo* discourse that there must have been considerable anxiety about it, especially in light of the hygiene craze discussed in the previous chapter. The following comment made by Segovia, in which he acuses women of being the primary carriers of this particular disease, is typical of the medically-charged language used to condemn the love of luxury:

> Son más frecuentes en las personas de vuestro sexo los casos del hidrópico frenesí del lujo. Y me atrevo a decir más todavía: las mujeres, y solamente las mujeres, son las que propagan ese funesto contagio, así como también son ellas las únicas que pueden contener el torrente de tan pernicioso desenfreno. (cited in Aldaraca 1991: 104).

Segovia's comment supports the popular belief that *lujo* was primarily a problem among women. Acuña, for instance, describes *lujo* as a cancer of urban life: "Esta carcoma, este mal invasor, repugnante siempre en los grandes centros de las naciones" (Acuña 1882: 5-6). While Acuña paints a picture of invasiveness, Segovia's choice of analogies is perhaps more apt given that *hidropesía* is the harmful accumulation of fluid that cannot be discharged, that is, that flow is impeded within the body, and his description of *lujo* as a "torrente de tan pernicioso desenfreno" reiterates this idea of flow and excess. Typical of the anti-*lujo* discourse, which represents *lujo* as an imbalance, this passage depicts an excess of desire overflowing in the form of material finery.

In discussing the dangers of *lujo* Acuña describes it as a desire driven by passions–"apasionamiento ridículo" (Acuña 1882: 28) and "pasión hacia las apariencias" (Acuña 1882: 29)–and she even argues that *lujo* transforms the home from a "santuario de Dios" into an "apeadero de los vicios y recinto de las pasiones" (Acuña 1882: 28-29). By repeating the term "pasión" Acuña reiterates the belief that *lujo* was a moral problem, one which could quickly spiral out of control and lead to sexual promiscuity or prostitution. *Lujo* was viewed as such a threat to the feminine ideal that it was repeatedly condemned in women's magazines, conduct manuals, public speeches and literature. *Lujo* carried unfavourable connotations and was often linked with deviant femininity. Aldaraca devotes an entire chapter to the subject of *el lujo* in her study *El ángel del ho-*

gar: Galdós and the Ideology of Domesticity in Spain (1991), noting how *lujo* was invariably linked with *lujuria* in the existing gender discourse:

> In the minds of Spanish Restoration moralists, Fashion, like Don Juan, is endowed with fatal seductive power, capable of scaling the barricade of bourgeois domesticity and penetrating into its inner-most core which is located, and it comes as no surprise, in the bedroom. (Aldaraca 1991: 115)

Given this link between *lujo* and *lujuria*, it is easy to see, in the case of Isidora, why an obsession with fine clothing would be viewed as a precursor to prostitution.

The *lujo*/prostitution link can also be found in the language of flow. For both Segovia and Acuña, at the heart of the *lujo* problem is the gulf between needs and desires. Homes may abound with material riches yet "carecer de los más indispensables objetos" (Acuña 1882: 29). Acuña suggests that for a woman to drive the passion for *lujo* out of her home and her heart, she must "suprimir en sus costumbres, no lo preciso, sino lo superfluo" (Acuña 1882: 31). Acuña repeats her solution a number of times: "Desterrar […] lo superfluo, y aun de lo necesario dejar lo estrictamente preciso" (Acuña 1882: 36). Her use of the word "superfluo", which she uses on more than one occasion to describe the problem of *lujo*, highlights a broader concern about flow and excess.

The imagery of flow, which is not describing circulation but a unidirectional current, appears in the novel when the narrator describes Isidora's home and habits: "En la casa reina una abundancia incongruente. Suelen escasear, y aun faltar del todo, las cosas necesarias" (Pérez Galdós 2000a: 294). And later: "tus apetitos de lujo toman la delantera a tus débiles cálculos, y empiezas a gastar en caprichos, dejando sin atender las deudas sagradas" (Pérez Galdós 2000a: 302). Given the number of articles and books published on the subject early on in the second half of the century, the word *lujo* would not have gone unnoticed by Galdós's reader. It appears forty-two times in *La desheredada*, usually in connection with Isidora, and because of the overwhelming negative connotations of the term these references serve to bias the readers against the protagonist. The novel echoes the anti-*lujo* attitude of Acuña and Segovia when Miquis discusses Isidora's problems as if he were diagnosing an illness: "Estás enferma, estás llagada", Miquis tells Isidora, "Pues he de curarte"; and his cure is simple: "Huye de esas peligrosas alturas, y vuelve los ojos al valle ameno que está abajo" (Pérez Galdós 2000a: 388). This language of illness continues when Miquis calls Isidora's "idea del marquesado" a threatening "cáncer" in need of removal (Pérez Galdós 2000a: 391). Isidora's surrender to prostitution is not the illness itself but the final result of her true sickness, which is her "apetitos de lujo" (Pérez Galdós 2000a: 302) or overwhelming desire for distinction.

A PORTRAIT OF DESIRE

Isidora's social agenda is neatly encoded in the form of a painting. In a novel where the protagonist peruses the masterpieces housed in the Prado (Pérez Galdós 2000a: 117) and where one of Velázquez's works hangs on the wall of the Aransis family home (Pérez Galdós 2000a: 233), it is a portrait of a dead woman that figures most prominently. It is no ordinary portrait but one characterised as being "tan fina, tan conforme con la distinción, elegancia y gracia" of the individual it represents (Pérez Galdós 2000a: 201). The portrait in question is that of the Marquesa's daughter, the woman who Isidora believes to be her true mother. Twice the portrait appears in the narrative, once when the Marquesa de Aransis contemplates her deceased daughter (Pérez Galdós 2000a: 201) and again when Isidora is taking a tour of the Aransis home. But the text also alludes to the portrait in the pivotal passage when Isidora reveals her belief that the Marquesa is her long-lost grandmother. Isidora believes her own face, like the portrait, mirrors the face of the marchioness's daughter and when the Marquesa de Aransis fails to believe Isidora is who she claims to be, she dramatically draws her veil back to expose her face: "¿Para qué leyes? Soy mi propio testigo y mi cara proclama un derecho. Soy el retrato vivo de mi madre" (Pérez Galdós 2000a: 268). Isidora's statement that her countenance trumps the law in proving her heritage reveals her confidence in the reliability of visible identities in determining worth and displaying desires. In a period when faith in physiognomic typing is extremely high Isidora's belief that her resemblance to the Marquesa's daughter in the portrait is proof enough of her nobility is perhaps understandable.

That Isidora is attempting to achieve distinction by proving she is an illegitimate child is not without its irony, nor is it without precedent. Isidora's reference to the legal system and her subsequent *pleito de filiación* provides a substantive example of the uneasiness surrounding social relations and highlights a significant topic of debate in eighteenth- and nineteenth-century Spanish juridical discourse, that of legitimacy. In her book *Public Lives, Private Secrets: Gender, Honour, Sexuality and Illegitimacy in Colonial Spanish America* (1999) Ann Twinam argues that the issue of illegitimacy was a source of deep anxiety in the Hispanic world, both on the Peninsula and in the colonies. With scores of individuals petitioning the legal system for legitimization of possible noble rank through so-called *cédulas de gracias al sacar*, a sizeable corpus of legal reforms was instituted, many of which were contained in the Bourbon Reforms of 1759-1808, to determine under what conditions such illegitimate births should be re-inscribed as legitimate. The ramifications of such cases were great, with honour, social benefits and huge inheritances at stake. Isidora's case differs from most petitions which dealt with individuals unofficially recognized by society as noble who merely wanted official documents to reflect this. Isidora, on the other hand, does not already inhabit the social sphere of the aristocracy but is attempting to cross this closed frontier. As such, she poses a greater threat and her bid for distinction is all the more desperate.

Not only does Isidora want the Marquesa to recognize her as a granddaughter, she also wants Joaquín Pez to recognize *Riquín* as his son (Pérez Galdós 2000a: 345). No reason is given as to why Isidora wants him to do so, but one possibility is that illegitimates usually benefited when parents who had denied them official recognition on a baptismal certificate eventually acknowledged their blood ties. Even if they were not honoured members of their families, they were sheltered under the family name and could call upon the patronage of their often influential kin (Twinam 1999: 138). This argument is clearly relevant in the case of *Riquín*, whose ties to the nepotistic Pez clan would be sure to provide infinitely more opportunities than he would enjoy if he continues to be recognized only as the son of Isidora. That this is Isidora's principal motivation behind the plea can be seen by the fact that she has renounced her hope of marrying Joaquín (Pérez Galdós 2000a: 419), making it unlikely that she herself has anything to gain.

Her effort to improve Riquín's future through legitimacy hints at a possible financial motivation behind her own petition. Recognition by the Marquesa would be sure to provide greater wealth than anything the Pez family could provide for *Riquín*, suggesting the latter option is second best and that she is acting out of desperation. Due to a complex combination of circumstances, which Twinam explains in her discussion of Spanish inheritance laws (Twinam 1999: 220-21)–such as the Marquesa's apparent lack of other children, her daughter's single status at the time of the births, that the line is maternal rather than paternal, and the fact that the purported father was not married nor a member of the clergy–Isidora and Mariano, if confirmed as *hijos naturales*, would be the primary heirs of the Aransis estate despite their illegitimacy. Isidora clearly has this inheritance in her sights as she frequently fantasizes about how she will spend it once it is hers. While this may explain Isidora's possible motivations for pursuing the filiation claim with such determination, it also offers a possible motive for the Marquesa's reluctance to entertain the possibility. With so much to lose, she would naturally want to defend her wealth for more respectable friends and family.

All of Isidora's ambitions are placed in the portrait of the Marquesa's daughter. Like the pretences of those parading down the Castellana, the portrait is a visual representation of Isidora's anxieties and hopes, representing who she longs to be as well as who she does not want to be. Like so many in Madrid, Isidora is convinced that by appearing the part, whether by wearing the right clothes or by being seen in the right places, her quest for distinction will come true. This possibility seems unlikely given the many negative appraisals of putting on appearances and the fact that Isidora's conviction that she is of noble birth is legally proved to be unfounded. Little to no information is presented in the novel about the actual details of the legal proceedings of her case. We are told, through Miquis's father-in-law, Muñoz y Nones, that "la falsificación [de sus papeles] es tan clara, tan evidente como la luz del mediodía", and that the tribunal has found her claim "categóricamente" without basis (Pérez Galdós 2000a: 457). Such emphatic language, combined with the highly favourable picture painted of Muñoz y Nones's character, suggest that the court's ruling is above suspicion and that, in fact, Isidora is not the Marquesa's granddaughter, providing one explanation of the novel's title. But Isidora is also disinherited from the social world. Throughout the novel she is pushed further toward the margins. As a poor orphan she is excluded from many social spaces. As a dishonoured, single mother she cannot penetrate those social circles reserved for "respectable" members of society. By taking the final step to prostitution she essentially loses her place altogether within mainstream society.

It is a cruel irony that Isidora becomes socially disinherited as the result of her biological inheritance. Isidora's fall is initiated by an insane father and advanced by her fanciful uncle, but it is ultimately fulfilled by her very own delusions of grandeur. She is caught up in the type of "family romance" identified by Freud, where children become dissatisfied with their familial relationships and thus imagine that they are actually the offspring of far more significant individuals and have simply been adopted by the parents from whom they wish to distance themselves (Freud 1991: 221-25). Her motivation for believing such a delusion is compelling; the idea that she was actually the child of a prematurely deceased mother and an insane father is admittedly unattractive, but not even the false paper trail forged by her father nor her own exaggerated sense of self worth were enough to obfuscate the implications of her true parentage. In an age when degenerative conditions–of which her father's mental illness, her son's macrocephaly and her brother's criminal disposition are paradigmatic examples–were believed to be hereditary, Isidora's own lineage can be of little doubt. She has even inherited her father's aspirations and "insaciables apetitos" (Pérez Galdós 2000a: 82, 464). She does not bear the physical stigmata of the lunatic, the diseased or the criminal but her degenerative state is no less real. With increasingly strong evidence suggesting Isidora comes from "bad blood", her dizzying descent into Madrid's seedy underworld can be interpreted as the inevitable outcome of her degeneracy magnified by a squalid urban setting. By depicting Isidora as an unproductive "enferma" who suffers from a lust for *lujo*, the text presents her as a parasitic drain on society. By becoming a prostitute, Isidora becomes a literal drain, the model of female degeneracy *par excellence*, and as such she falls within the very category from which she had tried so hard to escape.

Based on such evidence we can justifiably label Isidora as a degenerate. But while this may be true, there is cause for doubt; episodes which would lead us to believe that something about her–her great beauty, her charm, her imaginative capacity–extends beyond such a classificatory system. As noted earlier, the Marquesa, a powerful and respected woman who knew that Isidora was not who she claimed to be, was nevertheless taken aback by the young protagonist's "distinción innegable" (Pérez Galdós 2000a: 268). Similarly, just days before his wedding to the daughter of Muñoz y Nones, a brief encounter with Isidora stirs dormant emotions within Miquis, emotions that nearly cause him to slip and deny his engagement (Pérez Galdós 2000a: 393). If Miquis, the embodiment of reason who earlier in the narrative so easily exposed the pretensions of social aspirants as false and unfounded, could still waiver in her presence, why should Isidora not give a moment's pause to the reader? Despite her obvious moral failings, one cannot contemplate Isidora's emotional, physical, and spiritual complexities without wondering just how reliable any social map–whether based on science or fashion–can truly be. It is a suspicion that proves well-founded when we eventually see Isidora again as a selfless companion to a dying painter in *Torquemada en la hoguera* (1889).

CHAPTER 3

MAPPING GENDER IN *TORMENTO* AND *LA DE BRINGAS*

> What are little boys made of?
> Snips and snails, and puppy dog tails,
> That's what little boys are made of.
>
> What are little girls made of?
> Sugar and spice, and everything nice,
> That's what little girls are made of.

GENDER identities in Spain, like class distinctions, were affected by the rise of the middle classes during the latter half of the nineteenth century. In *Desire and Domestic Fiction* (1987), Nancy Armstrong argues that social insecurities led Europe's bourgeoisie to seek out ways of transferring attention away from a preoccupation with noble birth in order to validate and facilitate their own emergence as an entity. One solution was to focus on gender as the primary distinguishing feature of an individual.[1] Drawing on contemporary theories about gender as well as nineteenth-century sources of gender discourse–such as dictionaries, conduct manuals and the press–this chapter will focus on the principal figures of Galdós's *Tormento* and *La de Bringas* in order to see whether these characters deviate from or embody the cultural ideals of masculinity and femininity in vogue at the time. Specifically, the two principal female characters of these novels will be viewed against the ideal

---

[1] While I believe Armstrong's hypothesis is valid, I think it is too sweeping to suggest gender became the *primary* distinguishing feature of individuals. I would argue that other distinguishing features, such as race, were equally important as social groups struggled to gain legitimacy.

that dominated the gender discourse of the period, the *ángel del hogar* figure, while the male characters will be examined according to a more general model of masculinity. As this analysis will show, Galdós's work is not merely a reflection of Spanish gender norms but an active critique of those norms as well.

Fashioning Gender

Simone de Beauvoir famously stated that "one is not born a woman, but rather becomes one" (Beauvoir 1953: 267). The same could be said of men. The theory that gender and sex are not innate qualities but identities built through experience and social pressures has gained greater credibility and popularity in recent decades through the work of feminist and post-modern theorists. Following Foucault, who argued that the human subject is a cultural construct produced by discourse, Judith Butler argues that gender identity represents a "cultural fiction" formed by the dominant ideology of any given society. Gender, she concludes, depends on what you *do* at particular times rather than a universal *who you are*, with the codes of "proper" gender conduct varying from culture to culture. Butler's emphasis on the activities of gender identity is encapsulated in the concept of performativity, which she defines as the compulsory and repetitive enactment of discursively produced gender norms: "Gender is the repeated stylization of the body", she explains, "a set of repeated acts within a highly rigid regulatory frame that congeal over time to produce the appearance of substance, of a natural sort of being" (Butler 1990: 33). Butler's statement highlights two important aspects about gender. The first is that gender is expressed through perceivable (typically visual) signs, "the *appearance* of substance", which she goes on to describe in greater detail:

> Acts, gestures and desire produce the effect of an internal core or substance, but produce this *on the surface* of the body. [...] Such acts, gestures, enactments, generally construed, are *performative* in the sense that the essence or identity that they otherwise purport to express are *fabrications* manufactured and sustained through corporeal signs and other discursive means. (Butler 1990: 136)

The physical signs to which she alludes include a vast array of visible markers–physical gestures, dress and grooming being the most common.

A second key point made by Butler is that performative acts operate within a "highly rigid regulatory frame" (Butler 1990: 33). The gender roles we enact are not anchored in biology, as was previously believed, but in the social dictates of the time. But this relativity should not be mistaken for autonomy. As Cindy Patton explains: "[Performance] involves deployment of signs which have already attained meaning and/or standard usage within the legitimated discourse and crystallized practices of a 'social' [context]" (Patton 1995: 182). Medical, religious and popular discourses tell us what masculinity and femininity look like and we set about (usually unwittingly) moulding our appearance, behaviour and thoughts accordingly. Within the gender wardrobe, there are a limited number of costumes permitted by the established discourses of a given society. Failure to wear the right costume can potentially lead to social exclusion.

Given the view that gender construction is a cultural process that springs from one's society, it becomes necessary to determine the unique cultural forces at work in late nineteenth-century Spain. What did it mean to be a man or woman in the Madrid of Galdós? Only by answering this question will we have a standard against which to measure the characters in *Tormento* and *La de Bringas*.

Discursive trends reflect intense cultural anxieties. Just as the social disquiet described in the previous chapters was a reaction to eroding class boundaries, so too was the gender discourse of nineteenth-century Spain a symptom of anxiety. As a number of scholars have recently shown, nineteenth-century Spanish society was characterised by a collective obsession with gender. Catherine Jagoe believes such anxiety was in part due to the aristocracy's lax observance of gender norms:

> The notion of men and women as radically different was attractive to those who saw aristocratic life as tending towards a dangerous blurring of gender lines, as the fashionable court ladies became more brazen and the *petimetres* (eighteenth-century dandies) more effete and feminized, absorbed by dress and gossip. (Jagoe 1994: 19)

Jagoe's comment identifies female docility, or lack thereof, and fashion as two areas of particular importance in the gender discourse, and indeed these topics are of particular importance in both *Tormento* and *La de Bringas*.

The desire to establish firmer gender boundaries was somewhat extreme, as reactionary instincts tend to be. Gender came to be understood in increasingly polarized terms and the volume of discursive material establishing this divide was immense. Femininity in particular received intense scrutiny by social critics, the medical profession, religious authorities, and literary authors. One gets an idea of just how rife this scrutiny was from the abundance of prescriptive writing on the subject, and with titles like *El ángel del hogar* (Sinués de Marco 1859), *La mujer bajo el punto de vista filosófico, social y moral* (Alonso y Rubio 1863), "La misión de la mujer en la sociedad" (Pi y Margall 1869), and "La misión de la mujer" (Gassó y Ortiz 1878), one can get an idea of the type of domestic femininity promoted by such works. The question of masculinity, by contrast, is conspicuously absent from nineteenth-century Spanish gender discourse and, to a large degree, from current scholarship.

Rather than claiming that gender roles were divinely ordained, as was previously the case, the gender discourse of the nineteenth century proffered the concept of essential differences, which justified the roles of men and women by suggesting that these roles were simply natural to their sex. Writing in 1853, physician Pedro Felipe Monlau described the anatomical, physical, and psychological differences that constitute the respective natures of man and woman:

> El hombre es ardiente, altivo, robusto, velludo, osado, pródigo y dominador. Su carácter es ordinariamente expansivo, bullidor; su textura es fibrosa, recia, compacta; sus músculos son fornidos, angulosos; sus fuertes crines, su barba negra y poblada, y su pecho velludo, exhalan el fuego que le abrasa; su genio sublime e impetuoso le lanza a los altos, y le hace aspirar a la inmortalidad. [...] La textura general de todas las partes del cuerpo [de la mujer] es más floja y más blanda. La mujer está dotada de una sensibilidad mayor; sus sentidos son más delicados y finos. Predominan en la mujer las facultades afectivas, así como en el hombre las intelectuales. (Monlau 1998: 389-90)

In a post-Darwinian era these characteristics were seen as evidence that the natural habitat of woman was the home and that of man was the public sphere. That the public/private divide was crucial to the formation of gender norms in nineteenth-century Spain has been thoroughly examined by Labanyi (2000: 31-87), Charnon-Deutsch (2000: 53-84), Jagoe, Blanco and Enríquez de Salamanca (1998), Jagoe (1994: 15-31), and Aldaraca (1991). As each of these studies indicates, the gender discourse of the period presented a paragon of femininity that was commonly referred to as the *ángel del hogar*. The *ángel del hogar* figure–so called because of María del Pilar Sinués de Marco's best-selling work *El ángel del hogar* (1859)–is not entirely new to those familiar with the discursive treatment of woman in Spanish history. In many ways the nineteenth-century domestic angel resembles the ideal Christian wife described by Juan Luis Vives in his *Instrucción de la mujer cristiana* (1524) and by Fray Luis de León in *La perfecta casada* (1583). Where the nineteenth-century ideal differs from its sixteenth-century predecessors is in the motivating force behind the domestication of woman. For Fray Luis and Juan Luis Vives, woman's lustful nature and weaker moral constitution meant that she posed a danger to man's honour. Only by confining her to the home could man be sure that she would not damage the integrity of the patriarchal order. Within the context of nineteenth-century society, however, woman was not a domestic prisoner, but a domestic saviour (Jagoe 1994: 24-25). Tainted by commerce and politics, man bore the label of fallen creature, while woman's spiritual and moral superiority made family and home an almost sacred refuge, an Edenic haven from the harrowing public realm.

The prominence of the *ángel del hogar* figure in the discourse of the period signals the beginning of a new gender ideology in Spain, one that is tied to the emergence of the middle classes. Jagoe notes that the concept of feminine domesticity was an ideal that marked off the middle classes from the aristocracy and the working classes despite the fact that writers presented it as woman's essential nature regardless of class lines (Jagoe 1994: 21). Because the domestic angel did not engage in any form of productive labour–thereby testifying to the success and social standing of the husband–working-class women, most of whom were drawn away from the domestic hearth by pure necessity, working in agriculture, industry, or service, were conveniently barred from the ideal. Similarly, the admonitions to lead a secluded and reserved existence also differentiated the *ángel del hogar* from the aristocratic lady, who, Jagoe explains:

> had begun entertaining on a lavish scale in her home and behaving with less public restraint than had previously been demanded of her. [...] Women began the practice of daily visiting and attending public entertainments such as the theatre and the opera, all of which gave the bourgeoisie an impression of licentious freedom on the part of the great ladies of Spain. (Jagoe 1994: 21)

The domestic angel was an ideal for all women to aspire to, but one which only certain segments of society could easily achieve. By couching the feminine ideal in a language that was at once all inviting and yet exclusive, Spain's gender discourse illustrated the superiority of the middle classes and diverted attention from the fact that they were aspirational by legitimizing their ascendancy.

Being readily available and easily interpreted, clothing was one of the most common currencies used to establish social distinction, and given the class influences that shaped the discursive trends of period, it comes as no surprise that fashion figured prominently in the formation of gender lines. Alison Sinclair's computerized handbook of eighteenth- and nineteenth-century Madrid periodicals lists a significant number of journals devoted to the subject of fashion (Sinclair 1984: 438-39). Without exception, all of these periodicals appear under the rubric of "women's papers", suggesting that fashion was a purely feminine interest.[2] In the year Galdós wrote *Tormento* and *La de Bringas*, virtually every issue of the mainstream newspaper *La Época* featured an advert urging women to subscribe to one fashion magazine or another. The proliferation of such fashion magazines—which were replete with illustrations, sewing patterns, and articles—helped dictate the latest styles and influence the spending of the middle class. Fashion magazines intersected with and complemented other popular forms of print such as conduct

---

[2] The absence of magazines explicitly devoted to men's fashion from the Spanish press does not reflect trends in Europe generally. In France and England, for instance, periodicals such as *Journal des tailleurs* and *The Gentleman's Magazine of Fashion* discussed and shaped men's fashions during this same period. However, even in these countries the number of publications dealing with men's fashion was miniscule when compared to the number of women's fashion magazines.

manuals. In Rementería y Fica's popular conduct book *Nuevo manual de urbanidad, cortesanía, decoro y etiqueta, o el hombre fino*, which went through numerous reprintings before the end of the century, the author states that women's clothes are meant to "adornar" rather than simply "vestir" (Rementería y Fica 1850: 27), the implication being that men's clothing is limited to functionality while women's clothing has a decorative or specular role.

As indicated in the above citations, attitudes towards men's fashion contrasted sharply with ideas about women's fashion. Unlike his advice to women, which places the decorative role of fashion above its practicality, Rementería y Fica's instruction to men is to "seguir la moda de lejos", explaining that their clothing should be characterised by a "severa sencillez" and a concern for "el aseo y la comodidad" (Rementería y Fica 1850: 31). More often than not men's fashion was simply ignored by the press or relegated to the back pages. One such article, notable for its brevity and ironic tone, exemplifies the wry disregard reserved for the subject of men's fashion. In an article no more than a couple of inches long and lumped under the heading "Crónica" along with other short articles on a variety of subjects, one finds a commentary on the *frac*. Noting that the Frenchman Jules Claretie published an extensive article in *Le Temps* on the *frac*, the author of this article mockingly acknowledges the importance of such a piece: "Se comprende, porque el frac es por sí mismo un artículo de primera necesidad", adding that:

> Entre las cuarto paredes de vuestra casa podéis vivir como mejor os acomodéis, sin muebles, sin adornos y hasta sin lecho; podéis comer lo que os plazca, garbanzos o verdura; podéis estar en mangas de camisa, o si os parece, sin ella; pero en sociedad, el frac es necesario, indispensable, indiscutible. (*Crónica*, 7 April, 1884)

By exaggerating the importance of the *frac* the author humorously undermines the validity of his own article while simultaneously invoking the mocking attitude expressed by notable writers such as Larra, whose sardonic comments on fashion were well known. The writer of this piece goes on to say that the abolition of capital punishment would prove less controversial than the idea of abolishing the *frac* from contemporary styles of dress. The short piece ends with the author indicating which colour *frac* men should wear, varying the colour according each man's character or status. It appears, if this article is any indicator, that efforts at prescribing men's dress were treated as a joke rather than a serious topic. The brevity of the article and the clear sarcasm denote something midway between indifference and hostility toward the subject.

Galdós's own musings on the subject of men's fashion convey a similar satirical disdain. In an essay simply titled "El elegante", Galdós broaches the subject of men's fashion but only for the purpose of ridicule. The opening paragraph of "El elegante" reveals an ironic, almost acerbic tone:

> ¡*Modas de hombre!* Siempre que veo en algún periódico, al frente de un artículo de actualidad esta frase tiemblo de gozo [...] Creo que de cuantos problemas agitan la conciencia humana, ninguno es tan grave como el de nuestro vestido, el más incómodo, el más antiestético y dispendioso que la humanidad haya podido inventar. (Pérez Galdós 1923: 231)

Galdós's irony is immediately felt when he states that he trembles with joy upon seeing an article about men's fashion. Given the unmistakable tone of the passage, the suggestion that clothing is in any way relevant to the greater good of society comes across as comical and should be read as a not so subtle intimation that men ought to forget about the latest styles and instead worry about more pressing matters such as politics, economics and philosophy.

Galdós does not limit his satirical wit merely to complaining about the ugliness and discomfort of men's fashion. He also plays with gender stereotypes as he offers a solution to this "interesantísima cuestión": "Dejemos a la mujer el reino gracioso de la moda. Varíen ellas sus trajes en cada estación para añadir nuevas seducciones a su belleza; pero concretémonos nosotros, sexo fuerte y grave, a cubrir la mísera humanidad con todo el decoro y toda la comodidad compatibles con una estética severa. Vistámonos de frailes" (Pérez Galdós 1923: 340). Like any good work of satire, Galdós's proposal that men adopt the robes of friars as the new uniform of masculinity is purposefully outlandish. Because of the physical similarities between religious vestments and women's dresses, his statement can be read as an allusion to the effeminacy of religion and, more generally, to the distinct spheres of masculinity and femininity. But whatever the subtle intentions of the author, the general aim of the essay is to ridicule the subject of men's fashion. Like the previously mentioned *frac* article, Galdós uses a mocking tone and an absurd proposal in his own article to depict fashion as a topic unworthy of man's consideration.

It is a virtual mainstay of fashion history that nineteenth-century men eschewed fashion in favour of an intentionally drab and conservative appearance. Certain critics, like Diana Crane (2000: 16–19), oppose this assertion, arguing that men's fashions did change, though not as often or as radically as women's fashions. Crane, however, does not distinguish between "traditional" men's fashions and "alternative" men's fashions, which would take into account the clothing and styles of the dandy. In this light, scholars identifying examples of non-adherence or adherence to men's fashion trends in the nineteenth century should be prepared to qualify their claims, distinguishing between those men aspiring to a model of conventional masculinity and those purposefully following an alternative standard. For the most part, conventional masculinity did not permit significant adherence to fashion trends as evinced by the ubiquity of black suits among most men.

Thorstein Veblen explains the opposing attitudes toward women's and men's fashion by attributing the difference to the unique spheres men and women were meant to occupy. Because men went out into public to work, their dress called for pragmatism. Women, he contends, not only occupy the home but symbolize it as well–they are a visual representation of family life and everything this entails. In a culture where social groups strive to belong to the "leisure class", even if only in appearance, dress offers the ideal expression of pecuniary standing because it is always visible. Thus, the well-dressed woman acts as a quick indicator of her family's taste and financial position (Veblen 1990: 119–26). In *La de Bringas* Rosalía justifies her spending and enthusiasm for clothes in very similar terms: "Si se tratara de mí sola, me importaría poco. Pero es por él, por él... para que no digan que me visto de tarasca. [...] ¿Cómo ha de hacer carrera un hombre semejante, un hombre que así discurre, un hombre que de este modo procede?" (Pérez Galdós 2001a: 173). Such an explanation does little, however, to explain why a patriarchal society would encourage the visibility of woman, thereby drawing her out of the home and into the public sphere (after all, being visible requires an audience). The idea of woman displayed as object rather than concealed as precious possession seems to contradict the *ángel del hogar* discourse. Nor does Veblen's reasoning account for the underlying hostility and anxiety of male critics like Galdós when it comes to men's fashion. One explanation is that by encouraging women to dress conspicuously and by ignoring fashion themselves, men divert the anxiety associated with becoming an object of the gaze. If one assumes, as many have, that the gazing subject occupies a (masculine) position of power while the object of the gaze is situated in an inferior (feminine) position, then for a man to be caught in the Other's gaze would be tantamount to emasculation. This might explain the preference for conservative black clothing among men, which seemed to offer an escape from the gaze by saying "Don't see me! I efface myself" (Harvey 1995: 13). Thus the feminine ideal is, to a certain extent, sacrificed in order to alleviate male anxiety.

The nineteenth-century man who shunned fashion in order to preserve his masculinity had a model against which to base this action: the dandy. The Spanish dandy, or *petimetre* as he was known, emerged from the margins of masculinity around the late eighteenth and early nineteenth centuries. Diego Torres Villarroel describes *petimetres* as "machos desnudos y hembras vestidas" (Torres Villarroel 1796: X, 29), while Juan Fernández de Rojas categorises them as "enteramente opuesto al hombre" (Fernández de Rojas 1795: 27). Writing at the very end of the eighteenth century, both of these authors signal the opposition between dandyism and masculinity, an opposition based in large part, as Torres Villarroel's comment insinuates, on the *petimetre*'s preoccupation with fashion. In her excellent analysis of the *petimetre*, Rebecca Haidt notes that the motivation behind this obsession with clothing is the desire to be seen (Haidt 1998: 109-112). Because he differs from "real" men, who are ideally shaped by war and work and avoid visual attention when possible, the *petimetre* is a prime example of gendered alterity (Haidt 1998: 109). In attempting to attract the Other's gaze, the *petimetre* exhibits a behaviour that is distinctively un-masculine. The gaze objectifies and subjects, something a "real" man would never allow to happen to himself. What this model of un-masculinity provides is a type of negative measuring stick upon which conventional masculinity, embodied in the character of Agustín Caballero, can be checked.

FALLEN ANGELS

Given the class impetus behind the gender ideology at the time it is unsurprising that Galdós, an author whose work is self-consciously concerned with charting and critiquing the ascendancy of Madrid's middle class, should give considerable attention to the subject of gender in his novels. The novels examined in the present chapter, *Tormento* and its sequel, *La de Bringas*, provide a gallery of divergent gender identities. *Tormento* is set in Madrid between 1867 and 1868 (prior to the revolution) and relates the story of Amparo Sánchez Emperador, a recently orphaned woman who lives with her sister and helps out in the home of a distant relative, Rosalía de Bringas. Despite her apparent adherence to the hegemonic gender ideology of the period, she is barred from being a true *ángel del hogar* due to the fact that she once had a sexual relationship with a priest, a secret that constitutes a threat to her possible engagement to a wealthy *americano* by the name of Agustín Caballero. In Galdós's follow-up novel, *La de Bringas*, Spain's bourgeois gender ideology continues to provide Galdós with literary ammunition as he shifts his focus entirely onto the Bringas family. Set in the months leading up to the revolution of 1868, the novel details Rosalía's efforts to conceal a debt from her husband, a debt incurred when she succumbs to her excessive appetite for luxurious materials. Both narratives provide numerous points of contrast between Amparo and Rosalía as well as among the various male characters.

In many respects Amparo epitomizes the *ángel del hogar* ideal. Her name, derived from *amparar*, suggests something or someone that protects "en sentido material o espiritual [...] a los débiles y desvalidos" (Moliner 1998: I, 169), possibly relating to some Virgen del Amparo. This dual emphasis on spiritual and material safety is certainly in keeping with the *ángel del hogar* figure and her natural habitat, the home, whose womb-like enclosure provides a sanctuary for man from the perils of the outside world, as described in *El matrimonio* (1875):

> El uno vuelve siempre en medio de los suyos con la frente encorvada por las preocupaciones del día, abrumado por los azares de la vida pública; la otra desempeña el sacerdocio sublime del santuario doméstico y prepara allí al hombre horas de alegría y de consuelo. (Sánchez de Toca 1875: I, 165)

Amparo is neither wife nor mother, strictly speaking, but she does engage in maternal/spousal activities such as caring for the Bringas children when their parents go to the theatre, looking after her younger sister Refugio, and even cleaning and cooking in Pedro Polo's home. Such activities show that Amparo is maternal in nature and suggest a link with the *ángel del hogar* ideal. She herself seems to confirm this domestic-angel status when she explains that her ultimate aspiration is "la tranquilidad, el orden, estarme quietecita en mi casa, ver poca gente, tener una familia a quien querer y que me quiera a mí" (Pérez Galdós 2002a: 64).

Comments made by and about Amparo distinguish her from unacceptable variants of feminine behaviour. She tells Refugio that rather than sallying out into the public sphere to earn money, a good woman should stay at home and sew (Pérez Galdós 2002a: 82). Her fiancé, Agustín, writes a letter to his friend in America extolling her beauty and modesty while condemning the young ladies of Madrid who dress beyond their means in order to appear wealthy (Pérez Galdós 2002a: 162). Such comparisons between Amparo and other women in Madrid also establish a clear contrast between her and Rosalía. Unlike Rosalía, whose expensive tastes will prove problematic in *La de Bringas*, Amparo prefers "lo útil a lo brillante" (Pérez Galdós 2002a: 176). While Rosalía fantasises about the wardrobe she could purchase with Agustín's immense fortune (2002a: 48-49), Amparo adopts more of a make-do-and-mend outlook: "a ella no le gustaba dar dinerales a las modistas, y aunque tuviera todos los millones de Rothschild, no emplearía en trapos sino una cantidad prudente. Además, sabía arreglarse sus vestidos" (Pérez Galdós 2002a: 193). In shunning the excessive consumption of luxurious goods, commonly referred to as *lujo* in Spain's gender discourse, Amparo has an attitude and behaviour that are very much in keeping with the ideology of domesticity.

The manner in which Rosalía is depicted in *La de Bringas* corroborates Aldaraca's previously cited observation about the connection between *lujo* and *lujuria*. Rosalía's reaction to clothing is exaggerated and visceral, described as "febril" and even "éxtasis" (Pérez Galdós 2001a: 94, 95). The word most frequently used to describe Rosalía's love of clothing is *pasión*: "se había *apasionado* grandemente por los vestidos [...] Los regalitos de Agustín Caballero [...] despertaron en Rosalía aquella *pasión* del vestir" (Pérez Galdós 2001a: 92). The narrator goes on to compare Rosalía to Eve in the Garden of Eden:

> La prudencia de Thiers no pudo poner un freno a los apetitos de lujo [...]. Mientras no se probó la fruta, prohibida por aquel dios doméstico, todo marchaba muy bien. Pero la manzana fue mordida, sin que el demonio tomara aquí forma de serpiente [...]. Los regalitos [de Agustín] fueron la fruta cuya dulzura le quitó la inocencia, y por culpa de ellos un ángel con espada de raso me la echó de aquel Paraíso en que Bringas la tenía tan sujeta. (Pérez Galdós 2001a: 93)

This allusion is unambiguous (the narrator goes so far as to call the *manteleta* that Rosalía purchases on credit a "manzana de Eva" (Pérez Galdós 2001a: 98). Like Eve's fall from grace, Rosalía, as a result of her passion for fashion, is a fallen angel.

With this connection between *lujo* and *lujuria* in mind, it may come as no surprise to the reader of *Tormento* and *La de Bringas* that Rosalía, who shows an unquenchable penchant for fine clothes from the very beginning, eventually falls into a series of adulterous affairs as a means of repaying her debts. Rosalía's desire to imitate the aristocratic ladies with whom she interacts effectively distances her from the role of domestic angel, whose ideals were meant to serve as a transparent countermeasure to the decadent behaviour of the aristocratic lady. One might even be tempted to attribute Amparo's happy ending to her rejection of *lujo* and her adherence to the *ángel del hogar* ideal, were it not for one glaring detail. It is impossible to accept Amparo as an *ángel del hogar* given the protagonist's brief affair with the defrocked priest, Pedro Polo. While the incident (which occurs prior to the events of this novel) may indeed be "la única mancha de su vida" (Pérez Galdós 2002a: 119), in matters of sexual chastity current behaviour is not enough to cancel out history. The significance of this sin within the context of Spain's hegemonic gender ideology, according to which a true angel's sexual purity is never in doubt, is such that it destroys the possibility that she will attain the ideal. Her affair with Polo is the ultimate bar to her being an angel as it cannot be undone in the way that excessive spending can be remedied. Amparo is clearly no angel, but in a curious moral twist her misdeed provides her with an opportunity to be with Agustín without jeopardizing his masculinity, as I shall explain later in my discussion of the male characters.

Rosalía, with her spendthrift ways, love of pomp, and lack of respect for her husband, stands in sharp contrast to modest and meek

Amparo. Rosalía's non-conformity to the hegemonic gender ideology is neatly illustrated by material allusions and a critical narrative tone throughout the novels. One such episode appears in the final three paragraphs of the sixteenth chapter of *La de Bringas*. This passage describes the morning walks of Pez, Rosalía and her two younger children, Isabel and Alfonso, as they amble about the northeast area of the Parque del Retiro known as the Reservado. A close examination of the objects and events depicted in this scene will confirm Jonathan Culler's observation that, "what appears to be a reference to an object, a state of affairs, etc., can and should be read as a reference to other texts and to the clichés and descriptive systems of a culture that result from the repetition of connections and associations in texts" (Culler 1981: 105). The obvious influence of the *ángel del hogar* discourse on this novel and its prequel imparts a unique significance to the buildings and landscape of the park and the behaviour of the characters. These details suggest that Rosalía is incapable of abiding by the norms of "proper" femininity.

Unlike the rest of the Parque del Retiro, the Reservado was not open to the public but, as the name suggests, was reserved for members of court. The Pez-Bringas group gains entrance to this private area because the Bringas family lives in one of the palace apartments–or, as the gatekeeper says, "por ser Rosalía *de la casa*" (Pérez Galdós 2001a: 124). The reference here to the palace as being "la casa", and the exclusive Reservado as being an extension of that house, conjures up images of family and domesticity and reinforces the private/public dichotomy associated with the domestic sphere. Significantly, it is through Rosalía that Pez gains access to this private domain. Because Francisco is notably absent from this domestic parallel, with Pez seemingly occupying his place, the connotations of home and family highlight an adulterous dynamic between Rosalía and Pez that becomes more apparent as the chapter progresses. Francisco's absence, along with the garden setting and Pez's flattering words later on, is also reminiscent of Eve's temptation by the serpent in the Garden of Eden.[3]

Reference to a number of different "casitas"–la casita del Pobre, la casita del Contrabandista, la casita del Pescador, la casita de Fieras–in this same paragraph continues the theme of troubled do-

---

[3] For a comprehensive discussion of the Eden-Retiro link see Daniel Frost's "Public Gardens and Private Affairs in the Spanish Realist Novel" (2005).

mesticity, as these buildings allude to various aspects of Rosalía's and Pez's domestic situations. Beginning with the Casa del Pobre, one can quickly appreciate its textual and historical significance. At a textual level the reference recalls numerous insinuations about the penurious lifestyle of the Bringas family as a consequence of Francisco's niggardliness. The name also applies to the Pez family which, despite a well-kept façade, is impoverished, as Rosalía finds out only after she tries to prostitute herself to Pez in order to pay off her debt. The name of this building also resonates with the historical context of the novel. In the period leading up to the Revolution of 1868 Spain had slipped into an economic decline. Isabel II offered to sell the goods of the National Patrimony, of which the Reservado formed a part, in order to alleviate the nation's financial problems. Her critics reacted to the proposal with outrage. Not only did the National Patrimony belong to the crown and not to Isabel, but she had also planned to keep twenty-five percent of the proceeds for herself (Blanco and Blanco Aguinaga 2001: 13, note 11).

The Casa del Contrabandista is another name with intratextual significance that applies to both Rosalía and Pez. On separate occasions the word *contrabando* is used to describe women's clothing. Because Rosalía's "pasión del vestir" conflicts with Francisco's severe budget, she hides her ribbons, buttons and bits of fabric in the *Camón* where she and Milagros rummage through them without being noticed. On one occasion when Francisco approaches the room Milagros exclaims: "¡Ay, amiga!, su marido de usted parece la Aduana, por lo que persigue los trapos... Escondamos el contrabando" (Pérez Galdós 2001a: 97). In comparing Rosalía's behaviour in the *Camón* to the illegal activity of smuggling contraband, the text would seem to suggest that her interest in clothing is inappropriate. It also suggests that Francisco, associated with the Aduana and thus with the law, is justified in restricting the purchase of clothing. In Pez's case the association between the Aduana and clothing/contraband is literal. Every year when he and his family go on holiday his daughters and other female friends ask Pez to use his influence to smuggle dresses across the border in order to avoid paying tariffs (Pérez Galdós 2001a: 231). His smuggling of dresses is just one aspect of Pez's own passion for fashion, which, according to the gender discourse of the day, is decidedly un-masculine. Given the condemnation of men's fashion in Spain's gender discourse,

Pez would be expected to distance himself from the minutiae of fashion. However, not only does he help others stay up to date on the current trends but he too takes great care in his appearance by sporting the latest styles:

> Aquel aire elegante, aquella levita negra cerrada, sin una mota, planchada, estirada, cual si hubiera nacido en la misma piel del sujeto; aquellos cuellos como el ampo de la nieve, altos, tiesos; aquel pantalón que parecía estrenado el mismo día; aquellas manos de mujer cuidadas con esmero... (Pérez Galdós 2001a: 170-71)

The mention of Pez's feminine hands in conjunction with the clothing, as well as the description of the *levita* as being "nacido en la misma piel del sujeto", reflect the attitude that clothing is but an extension of one's body: "la vestidura", suggests Galdós in a speech to the Real Academia Española, "diseña los últimos trazos externos de la personalidad" (Pérez Galdós 1972: 176). Such an attitude is in keeping with the physiognomic mentality that outer appearances reflect an inner reality. In interpreting the underlying reality of Pez's appearance, one is led to assume that he is not a real man.

In mentioning the Casa del Pescador, Galdós underscores an aspect of Rosalía's relationship with Pez that, at this point in the narrative, may appear counterintuitive. Given Pez's surname we can see the Casa del Pescador as foreshadowing the final sexual encounter between him and Rosalía. In this same chapter, as elsewhere in the novel, Pez goes about seducing Rosalía. Eventually, however, it is Rosalía who initiates their adulterous meeting (in Chapter 43), assuming the role of fisher while Pez is the catch. This reading of the allusion is made explicit when she later discovers that Pez has no money to give her following their sexual encounter: "Hacía propósito de no volver a pescar alimañas de tan poca sustancia, y se figuraba tendiendo sus redes en mares anchos y batidos, por cuyas aguas cruzaban gallardos tiburones, pomposos ballenatos y peces de verdadero fuste" (Pérez Galdós 2001a: 295-96). As this passage illustrates, Rosalía not only acts as the aggressor in her relationship with Pez, but she intends to prostitute herself again in the future. By assuming an active role in her sexual encounters Rosalía deviates significantly from the *ángel del hogar* pattern of sexual passivity; she adopts the role of predator instead of prey and thus fails to adhere to the woman-as-sexual-object stereotype or the model of the angel as asexual being.

The last of the *casas* mentioned in the passage, the Casa de Fieras, is a wide-reaching allusion that resonates not only with this text but with adultery novels in general. Conjuring up images of caged animals, the mention of the Casa de Fieras here anticipates a similar phrase used by the narrator at the end of the chapter to describe Rosalía's and Pez's marital frustrations: "es rarísimo hallar dos caracteres en completo acomodo y compenetración dentro de la jaula del matrimonio" (Pérez Galdós 2001a: 127). In signalling a dichotomy between nature (wild animal) and civilization (the caged or domesticated animal) and relating that opposition to marriage, a relationship analysed in great detail by Tony Tanner in *Adultery in the Novel* (1979) and extended by Labanyi (1986) in her analysis of *La Regenta*, this reference provides a way of interpreting the rest of the chapter. However, it should first be noted that the context in which the Casa de Fieras is mentioned differs from that of the other "casas". During their morning walks, we read that Rosalía and her group visit the "casas" mentioned above. The Casa de Fieras, however, is only mentioned in relation to the Montaña Artificial and other "regios caprichos" which the narrator describes as "el colmo del artificio" and as a "tontería pura" (Pérez Galdós 2001a: 125). The reference to these "regios caprichos" recalls the purpose for which the park was initially designed. Since its creation in the seventeenth century, the Retiro was a place where the royal family and other members of court could find refuge from the realities of everyday life. Mock naval battles on the lake, labyrinthine gardens, and manmade objects in imitation of nature were ideal for entertainment, recreation and privacy. In short, it was an ideal form of escapism. Such references highlight the theatrical dynamic of the episode and especially of Rosalía's and Pez's actions.[4] But the judgmental language used by the narrator to describe these locations reveals him to be far from objective.

Within the context of European literature the Retiro setting is one of so many liminal spaces where the traditional rules of social conduct seem out of place and where forbidden passions can develop unhindered. In his study of adultery in the novel Tanner explains that Rousseau's notion of the social contract established clear

---

[4] For a history of the Parque del Retiro see Brown and Elliott (2003).

ideological boundaries between nature and society. Marriage is paradigmatic of the social contract whereas adultery poses a problem because it blurs the nature/society distinction (1979: 16-19). As a small piece of nature set apart from the city streets of Madrid, the Retiro park is an ideal setting for a novelistic treatment of adultery because landscaped gardens "constitute perfect images of this blurring of distinctions between what is inside society (city) and what is outside it (country)" (Labanyi 1986: 55). In this light, the description of Rosalía and Pez walking freely about the park would suggest that they are heading down the road of adulterous love: "Rosalía y don Manuel, influidos favorablemente por la gala de la vegetación, la frescura del aire y el picor del sol de mayo, se reverdecían, y a ratos casi eran tan chiquillos como los chiquillos, es decir, que charlaban atolondradamente, y su andar no era siempre todo lo mesurado que corresponde a personas graves" (Pérez Galdós 2001a: 125). The impression that the couple is caught up in a prelapsarian return to innocence, in which social propriety becomes meaningless, is called into question, however, by the narrator's evocation of the "regios caprichos" in the previous paragraph, which imply farce and artificiality. That the couple's adaptation to the environment is simply a case of self-imaging can be assumed if one recalls a similar episode from Chapter 13 in which Rosalía and Pez stroll along the palace terrace:

> El paseo por sitio tan monumental halagaba la fantasía de la dama, trayéndole reminiscencias de aquellos fondos arquitectónicos que Rubens, Veronés, Vanlóo y otros pintores ponen en sus cuadros, con lo que magnifican las figuras y les dan un aire muy aristocrático. Pez y Rosalía se suponían destacados elegantemente sobre aquel fondo de balaustradas, molduras, archivoltas y jarrones, suposición que, sin pensarlo, les compelía a armonizar su postura y aun su paso con la majestad de la escena. (Pérez Galdós 2001a: 106)

As with the park, the setting in this scene suggests a blurring of boundaries. The palace terrace is both inside and outside, within the home and outside of it. As Labanyi and Tanner note, balconies, like parks, are a common location in literature for extramarital activities. In both settings the couple seems taken with delusions of grandeur ("*se suponían* destacados elegantemente") as they identify with desirable role models–painted figures in the quotation just given and members of the royal court who used the Retiro for recreation in the case of the primary passage. The settings become theatrical stages upon which they enact impromptu performances of questionable taste.

The narrator's use of free indirect discourse and subjective language further undermines the romantic overtones of the passage. Throughout *La de Bringas* Galdós uses ellipses to signal changes from basic narration to free indirect discourse and back again (Jagoe 1996: xxxv). It is worth viewing a rather lengthy excerpt as it provides an example of this technique as well as instances of the narrator's biased tone:

> ¡Cuántas veces tenemos en la mano, sin percatarnos de ello, el remedio de inveterados males!... La fácil palabra de Pez, saltando de un concepto a otro, llegó al capítulo de las lisonjas, que en aquel caso eran muy fundadas, y allí fue el ponderar la frescura y gracia de la dama. ¡Qué bien le sentaba todo lo que se ponía, y qué majestad en su porte! Pocas personas poseían como ella el arte de vestirse y el secreto de hacer elegante cuanto usara... Estas bocanadas de incienso ahogaban a Rosalía, quiero decir, que el depósito de la vanidad (cierta vejiga que los fatuos tienen en el pecho) se le inflaba extraordinariamente y apenas le permitía respirar. (Pérez Galdós 2001a: 125)

The first ellipsis demarcates a change from the voice of the narrator to free indirect discourse, focalised through Pez, and the second ellipsis signals a return to the narrator's voice. In the portion focalised through Pez, the text mentions the "capítulo de las lisonjas", suggesting that Pez is operating from rote, reciting lines from his book of seduction rather than showering Rosalía with spontaneous compliments. Significantly, Pez views Rosalía's fashion fixation as the best way of gaining her trust and affection, corroborating the *ángel del hogar* discourse, which cites *lujo* as a precursor to sexual promiscuity. We know that Rosalía reacts passionately, perhaps even erotically, to clothing (Pérez Galdós 2001a: 92-95), and that Rosalía's attraction to Pez is based in part on his sense of style (Pérez Galdós 2001a: 170-71). Together, plus the fact she feels that no one can sympathise with her as completely as Pez does–"¿quién, sino el mismo Pez, podría recoger sus palabras, impregnadas de un cierto desconsuelo y melancolía dulce?" (Pérez Galdós 2001a: 126) –these details signal the inevitability of Rosalía's infidelity.

Following the second transition, from free indirect discourse back to the voice of the narrator, the compliments cease and Rosalía is depicted with less-favourable language. Suggesting that her vanity is unfounded by calling her a *fatua*, the narrator humorously attributes her difficulty breathing to a bladder that is filled by sentiments of self-importance. These disparaging comments, coupled with the artificiality of the couple's behaviour, make it impossible for the reader to get caught up in the supposedly romantic atmosphere that encompasses Rosalía and Pez. The episode comes across not as a romantic foray of two potential lovers but as a comic sham between two actors. As a result the reader is unlikely to experience any sympathy for the budding romance between Pez and Rosalía. While this in itself does not constitute a condemnation of their adulterous relationship–something we would hardly expect from a narrator who will have a similar liaison with Rosalía–it reduces the affair to something calculated and fundamentally unromantic and hence even more out of line with the gender ideology than is Amparo's relationship with Polo.

MODELS OF MASCULINITY

For the most part, scholars tend to overlook the subject of masculinity when studying gender in the work of Galdós, concentrating instead on the *ángel del hogar* figure and other aspects of femininity.[5] One might argue that this is because the masculine pole of the sex/gender system is an unproblematic default position against which femininity is measured. The problem with such a view is that it not only glosses over a potentially rich area of scholarship, but in

---

[5] This trend seems to be changing. Michael Iarocci's article "Virile Nation: Figuring History in Galdós's *Trafalgar*" (2003) concentrates entirely on the subject of masculinity. Iarocci's argument that "the performance of masculinity through courageous action on the battlefield is central to a full understanding of the novel's representation of history" (Iarocci 2003: 190) offers an innovative way to read *Trafalgar*, and other novels about warfare, but the article also suggests the need to give the question of masculinity a more central place in Galdós studies generally. Also, Eva María Copeland will soon publish a book on the subject of masculinity in nineteenth-century Spanish discourse and literature.

doing so it does a disservice to Galdós and his contemporaries, whose portrayal of masculinity is anything but unproblematic.

As with the two female characters, a comparison of Agustín and Francisco shows that they occupy quite different positions on the gender spectrum. While Francisco, as we shall see, lacks the characteristics traditionally associated with masculinity Agustín certainly does not. An initial judgment of Agustín's masculinity can be made from the details revealed during his first appearance in *Tormento* in the fifth chapter. Initially, the reader must rely on a brief dialogue between Agustín and Rosalía for a picture of Agustín before the narrator presents him directly. After greeting her cousin, Rosalía enquires whether or not Agustín has gone for his morning ride on horseback. This seemingly innocuous question is a subtle affirmation of Agustín's masculinity, as horseback riding is a symbol of masculinity dating back centuries. In revealing Agustín as a habitual equestrian, Galdós gives his character an air of manliness in one swift act of characterisation. The detail also provides a tangible manifestation of Agustín's surname, Caballero. That he lives up to one definition of his name–"persona que va a caballo" (Moliner 1998: I, 435)–implies the probability, or at least the possibility, that he will embody other meanings and allusions associated with the term *caballero* as well, such as the chivalric knight errant who rescues the damsel in distress, an allusion that will become clearer in connection with the wild-man tradition embodied by Pedro Polo and discussed below.

Rosalía's next comments about Agustín's appearance carry connotations of the masculinity/fashion dichotomy discussed above. Rosalía tells Agustín to fix his tie, which he wears askew, while gently chiding him about his appearance: "¡Ay, qué desgarbado eres! Si te dejases gobernar, qué pronto serías otro" (Pérez Galdós 2002a: 39). As one might expect from a "real man", Agustín brushes aside any concern for these social "melindres", explaining that he has not looked into a mirror in fifteen years (Pérez Galdós 2002a: 39). Agustín's response, particularly his use of the term *melindres*, falls in line with the common stereotype that men concerned with fashion are not really men at all, but effeminate dandies.

The allusion is broadened by the narrator who, in describing Agustín for the first time, highlights dichotomous relationships between masculinity and society and between frontier and civilization. The narrator describes Agustín as someone whose body displays signs of decadence from living a "penosa vida" in America: "Siempre vi en Caballero una vigorosa constitución física, medio vencida en ásperas luchas con la Naturaleza y los hombres, una fuerte salud gastada en mil pruebas, una hermosura tostada al sol" (Pérez Galdós 2002a: 40). Agustín's hardships in America have made him painfully out of place in "la afeminada sociedad" of a modern city (Pérez Galdós 2002a: 40). This somewhat romantic vision of America as a place of untamed wilderness full of adversity and danger–the "hard and heavy phenomena" that Lionel Tiger views as contributing to the formation of masculinity (Tiger 1969: 211)–provides the ideal genesis for the only "real" man in the novel.

The frontier enterprise was thus conceived of as being a masculine experience and is frequently defined in opposition to civilization. Male freedom and aspiration versus female domesticity, wilderness versus civilization, violence and danger versus the safe and tamed, these were oppositions that made sense within the hegemonic gender paradigm of the nineteenth century. In this light we can read Caballero's time spent on the Mexican-American border as belonging to an ideological tradition in which the frontiersman is seen as an exemplar of masculinity. In an extensive analysis of modern masculinity, Connell notes that the frontiersman is a paradigm of manliness in most Western cultures (Connell 1995: 185; 194). Connell traces this tradition back to Western imperialism:

> Empire was a gendered enterprise from the start, initially an outcome of the segregated men's occupations of soldiering and sea trading [...] The men who applied force at the colonial frontier, the "conquistadores" as they were called in the Spanish case, were perhaps the first group to become defined as a masculine cultural type in the modern sense. The conquistador was a figure displaced from customary social relationships, often extremely violent in the search for land, gold and converts, and difficult for the imperial state to control [...] Loss of control at the frontier is a recurring theme in the history of empires, and is closely connected with the making of masculine exemplars. (Connell 1995: 187)

As the inverse of the city man, who is well versed in codes of conduct, the frontiersman is savage, indomitable and painfully out of place in society. Agustín's first appearance in the novel relates to this tradition. He is portrayed as a modern conquistador, an "apostolado colonizador" in the words of the narrator, who has travelled around the world to find riches. The narrator's comment that Agustín possesses a character "más propia del salvaje que del cortesano" (Pérez Galdós 2002a: 41), and Rosalía's mental references to her cousin as a "salvaje", "pedazo de bárbaro" and "animal", only affirm the correlation between Agustín and this model of "primitive" masculinity (Pérez Galdós 2002a: 48-49).

Marriage also figures into the dichotomy between feminine society and masculine frontier. Implied in Rosalía's comment to Agustín, "Si te dejase gobernar", is the popular cliché that a feminine touch makes a man less rough around the edges. Before learning of Amparo's relationship with Polo, Caballero eagerly embraces the idea of settling down:

> Aquel buen hombre, que se había pasado lo mejor de su vida en un trabajo árido, siendo en él una misma persona el comerciante y el aventurero, tenía, al entregarse al descanso, la pasión del orden [...] Por lo mismo que había pasado lo mejor de su vida en medio del desorden, sentía al llegar a la edad madura, vehemente anhelo de rodearse de paz y de asegurarla arrimándose a las instituciones y a las ideas que la llevan consigo. Por esto aspiraba a la familia, al matrimonio, y quería que fuera su casa firmísimo asiento de las leyes morales. La religión, como elemento de orden, también le seducía, y un hombre que en América no se había acordado de adorar a Dios con ningún rito, declarábase en España sincero católico. (Pérez Galdós 2002a: 158-59)

Caballero equates the frontier with adventure and chaos but the city he associates with order and peace, and he views the home, marriage, and religion as emblematic of that order. Quoting at length from eighteenth-century social anthropologist Giambattista Vico, Tanner argues that marriage is that which marks "man's transition from chaos to order [...] the shift from the nomadic to the settled state, from man as savage giant to man as articulate citizen [...] from the state of nature to that of culture" (Tanner 1979: 58-59). However, this process of domestication comes at a price. Because masculinity is typically juxtaposed with a feminizing social order, as suggested in the quotations above, marriage, by which man and woman enter into a social contract, requires man to give up his independent masculinity.

Ironically, Agustín, who in many ways embodies the ideals of masculinity, seems perfectly content to trade his independence, and thus his masculinity, for domestic tranquillity. In fact, glimpses into Agustín's thoughts reveal that he views family life and domestication as something positive, a prize for years of hardships on the frontier. A problem arises, however, when Agustín discover that Amparo is not the virtuous angel he made her out to be. In the final chapters of *Tormento* Agustín begins to see himself as a noble savage who cannot adapt to civilization:

> ¿Por qué no te quedaste en Brownsville, bruto? ¿Quién te mete a ti en la civilización? Ya lo ves... a las primeras de cambio y te han engañado. Juegan todos contigo, como con un chiquillo o con un salvaje [...] Este mundo no es para ti. Tu mundo es el río Grande del Norte y la Sierra Madre; tu sociedad las turbas de indios bravos y de aventureros feroces; tu trato social el revólver, tu ideal el dinero. (Pérez Galdós 2002a: 277)

Curiously, Agustín's frontiersman persona (and, by extension, his primitive masculinity) is reborn by the knowledge that Amparo is not an *ángel del hogar*. This detail is enough to dissuade Agustín from marrying her, but it does not stop him from wanting to be with her: "Mi mujer no... Pero pasará el tiempo, el tiempo indulgente, y será mujer de otro. Otro morderá en lo sano, pues mucho hay sano todavía, mucho que convida, mucho que está diciendo: *comedme*" (Pérez Galdós 2002a: 299). Here eating serves as a metaphor for sexual activity, as it frequently has in cultural practices as well as in literary works. As Agustín becomes aware of his passions he assumes the traditional male role of agent, here illustrated as a sexual consumer, and Amparo that of feminine object to be devoured. Following the traditional gender associations of this metaphor, Amparo is clearly an object to be consumed at the sexual table while Agustín is a subject with an appetite.

As readers we should not fail to recognize the irony of this situation. Amparo's "mancha" may prevent her from being a true *ángel del hogar* but she is undoubtedly the nearest thing to it in the book. And yet it is that very blemish that leads to a reawakening of Agustín's dormant masculinity, suggesting that in situations where the rules of feminine propriety conflict with the paradigm of masculine behaviour the feminine ideal is sacrificed in order to maintain the integrity of the masculine ideal. At the end of the novel

Agustín and Amparo run off and live together without getting married. Doing so allows Agustín to keep his masculinity intact by avoiding marriage. Amparo, meanwhile, is pushed further away from the *ángel del hogar* ideal. And while departing from the ideal will inevitably lead to social ostracisation, it frees her from a constrictive ideal and grants her a degree of agency.

Francisco Bringas represents a very different picture of masculinity. Francisco is first introduced in a prolepsis in the second chapter of *Tormento*: "se nos aparece, dando el brazo a un criado, arrastrando los pies, hecho una curva, con media cara dentro de una bufanda, casi sin vista, tembloroso" (Pérez Galdós 2002a: 16). Not really a portrait of virile strength, but even the younger Francisco seen in the rest of the novel cannot stand up to Spanish society's model of masculinity embodied by Agustín. Francisco is depicted as a model of social propriety. In terms of home and family, the narrator depicts Francisco as a domesticated man, a characterisation that places his masculinity in serious doubt. Known for administering his "asuntos domésticos con intachable régimen", he dedicates his free hours to "diversos menesteres domésticos de indudable provecho" (Pérez Galdós 2002a: 16-17). He not only cooks and cleans, but he does so better than his wife (Pérez Galdós 2002a: 18). In short, he is an "excelentísimo padre de familia" as well as an "amo hacendoso y listo" (Pérez Galdós 2002a: 18, 20), traits better suited to a domestic angel than to a "real man".

Similarly, this early description of Francisco shows him to be lacking in the habits and motivations stereotypically associated with masculinity. Whereas smoking and beards are both perennial symbols of masculinity, Francisco does not smoke and is clean shaven (Pérez Galdós 2002a: 17, 21). The fact that Francisco "no sentía ambición" (Pérez Galdós 2002a: 17) is also a significant detail given the salient facets of masculinity as they are set out in the *Diccionario de Educación*: Espigado Tocino states that a man should "ambicionar lo que no tiene, jamás contentarse con la posición que ocupa y no doblegarse ante voluntad ajena" (Espigado Tocino 1995: 138). Francisco's lack of ambition will become one of Rosalía's chief complaints against her husband in *La de Bringas* (Pérez Galdós 2001a: 129-30).

Whereas Agustín's domestication is a desire that never amounts to anything tangible, Francisco's domestication is so complete that the reader rarely sees him outside the home (something that holds true in both novels). In *La de Bringas* his reluctance to leave the home and enter the public sphere, as when he repeatedly sends Rosalía to Milagros's *tertulias* alone, borders on agoraphobia. His retreat inward becomes more acute as the narrative progresses. He gradually moves from public (his workplace), to semi-public (the salon where social visits take place), to private (his makeshift *despacho*), to complete, albeit symbolic, isolation (his blindness) from which he never fully recovers. This transition from outer to inner is intensified by the fact that his home is situated within another building, the palace. If the frontiersman, with his freedom, mobility, and outward focus, epitomizes masculinity, then Francisco's ever-deepening withdrawal from the public sphere signifies a lack of masculine qualities.

Returning once again to the Retiro scene in Chapter 16 of *La de Bringas*, we see more information, focalised through Rosalía, about Francisco's suspect masculinity. In complaining about her husband's avarice, Rosalía does manage to point out what she considers to be some of his finer points. Francisco, she explains, is a good father, "bueno y cariñoso, honrado como pocos", he does not frequent the *casino*, the male domain par excellence, nor does he gamble, drink, or associate with immoral women. And most importantly, according to Rosalía, he is "de genio tan pacífico, que [...] se hacía de él lo que se quería" (Pérez Galdós 2001a: 127). Rosalía's description of her husband goes against the popular model of masculinity in nineteenth-century Spain described by Espigado Tocino: "un hombre que crea merecer dicho apelativo jamás deberá ser débil, sensible, afectuoso, abnegado, caritativo, caprichoso, presuntuoso, vanidoso, frívolo, charlatán, delicado, cordial, dulce, condescendiente, paciente" (Espigado Tocino 1995: 138).

The ultimate evidence of Francisco's un-masculinity is his blindness. Taking a stance that is accepted by most students of gender studies, Luce Irigaray argues that "investment in the look is not as privileged in women as in men" (Irigaray 1978: 50). This gendering of the gaze, she explains, is due to the intertwining of knowledge, power and looking: "More than any other sense, the eye objectifies and it masters" (Irigaray 1978: 50). About midway through *La de Bringas* Francisco loses his vision as a result of eye-strain from working on his hair picture. Francisco's loss of sight is essentially a loss of power, evinced by the way others in the house ignore his dictates: "Me parece que desde que estoy así no se hacen muchas

cosas que tengo ordenadas" (Pérez Galdós 2001a: 179). In what clearly represents an abdication of domestic power and a gender-role reversal, Francisco's blindness requires him to turn over the administration of the family purse to Rosalía. Blindness also carries connotations of psycho-sexual significance. In one of his most well-known essays, "The Uncanny" (1919), Freud investigates the symbolic implications of blindness in E.T.A. Hoffmann's story "The Sandman" (1817). In his analysis of the text Freud identifies the protagonist's blindness as a symbol of castration, an understandable interpretation given vision's historical status as the noblest of the senses and a source of power with regard to intersubjective relations (Jay 1993). Though Francisco's blindness, which renders him totally passive and lacking in knowledge, is not the sole cause of his cuckoldry, it is certainly a contributing factor and it is on this account that his blindness is in clearest opposition to his masculinity: "The cuckold provides the counter-example to the successful man who would otherwise embody the norms and ideals of the patriarchal society. The cuckold represents a fissure in the presentation of hegemonic masculinity in the patriarchal society that produces him" (Sinclair 1993: 56). Francisco's role as deceived husband is further emphasized by his name, which he shares with a cuckold taken from real life, Francisco, the husband of Isabel II. As the epitome of the un-masculine man, Francisco places Agustín in relief and highlights the manner in which the latter embodies the standards of masculinity.

We can compare Pedro Polo's hyper-masculinity with Agustín's traditional sort of masculinity and Francisco's utter lack of masculinity. Polo's transformation from a despairing and sickly apostate to a robust and brutal man following his stay in the country justifies his place in the present discussion. Like Agustín, Polo's metamorphosis during his time away from Madrid results in a savage type of masculinity that differs significantly from that of the "civilized man". His thick beard, powerful physique, and aggressive personality link him with masculine figures like the medieval wild man or the degenerate criminal and contribute to the juxtaposition between nature and culture. While one can interpret Agustín's primitiveness as a desirable representation of masculinity within the cultural context, Polo's character highlights some of the negative aspects of the natural man.

When Polo first appears in the text he is described as someone

"ávida de sencillez y rusticidad primitivas" yet constrained by the artificiality of his religious vocation and society in general:

> Era un hombre que no podía prolongar más tiempo la falsificación de su ser y que corría derecho a reconstituirse en su natural forma y sentido, a restablecer su propio imperio personal, a hacer la revolución de sí mismo y derrocar y destruir todo lo que en sí hallara de artificial y postizo. (Pérez Galdós 2002a: 113)

He passes the time daydreaming about a manly existence: "Ya no era el desdichado señor, enfermo y triste, sino otro de muy diferente aspecto, aunque en sustancia el mismo. Iba a caballo, tenía barbas en el rostro, en la mano espada; era, en suma, un valiente y afortunado caudillo" (Pérez Galdós 2002a: 129-30). This fantasy, replete with masculine symbols such as the horse, beard, and sword, stands in stark contrast to the stereotypical effeminacy of clerical life that existed in the popular imagination and comes at a low point for Polo, when he is physically and emotionally fragile. The narrator's reference in the first citation to social existence as something unnatural and false is echoed later by Polo–"¡Malditos los que en el laberinto artificioso de las sociedades han derrocado la Naturaleza para poner en su lugar la pedantería" (Pérez Galdós 2002a: 189)–and again by Amparo when she sees Polo's radical transformation after his return from the country:

> Estaba tan transformado que casi no se le conocía al primer golpe de vista, pues se había dejado la barba, que era espesa, fuerte y rizada, y la vida del campo había sido eficaz y rápido agente de salud en aquella ruda naturaleza. El semblante rebosaba vigor, y sus miradas tenían todo el brillo de los mejores tiempos. Vestía chaquetón de paño pardo y llevaba en la cabeza gorra de piel. Ambas prendas le caían tan bien, que casi le hermoseaban. Más bien que un hombre disfrazado, era un hombre que había soltado el disfraz, apareciendo en su propio y adecuado aspecto. (Pérez Galdós 2002a: 217)

These three citations, appearing before, during, and after Polo's stay in the country, use negatively charged language–"falsificación", "artificial", "laberinto artificioso", "pedantería", "disfraz"–when describing city life and thus appear to lend weight to the Romantic ideal of the noble savage and the notion that a natural existence is superior to a social one. However, a closer look at Polo's transformation into a wild man suggests otherwise.

The underlying need for spiritual purification behind Polo's departure from Madrid, in addition to his hirsute, strong physique, and his brutal behaviour upon returning, are all steeped in a rich quasi-historical and artistic tradition dating back centuries. The tradition of the wild man, though codified in the art and literature of the Middle Ages, reaches back to the beginning of Western culture. Present in Greek mythology, Christian hagiography, and medieval literature, art and architecture, the so-called wild man has a wide-ranging and colourful past. Dwelling in the forests, mountains, and deserts of Europe, the wild man is distinguishable by his muscular build and fur-like body hair, both of which represent his inherent animality. Representations of the wild man are diverse, varying from vicious rapist to saintly ascetic. The one characteristic that remains constant in this mythology is the contrast between the wild man's existence and normal social life.

Given Polo's religious background and the spiritual impetus behind his brief rural sojourn, Bartra's analysis of religious wild men is particularly relevant (Bartra 1994: 52-62). Bartra presents medieval myths about wild anchorites who live in desert oases or mountain caves as one variant of the wild man tradition. Typically the wild anchorite is naked but covered by thick body hair and a long beard. He lives in complete solitude, excepting the wild animals that share his environment. A common motive for fleeing society to become an anchorite, as illustrated by the tale of the sinning monk of Thebes, involves a desire to avoid the sexual hazards of living in society.[6] In order to repent for his misdeeds, which arise from living around other humans, in particular women, and avoid future iniquities, the anchorite flees from society into the wilderness where he spends the rest of his life. Such retreats were viewed as a return to a prelapsarian state in which man could live an austere, asexual and angelic life without the temptations of civilization. This inversion of the biblical account of Adam–who was cast out of Eden for partaking of the forbidden fruit with Eve–meant that civilization, along

---

[6] The account of the Theban monk, as recounted by Bartra (1994: 56-57), involves a monk who fornicates with a nun and then flees to the desert in order to do penance. Once away from civilization he becomes hairy and lives with the animals in a desert cave for the remainder of his life.

with all of its material evils, could be removed from the anchorite's soul: "Adam was initially the perfect wild man and was then corrupted by sin. The anchorite, in contrast, was first the sinner and then achieved perfection in the form of a wild man in the desert" (Bartra 1994: 58). By fleeing society the corrupt man reclaims his wildness as well as his purity. The implication is that being wild is a more perfect state than being part of the social order.

Following this tradition, Nones orders Polo to the country so the latter can regain his physical strength and shed his licentious urges: "En esa finca, en ese paraíso te estarás hasta que yo te mande [...] Harás toda la penitencia que puedas, y fíjate bien en el plan de mortificaciones que te impongo [...] trabajar, alimentarte, fortalecer ese corpachón desmedrado. Quiero que empieces por ponerte en estado salvaje" (Pérez Galdós 2002a: 140-41). The remedy appears effective and Polo quickly recovers his health and physical strength. In a letter written to Amparo from the country Polo describes his return to primal simplicity, echoing Nones's comment about achieving a savage state and at the same time making explicit the allusion to the wild anchorite:

> El ejercicio, la caza, el aire puro, el continuo pasear, el trabajo saludable me han puesto en diez días como nuevo. Estoy hecho un salvaje, un verdadero hombre primitivo, un troglodita sin cuevas y un anacoreta sin cilicio [...] me recuerda más aún la inocencia y tosquedad de los tiempos patriarcales. Me figuro ser el papá Adán, solo en medio del Paraíso, antes de que le trajeran a Eva. (Pérez Galdós 2002a: 188)

However, his self-described transformation into an "anacoreta sin cilicio" and the comparison to Adam in the Garden of Eden reflect a physical transformation rather than any spiritual change, thus indicating that the remedy is only half-successful: "He recobrado mi agilidad de otras edades y un voraz apetito que me dice que aún soy hombre para mucho tiempo. Lo que no vuelve es la alegría ni la paz de mi espíritu [...] La bestia vive, el ser delicado muere" (Pérez Galdós 2002a: 189). In fleeing the city Polo has fallen short of the anchorite mission and instead has become a wild man of a more traditional sort.

After returning from the country Polo has one final encounter with Amparo. The terms used to describe Polo's state of mind and behaviour during this meeting–"bárbaro" (used five times), "fiera", "frenético", "salvaje ímpetu", "insano furor" (Pérez Galdós 2002a: 218-33)–make Aldaraca's likening of Polo to Rousseau's noble savage figure seem rather tolerant (Aldaraca 1991: 154). In contrast to the noble savage described by Rousseau, who is essentially good and free of all prejudices until corrupted by social institutions, Polo has gone from bad to worse as nature transforms him into an inhuman "bestia feroz" whose savagery is vividly illustrated by the way he assaults Amparo. Besides hoisting her into the air, blocking her path when she tries to leave, and dragging her violently away from the door, he also reveals his savagery by nearly suffocating her with a brutal embrace: "gritó el bruto con salvaje ímpetu de amor, estrechándola en sus brazos [...] iba oprimiendo más y más, hasta que Tormento, sofocada y sin respiración, dio un grito" (Pérez Galdós 2002a: 227). In this context the term "salvaje", used so often to describe Polo, loses the positive connotations it has when applied to Agustín.[7] Whereas Agustín displays a figurative savagery in his lack of social refinement and childlike naïveté, Polo's savagery is literal and vividly physical as he acts on carnal instinct alone. In this respect he resembles the degenerate criminal, described by Lombroso and other criminal anthropologists at the end of the nineteenth century, more than the noble savage.[8] Believed to be a case of atavism, the degenerate criminal was an antagonist to laws and other social contracts and was defined by his or her physical differences from that of normal, civilized individuals, something which gives Polo's statement that he is a "troglodita sin cuevas" an unfavourable nuance. Whereas the noble savage and even the wild man offered romantic contrasts to society, Lombroso's degenerate is decidedly undesirable.

Polo's behaviour also recalls more violent versions of the wild man: "the wild man was a monstrous force that nature had unleashed to assail civilized men with a bestial humanity, and who enwrapped whoever he so desired within his colossal embrace" (Bartra 1994: 100). The episode from *Tormento* described above resonates with numerous tales of wild men leading women off to the wilderness to be raped, although in such tales a knight errant usually intervenes. This tradition offers further interpretive possi-

---

[7] See page 97 of the present study for a discussion of Agustín as "salvaje".
[8] See Chapter 5 of this study for a detailed treatment of Lombroso's theories.

bilities with respect to Agustín's surname. In Spanish literature the vicious wild man's natural foe is the *caballero andante* who defends society/femininity from any force that might spoil it. Agustín does not intervene directly, as one might anticipate given this particular literary pattern; however, he still triumphs over Polo, his wild man foe, for in the end it is Agustín who gets the girl while Polo is ushered away from civilization for good.

In allowing the reader to see the dissimilarities between Agustín and Polo on the one hand and Agustín and Francisco on the other, the narrator is able to highlight the attractive qualities of Agustín's masculinity. Unlike Polo, who embodies the negatives and excesses of masculinity, Agustín's link with traditional masculinity is subtler and ultimately more attractive. As a man formed on the frontier, that space which is located at the point of contact between nature and society, Caballero has one foot in civilization and the other in the wild. This allows him to embody the positive qualities of both realms while the novel's other male characters embody the defects of both extremes.

Masculinity intact

It is to be expected that ways of visualizing difference will change according to discursive shifts, yet with respect to the gender ideology of the eighteenth and nineteenth centuries these discursive shifts merely led to new ways of justifying an existing binary rather than actually re-examining the validity of those differences.

It would be too strong to argue that Galdós's texts succeed in deconstructing the existing gender paradigms, but there is certainly a whiff of subversiveness in his representation of what constitutes acceptable masculinity and femininity. The very absence of ideal men and women from the pages of these novels exposes the unattainable nature of Spain's existing gender ideology. In *Tormento* the narrator's sympathies do not depend on adherence to the established ideals. Because the actions taken by Amparo and Agustín at the end of the narrative transgress the limits of conduct supported by the bourgeois gender discourse, and because their actions are viewed with sympathy by the narrator, the text undermines the authority of that discourse.

But if prescriptive discourse aimed at women is less about those very women targeted by the discourse and more about the fears and expectations of the men controlling the dissemination of that discourse (Charnon-Deutsch 2000: 3), then perhaps Galdós's novels are not as subversive as they initially seem. In some respects the safeguarding of masculinity appears to be the true lesson of the novel, as when Amparo's dreams are sacrificed so that Agustín will not have to marry a woman who is damaged goods, so to speak. Thus the text would simply be upholding the patriarchal order, albeit in a less typical fashion. But Caballero is no hero. On the surface Caballero seems to be the only male character, indeed the only character at all, who fully embodies the gender ideals of the day. But he vacillates throughout the text, opting one moment for marriage and social stability, and the freedoms of the frontier the next. Furthermore, his rejection of Amparo, although brief, may not sit well with readers who, thanks in large part to focalization, will have grown fond of the protagonist. Rather than redeem Amparo through marriage he is content to make her his mistress in order to prevent her being enjoyed by others ("Otro morderá en lo sano"). When the last line is read, the only clear conclusion we can make regarding gender is that the gender lines in nineteenth-century Madrid were not that clear at all.

CHAPTER 4

MAPPING THE FAMILY IN *FORTUNATA Y JACINTA*

> ¡Qué vasto cuadro ofrece esta clase, constantemente preocupada por la organización de la familia!
> –Benito Pérez Galdós

WHETHER as metaphor, symbol, model or simply an object of interest, the family is a fundamental component of our social landscape. Conservative ideology refers to the family unit as the "foundation of society" (Connell 1987: 121). For centuries the family has served as a metaphor for the nation (Saglia 1998). Many churches draw on the family as their structural model, complete with Fathers, Mothers, Brothers and Sisters. Traditional sociology considers the family to be the most basic of institutions ("Family" 1989: VII, 22). Psychoanalysis posits that an individual's psychological makeup is the product of family relations (Winnicot 1991; Klein 1988). Given this socially and symbolically rich history it should come as no surprise that the family model appears frequently in the discourse of nineteenth-century Spain. Families have been around as long as mankind, but it was not until the nineteenth century that the unitary nuclear family became the dominant family pattern. It is no coincidence that this development coincides with the rise of the middle class. By focussing on the treatment of family origins, family space and family relations in *Fortunata y Jacinta*, this chapter will look at the way in which the family tree doubled as a social map in nineteenth-century Spain.

Setting Roots

Throughout the second half of the nineteenth century the family was a ubiquitous topic of discussion in Spain's public discourse. Indeed, the subject of the family could be found in speeches, visual art, newspaper articles, conduct manuals, social studies, medical studies, religious tracts, political reforms, literary works, and numerous journals.[1] The variety and quantity of material produced begs the question: why so much interest in something as commonplace as the family? The answer lies in the fact that the rise of the middle class was accompanied by significant ideological changes that affected the way the family was perceived.

In her study of the bourgeois family in nineteenth-century Spain, Gracia Gómez Urdáñez observes how "the family microcosm reproduced the new pattern of social organisation and moral values" imposed by Spain's dominant class (Gómez Urdáñez 2005: 79). She goes on to explain that this single cell of society became "the basic structural element" for the nation and for society in general, and in turn these bore "the marks and characteristic of the action of the new ruling class" (Gómez Urdáñez 2005: 80). Jacques Donzelot describes the ideological value placed upon the family as follows:

> [In the nineteenth century] the family constituted a clear dividing line between defenders of the established order and those who contested it, between the capitalist and the socialist camp. [...] Who sided with the family? Mainly conservatives who favoured the restoration of an established order centering around the family, a return to an idealized former regime; but also liberals who saw the family as the protector of private property, of the bourgeois ethic of accumulation, as well as the guarantor of a barrier against the encroachments of the state. (Donzelot 1979: 5).

---

[1] By way of example see *La vida real: alegrías y tristezas de una familia* (1884) by María del Pilar Sinués de Marco, *Porvenir de la familia obrera* (1879), *Ligeros estudios sobre la sociedad y la familia* (Santivañes y Chávarri 1868), *La familia regulada con la doctrina de la Sagrada Escritura y Santos Padres de la Iglesia Católica* (1867) by Fr. Antonio Arbiol, *Origen de la familia: principales derechos y deberes consiguientes a esta institución* (1863) by Pedro Lavin y Olea, *Conferencias sobre la familia* (Félix 1863), *De la familia española* (1854) by Don José González de Tejada, and periodicals like *El Museo de las Familias* and *La Familia*.

This emphasis on the family unit is not so much a break from the previous social order, but a reworking of it. Even before the nineteenth century the family was seen as fundamental to society, but there existed a strong emphasis on kinship networks and family pedigrees as opposed to the nuclear family unit. With the rise of capitalism in the nineteenth century came a new way of seeing the family. Bloodlines, while not necessarily overlooked, were no longer the only criteria for determining social status as wealth (which was at that point concentrated in the hands of bourgeois family dynasties) became increasingly important (Cruz 2000).

Determined to set lasting roots in their elevated social sphere the new ruling class wanted it all, wealth and an attractive family pedigree. Consequently, the perpetuation of family lines became important for middle-class dynasties as they worked on two fronts to ensure their legacy lived on. On the one hand economic succession became increasingly important. With family businesses being passed from generation to generation, usually from father to son, "the bourgeoisie were concerned about the risk of future generations squandering their achievements" (Gómez Urdáñez 2005: 79).[2] Juanito Santa Cruz is clearly squandering his father's money, but Baldomero does not seem to mind. Determined to truly become part of the leisure class, Baldomero has given the family business to his nephews while Juanito is left free to do as he pleases.

In addition to amassed economic capital, the bourgeois family was also concerned with human capital. Gómez Urdáñez describes the middle-class father's interest in his children as a matter of social succession:

> Within the family, the children of both sexes were the human capital of an institution understood in terms of ownership. The family names, which were accompanied by a whole liturgy of honor, were an asset for the bourgeois family and marked and identified its position in society. So from the perspective of the

---

[2] This concern stemmed from what was known then as the *Buddenbrooks syndrome*, an expression that describes as "the decline of a family business due to the neglect of a third generation. For more on this see Gómez Urdáñez (2005: 79), Férnández Pérez's "La empresa familiar y el síndrome de Buddenbrook en la España contemporánea: el caso Rivière (1860-1979)" (1999) and Rose's "Beyond Buddenbrooks: the Family Firm and the Management of Succession in Nineteenth-Century Britain" (1993).

father, the behaviour of his children had to respond to the effort he invested in this capital. (Gómez Urdáñez 2005: 77)

In this way the social capital of the clan was maintained and perpetuated. With the family business in the hands of relatives, it appears to be an issue of social succession rather than economic succession that drives the Santa Cruz family's desire for "un muchacho que perpetuase la casta y les alegrase a todos" (Pérez Galdós 2002b: I, 239).

All of this suggests that the middle class's emphasis on family lines was forward-looking. But when viewed against the backdrop of the prevailing scientific theories on heredity, degeneration and eugenics, it is clear that the bourgeois family, despite a very real interest in its posterity, kept one eye on the past. This seems to be the more pressing concern in *Fortunata y Jacinta*. Family pedigrees are discussed, paternity is a constant concern, and the shadow of degeneracy surfaces time and again. As the subsequent sections of this chapter will demonstrate, a concern about heredity pervades the text.

Neither laymen nor men of science of the nineteenth century doubted the heritability of physical and mental characteristics. The theory that "like begets like" was common currency in the medical discourse and is echoed in *Fortunata y Jacinta* when the resemblance between Juanito and his illegitimate son is seen as sufficient proof of paternity (Pérez Galdós 2002b: II, 518). But many also subscribed to the theory that moral dispositions were passed from parent to child, or that moral faults could result in birth defects in the offender's offspring. Medical moralists coupled notions of acquired hereditary disease with Biblical prophecies about sins being passed from generation to generation (Waller 2003: 54). Psychiatrists such as Bénédict Morel and Henry Maudsley contended that mental illness was passed from parent to child. Phrenologists and criminal anthropologists seized on the idea of inherited physical, mental and moral characteristics with particular alacrity, arguing that certain races and social groups were more prone to degeneracy. As a consequence, the nineteenth century saw a surge in literature of all types warning against tainted family lines, including scores of advice manuals that cautioned families to avoid marrying the hereditarily sick (Waller 2003: 55).

Compounding this concern over family origins and specific to Spain was the culture of *hidalguía*, which, despite legal and political changes, remained very strong throughout the nineteenth century. As a relatively newborn entity, the middle class could not turn to noble ancestry to legitimate or enhance its newfound social prominence. It thus turned to strategic marriages, which brought with them well-established kinship networks, as one means of gaining this sought after legitimacy.[3] In *Los notables de Madrid* (2000) Jesús Cruz describes the eagerness with which members of the middle class pursued the symbolically valuable lineage of the "vieja aristocracia":

> La mayor parte de las familias ascendentes perseguían con premura la obtención de títulos nobiliarios y se recreaban en el uso de apellidos, escudos nobiliarios, genealogías, etc. Ser considerado noble en este período implicaba la posesión de capital simbólico y cultural y ayudaba a incrementar el prestigio y la dominación social. (Cruz 2000: 219-20)

In a clear example of economic capital being exchanged for cultural capital, members of Spain's middle class, buttressed by their great wealth, would marry into an increasingly impoverished aristocracy. Galdós's *Torquemada* series provides a classic literary illustration of this practice.

Fortunata y Jacinta contains an undeniable fascination with genealogy. The first two chapters follow in the tradition of the popular *Galería de españoles célebres contemporáneos* (Pastor Díaz and Cárdenas 1841-46) and other similar works, which were compilations of short biographies about Spanish "hombres de bien" written for a middle-class public. The individuals treated in such works were invariably introduced with a short description of the character's education and genealogical background, possibly to justify their presence in such a collection. Galdós begins his masterpiece in a similar vein, introducing Juanito Santa Cruz in the first chapter, including a brief overview of his education, and following up in the second chapter with the family's genealogy. This second chapter, entitled "Santa Cruz y Arnaiz: Vistazo histórico sobre el comercio matritense", not only evinces the novel's interest in genealogy–and

---

[3] Historians have provided ample evidence indicating that it was common practice in nineteenth-century Spain to marry strategically in order to obtain a title. See Cruz (2000), Héran (1990), Sierra (1992), McDonogh (1986) and Tuñón de Lara (1973).

flags up the central image of the family tree–but it also provides specific examples of the socio-economic motives for establishing family ties. As the chapter's title illustrates, family ties and socioeconomic relations formed one intertwining jumble of branches (Turner 1983).

It should be noted that the genealogical backdrop provided in the second chapter of *Fortunata y Jacinta* does differ from the *Galería de españoles célebres contemporáneos* in one very important respect. Whereas the genealogies traced in *Galería de españoles célebres contemporáneos* focused on the individuals' noble ancestry, the historical *vistazo* of the Santa Cruz and Arnaiz lines offers no connections with Madrid's noble families. In fact, one gets the impression that there is a certain amount of pride in the Santa Cruz family's humble beginnings and that this genealogical enterprise is more an act of creating than it is an act of recounting, providing a clear contrast to Isidora's desire to forget her own humble origin and insert herself into the *ancien régime* by claiming to be a forgotten branch of Marquesa de Aransis's family tree in *La desheredada*. Galdós's synopsis of the Santa Cruz/Arnaiz family histories repeatedly mentions parent/child relationships and discusses at length the inheritance of businesses. Words like *dinastía* and *reinado*, both of which are used to describe the Santa Cruz family business, the regal numbering of names–Baldomero I, Baldomero II–, the epithet of *Delfín* given to Juanito, even the incestuous union between Juanito and Jacinta, smacks of nobility and gives the impression that the Santa Cruz clan does not need to rely on members of the *ancien régime* for legitimacy because they are, in essence, the new aristocracy. The link between family lines and class is further highlighted by the fact that Fortunata, who metonymically represents "el pueblo" and is arguably the most important character of the novel, has no genealogy to speak of. This lack of lineage is encapsulated in the following statement, which highlights her orphan status: "¿Quién era la del huevo?... Pues una huérfana que vivía con su tía" (Pérez Galdós 2002b: I, 205). Other than the fact that she is incredibly beautiful, this is one of the only details Part I of the novel reveals about Fortunata.

Pruning and Grafting

The section of *Fortunata y Jacinta* that deals with Jacinta's visit to the impoverished slums of southern Madrid, the so-called *cuarto estado*, reflects many of the middle-class preoccupations associated with urban living that were discussed in Chapter 1. From the perspective of attitudes toward the perceived link between morality and domestic space, "Una visita al Cuarto Estado", with its description of delapidated apartments and the tenants living within, is one of the most illustrative chapters of the novel.

Like the spatial arrangement of the city, attitudes toward domestic space reflect the social preoccupations and aspirations of a given historical reality. Ruskin's classic essay "Of Queen's Gardens" (1864), which offers a standard bourgeois take on the significance of domestic space, argues that the home should be a sanctuary, a "place of peace; the shelter, not only from all injury, but from all terror, doubt, and division [...] a sacred place, a vestal temple" (cited in Jagoe 1994: 20). This citation highlights the fusion of the sacred and the domestic that formed the base of the *ángel del hogar* ideology.[4] Spanish discourse contains similar religiously infused descriptions of the home and woman's role in that home. Commenting on the domestication of woman in an article titled "La misión de la mujer" (1857), Ángela Grassi describes woman's place in the home as divinely ordained: "¡Cuán santa es la misión de la mujer! [...] Si la mujer misma hubiese podido escoger su misión sobre la tierra, no la hubiera elegido más bella que la que Dios la ha impuesto" (cited in Jagoe, et al. 1998: 55-56). Other times the topic was broached in a less diplomatic way, as in the case of Ramón García Sánchez's 1871 article for *La Mujer*: "La mujer ha nacido para sentir y amar la tranquilidad del hogar doméstico. En el momento en que abandone esta esfera ha perdido la categoría de ángel y arrojado a los azares de la suerte la corona de su virginidad" (Charnon-Deutsch 2000: 62). García Sánchez's warning invokes the *ángel del hogar* figure and also makes a link with female sexuality and the home. It also draws a clear line between the public sphere, man's domain, and the private sphere, woman's place. In explicating

---

[4] This rhetoric is linked to the spiritualization of women in nineteenth-century Spain, which Aldaraca discusses at length (1991: 55-87).

the importance of the private/public divide in nineteenth-century Spain, modern scholarship suggests that this binary reflects a general anxiety about boundaries in addition to specific concerns about gender roles and family life (Gómez Urdáñez 2005, Mathews 2003: 87-89, Labanyi 2000: 31-87, Charnon-Deutsch 2000: 53-84, Jagoe 1994: 15-17, and Aldaraca 1991: 28-32, 160-84).[5]

As I mentioned at the outset of the chapter, the family was considered to be the cornerstone of society, and Spain's middle classes viewed the boundary between private and public as crucial to the vitality and integrity of the family unit. At the forefront of *Fortunata y Jacinta* is the domestic disorder that results when this private/public division is breached through adultery. In the novel's ninth chapter, not long after her marriage to Juanito Santa Cruz, Jacinta begins to suspect that her husband fathered a son with Fortunata. This suspicion is confirmed by José Ido del Sagrario who comes to the Santa Cruz home selling subscriptions. Wanting to see the child first hand Jacinta decides to visit Ido, accompanied by Guillermina, in the *cuarto estado*. In order to get there Jacinta travels down the calle de Toledo, a descent which is both topographic and socioeconomic. This journey takes her from her familiar space of wealthy consumers down to the poverty stricken neighbourhood of the working class.

A comparison between these locations reveals a fundamental spatial element in the novel. In his 1897 speech to the Real Academia Española, Galdós notes that dwelling places are the external sign of the families living inside them (Pérez Galdós 1972: 175-76). In *Fortunata y Jacinta* living spaces reflect not only the tastes and lifestyle of the occupants, but also their position in society; a fact shown primarily through descriptions of two distinct living spaces–that of the Santa Cruz family and that of José Ido and the other residents of the *cuarto estado*. The Santa Cruz home is located in an affluent neighbourhood on the calle de Pontejos near the Puerta del Sol while the Ido apartment lies to the south in the destitute area known as the *cuarto estado*. The Santa Cruz family owns their home and lives on the ground floor, both indicative of wealth, whereas Ido's family rents a small apartment and lives on an upper

---

[5] For a look at the public/private divide in non-Spanish contexts see Fraser (1990), Davidoff and Hall (1987: 32-34, 264-69), and Ariès (1962: 390-404).

floor.[6] The description of the Santa Cruz home emphasizes its spaciousness: "era inmenso [...] la casa era tan grande, que los dos matrimonios vivían en ella holgadamente y les sobraba espacio" (Pérez Galdós 2002b: I, 247). By contrast, the narrator repeatedly makes reference to the dimensions of the living quarters in the *cuarto estado*, describing them as "estrecho", "oprimido" and "angosto" (Pérez Galdós 2002b: I, 323-25). The quality of the décor in the Santa Cruz home communicates wealth and the items described –beds, books, chairs and art– are metonymic indicators that this home belongs to a leisure class. The items in the Ido home connote labor rather than leisure. The only pieces of furniture mentioned are a sofa, "que no respondía de la seguridad de quien en él se sentase", and a couple of chairs that "eran también muy sospechosas" (Pérez Galdós 2002b: I, 326). The lack of adequate seating would seem to indicate that the family does not enjoy the privilege of relaxation, a conclusion corroborated by the fact that the only functional item in the room is a tabletop used for work (Pérez Galdós 2002b: I, 326).

The narrative tone in the passages describing the two living spaces betrays the narrator's identity as a member of the bourgeoisie and reveals the discomfort experienced by the middle class when faced with the disorder of space. John Sinnigen has stated that in Part I of the novel, in which the description of the Santa Cruz home appears, the narrator "is presenting the history of a class whose ideology and attitude he shares" (Sinnigen 1993: 118). The adjectives used to describe the Santa Cruz residence not only give a picture of that space but evaluate it as well. The narrator considers Juanito's *despacho* "una habitación muy bien puesta y cómoda", containing "dos hermosas librerías" (Pérez Galdós 2002b: I, 247). Jacinta's *gabinete* is "la estancia más bonita y elegante de la casa" and contains "unas acuarelas muy lindas" (Pérez Galdós 2002b: I, 247). His choice of words in these passages shows approval, yet at the same time the narrator does allow himself to make some criticisms concerning the décor, calling the salon "algo anticuado" and the wallpapering "de una arte dudosa" (Pérez Galdós 2002b: I, 247). But even in these instances his tone remains respectful. By contrast, the adjectives employed in the sketch of the people, objects and architecture

---

[6] For a discussion of the link between wealth and elevation of living quarters see Jagoe (1996: xxix).

of the *cuarto estado*–"feo", "miserable", "necios", "groseros", "repugnante", "tétrica", "nauseabundo", "horribles" (Pérez Galdós 2002b: I, 322-23)–convey disgust and even a certain degree of hostility. Later, the text refers to Ido's impoverished apartment as "la mansión de Ido" (Pérez Galdós 2002b: I, 325). This sarcasm and lack of sympathy connote a sense of discomfort on the part of the narrator, a discomfort which Jacinta experiences as well. When observing the edifice from within, Jacinta's reaction is so obvious that despite not uttering a word Guillermina can sense her friend's unease: "¿Qué, te asustas, niña bonita? –le dijo Guillermina–. ¿Pues qué creías tú que esto era el Teatro Real o la casa de Fernán-Núñez?" (Pérez Galdós 2002b: I, 323). Both the narrator's and Jacinta's reactions express a sense of anxiety concerning the disorder of the *cuarto estado*, be it in the form of filth, disrepair or the misplacement of objects and individuals in space.

This anxiety over disorder stems from the perceived relationship between order and morality. Foucault notes that the differentiation of domestic space at the end of the eighteenth century led to a "fixing" of the family and its activities: "by assigning [the family] a living space with a room that serves as kitchen and dining-room, a room for the parents which is the place of procreation, and a room for the children, one prescribes a form of morality for the family" (Foucault 1980: 149). In the Santa Cruz home order reigns. Everybody is assigned a designated space–Juanito and Baldomero each have a *despacho*, the ladies each have a *gabinete*, each couple has their own bedroom, the servants have separate quarters–and activities are assigned to these spaces–the *comedor* is for eating, the *salón* is used for receiving guests and socializing, etc. Thus space, and the activities carried out within that space, can be classified as private or public.

It should be noted, however, that the physical divisions found within the Santa Cruz home are somewhat superficial. Even within her own bedroom, the room which should be the most private of all, Jacinta is obligated to cover her husband's mouth to stifle a laugh so as not to awake Juanito's parents in a nearby bedroom: "su mujer le tapaba la boca para que no alborotase" (Pérez Galdós 2002b: I, 284). With others so close, the dividing walls and doors of the Santa Cruz home are, like so many other signs of bourgeois wealth and propriety, more show than substance. Jacinta's own living condition is just as claustrophobic as the overcrowding found in

Madrid's slums. Readers may wonder whether her uneasiness when visiting the *cuarto estado* is truly an example of elitism or simply the result of seeing her own lack of freedom mirrored in such a physical manner.

Clear divisions between private and public space and, it could be argued, a notion of middle-class morality are both absent from the *cuarto estado*. Instead, people, objects and activities mix indiscriminately in the same space. One of the first sights that Jacinta and Guillermina encounter upon arriving at their destination is a group of children of varying age and sex intermingling in the patio: "Los chicos eran de diversos tipos. Estaba el que va para la escuela con su cartera de estudio, y el pillete descalzo que no hace más que vagar. Por el vestido se diferenciaban poco, y menos aún por el lenguaje, que era duro y con inflexiones dejosas" (Pérez Galdós 2002b: I, 319). In comparing the two groups of children the text echoes contemporary discourse concerning the education of working-class children. According to Julia Varela, the enclosure of working class children in schools during the Restoration had a disciplinary component (in a Foucauldian sense):

> La institucionalización de una escuela para todos supone la aplicación de una serie de operaciones sobre los cuerpos de los niños que los convertirá en individuos sumisos, obedientes, disciplinados, buenos trabajadores del mañana [...] Los niños sufrirán este encierro del mismo modo que los vagabundos, los locos y las prostitutas, y serán separados del mundo de los adultos para sufrir en los hospicios, hospitales, casascuna, asilos, inclusas, etc., un régimen disciplinario que constituye el antecedente inmediato de la institución escolar. (Varela 1979: 225)[7]

However, the fact that Jacinta and Guillermina cannot distinguish between those children who do attend school and those that do not only serves to highlight the disorder of the *cuarto estado* while at the same time casting suspicion on the efficacy of that particular dividing practice as well as the middle class's ability to discriminate. Guillermina evokes this bourgeois call to "educate" the children of the working class moments later when she chastises Nicanora and

---

[7] In *Discipline and Punish* Foucault discusses schools at length as a technique of dividing and disciplining. See section titled "The organisation of geneses" (Foucault 1991: 156-162).

José Ido for not sending their children to school: "lo primero que tienen que hacer –indicó la Pacheco–, es poner en una escuela a esos dos tagarotes y a la berganta de su niña pequeña" (Pérez Galdós 2002b: I, 328). The pejorative manner in which Guillermina refers to the children indicates that her advice is motivated by class-interest rather than sympathy.

Still another manifestation of disorder in the *cuarto estado* is the mixing of private and public, such as the presence of household items in the public corridor: "Avanzaron por el corredor, y a cada paso un estorbo. Bien era un brasero que se estaba encendiendo, con el tubo de hierro sobre las brasas para hacer tiro; bien el montón de ruedos; ya una banasta de ropa; ya un cántaro de agua" (Pérez Galdós 2002b: I, 321-22). The public/private distinction becomes even more confused by a lack of boundaries. The physical barriers, primarily doors and windows, which separate the private sphere from the public, are left open so that smells and sounds, including a conjugal dispute, can be smelt and heard by everyone (Pérez Galdós 2002b: I, 322). Such a setting highlights the differences between a visual culture and other cultures dominated by other senses and echoes the class anxieties associated with such differences. While vision keeps objects at a distance, sounds and especially smells are dangerous because they cannot be contained, they escape and cross boundaries, and are considered primitive senses (Classen, et al. 1994: 4-5). Even as one moves into the living space proper, boundaries which separate the private from the public and various activities from one another are missing. In the Ido home cooking, socializing and work all take place in the same undifferentiated space (Pérez Galdós 2002b: I, 325).

The differentiation between public and private space contributed to the formation of an ideology of domesticity, which in turn contributed to a connection between the home and the female body. As Jagoe puts it: "Home, sweet home was idealized as a sanctuary, a womblike enclosure in which no conflict existed" (Jagoe 1994: 19). From the mid-nineteenth-century onwards, the distinction between work space and domestic space crystallized, resulting in a new configuration of gender relations and the view that the home was an exclusively feminine domain (Aldaraca 1991: 43-66; Jagoe 1994: 13-41; Fuentes Peris 1996-97: 36).[8] Not only did the

---

[8] This generalization holds true in the novel irrespective of social class. Both Barbarita and Nicanora exemplify the qualities of domestic overseer.

home communicate information regarding the family in general, as I have already indicated, but it served as a way to gauge the honour of the matriarch: "Es así que el mayor o menor orden de la casa emite mensajes relativos al grado de honradez de la mujer. Orden físico y orden moral se semantizan mútuamente, hasta el punto que la ausencia de uno de los términos puede comportar la pérdida o la modificación del otro" (Sánchez Pérez 1990: 90). As this passage suggests, the home was viewed as a metonymic indicator of the woman's, and by extension of the entire family's, moral standing.

Although the open doors in the *cuarto estado* represent disorder in a general sense, they also hint at earlier and later passages in the novel in which the image of the open door symbolizes loose sexual behaviour. The spatial arrangement of the home should, according to middle-class norms, dictate where sexual activities can take place by partitioning and erecting physical boundaries, which then represent moral boundaries. The bedroom is designated as the appropriate place for sexual relations and only between the people who share that space, husband and wife. In this context an open door suggests sexual promiscuity and infidelity. In this light the setting of Juanito's first encounter with Fortunata (Pérez Galdós 2002b: I, 182), through an open doorway, could be read as a sign of their future affairs. The clearest example of the open door as a symbol of sexual immorality occurs just after Fortunata's marriage to Maxi: "Fortunata se levantó y saliendo de la sala, se acercó a la puerta. En aquel acto, todo lo que constituye la entidad moral había desaparecido" (Pérez Galdós 2002b: I, 679). That same night, she has a dream in which she sees the unlocking and opening of doors. As Tsuchiya observes: "One need not have read Freud to discern the sexual symbolism of this dream" (Tsuchiya 1993: 69).

Still another example of the door as a moral boundary can be seen in fifth chapter of Part II, when Fortunata enters Las Micaelas, an institution for disciplining and rehabilitating prostitutes. Las Micaelas represents the antithesis of the *cuarto estado*. Its clearly demarcated boundaries, functional sites and classified bodies make it a paradigm of order and cleanliness.[9] When Fortunata arrives at

---

[9] Both Tsuchiya (1993) and Fuentes Peris (1996-97) have observed the parallel between Las Micaelas and Jeremy Bentham's panopticon. Whereas Tsuchiya takes Las Micaelas as a point of departure for showing how the family and society in general act as "local centers" of power, Fuentes Peris gives a detailed analysis of the functioning of the panoptic scheme within Las Micaelas as a means of controlling prostitution and filth.

Las Micaelas two nuns collect her and lead her into the interior of the edifice through a door. Maxi Rubín serves as focaliser for the passage:

> Vio desaparecer a su amada, a su ídolo, a su ilusión, por la puerta aquella pintada de blanco, que comunicaba la sala con el resto de la religiosa morada. Era una puerta como otra cualquiera; pero cuando se cerró otra vez, parecióle al enamorado chico cosa diferente de todo lo que contiene el mundo en el vastísimo reino de las puertas. (Pérez Galdós 2002b: I, 596)

The melodramatic tone, in addition to providing a humoristic glimpse at Maxi's character, makes the passage stand out and thus calls the reader's attention to an otherwise ordinary object. The door is a literal example of the inside/outside binary that forms the basis of social mapping. It isolates Fortunata visually and spatially from the reception area and from the entire outside world, and thus offers an illustration of what Stanley Cohen describes as "ceremonies of social exclusion":

> Prisoners were sent away or sent down, their "bodies" were symbolically received at the prison gate, then–stripped, washed and numbered–they entered another world. Those on the outside would wonder what went on behind the walls, those inside could try to imagine the "outside world". Inside/outside, guilty/innocent, freedom/captivity, imprisoned/released–these were all distinctions that made sense. (Cohen 1985: 57)

On one level Fortunata's passage through the door is a symbolic act of entombment from which she can hope to be spiritually and socially resurrected when she leaves. On another level this door can be contrasted with the open doors already discussed. As noted above, the open door where Juanito first meets Fortunata and the opening doors in her dream both symbolize licentiousness and in the *cuarto estado* the open, dirty doors indicate disorder. In contrast, the door at Las Micaelas is closed and white, both symbols of the very things that Fortunata has gone to Las Micaelas to learn –chastity and order.

A similar image of enclosure and division is the outer wall of Las Micaelas which slowly rises brick by brick: "Observó Maxi en los días sucesivos que cada hilada de ladrillos iba tapando discretamente aquella interesante parte de la interioridad monjil, como la ropa que extiende para velar las carnes descubiertas [...] al fin la masa constructiva lo tapó todo" (Pérez Galdós 2002b: I, 601). The simile comparing the rising wall to an article of clothing covering a naked body invokes the same concept of sexual chastity as the door, but it emphasizes to a greater degree the visual component of enclosure.

Jacinta's visit to the *cuarto estado* is, as it were, a confrontation with disorder and an attempt to restore order. In "Observaciones sobre la novela contemporánea en España" (1870), Galdós makes the link between family order and morality more explicit. In addition to his statement about the middle class's constant preoccupation with "la organización de la familia", cited at the beginning of the present chapter, Galdós also refers to adultery as "el vicio esencialmente desorganizador de la familia" (Pérez Galdós 1972: 123, 124). This notion of infidelity as a disorganising principle is precisely what Jacinta intends to remedy by adopting Juanín.

Jacinta's threat that Juanito will recognize and reclaim Juanín if Izquierdo refuses to turn the child over to her (Pérez Galdós 2002b: I, 359) conjures up images of a misplaced object that has now been found and needs restoring to its proper place. Indeed, for Jacinta the restoration of Juanín represents a return to stability. By adopting the young child she hopes to re-establish the boundaries that Juanito disrupted with his sexual escapades. In transplanting Juanín to her own home, where she already has a room set aside for the child, she is symbolically closing the door on Juanito's past and eliminating the one link between her own bourgeois world and that of the working class. However, far from restoring order the entire endeavour only results in greater disorder when Jacinta eventually realizes that Izquierdo has duped her into paying for a child that is not Juanito's.

Doña Bárbara employs two common images of disorder, disease and madness, when discussing Jacinta's desire to adopt Juanín: "Dice Juan que es manía; yo lo llamo ilusión, y las ilusiones se pegan como las viruelas. Las ideas fijas son contagiosas. Por eso, mira tú, por eso tengo yo tanto miedo de los locos y me asusto tanto de verme a su lado. Es que cuando alguno está cerca de mí y se pone a hacer visajes, me pongo yo a hacer lo mismo" (Pérez Galdós 2002b: I, 424). The same fear that Bárbara feels when in the company of the insane, the fear of contamination and indistinguishability, is what motivates the bourgeois to establish boundaries and employ dividing practices. In the case of Jacinta's visit to the *cuarto estado* she has failed to convert disorder/immorality into order/morality.

CORRUPT LINES

A significant portion of the criticism dealing with characterisation in *Fortunata y Jacinta* is devoted to identifying the real-life individuals upon whom Galdós based many of his characters.[10] Guillermina Pacheco has been linked with Ernestina Manuel de Villena (Braun 1970), Juanito Santa Cruz with Juan Valera (Chamberlin 1987), Plácido Estupiñá with José Luengo, a stallholder in the Plaza Mayor (Ribbans 1990),[11] Evaristo Feijóo with Galdós himself (Dash 1990), and Maximiliano Rubín with Maximilian Franz von Hapsburg (Chamberlin 2001). This emphasis on real-life models can slip into a rather simplified approach to literary creation and is therefore of limited value, for it is both inevitable and essential that literary characters evolve a great deal beyond their extratextual referents. This is especially true with respect to Maximiliano Rubín, who should be viewed as a reflection of society's concern over heredity and degeneracy, rather than a reflection of a historical figure.

In the preface to his *Traité des dégénérescences* (1857), psychologist Bénédict Morel recounts visiting numerous asylums throughout Europe after which he concludes that each patient was suffering from essentially the same disorder: degeneracy (Morel 1857: vi-vii). Pick defines the degenerate–as outlined in Morel's work–as "a given individual whose physiognomic contours could be traced out and distinguished from the healthy" (Pick 1989: 9). Morel was heavily influenced by Lavater's theory of physiognomy and subscribed to the same connection between exterior form and inner nature (Carlson 1985: 127). According to Morel, the degenerate would display signs and symptoms, which he called physical stigma-

---

[10] This is true of studies on other Galdosian novels as well. Varey, for instance, demonstrates the similarities between Francisco Bringas and French economist Adolphe Thiers (1967).

[11] Ribbans also identifies a second source for Estupiñá in Ramón Mesonero Romanos, while Chamberlin (2001) expands upon the narrator's comparison between Estupiñá and Rossini.

ta, of his degeneracy. Typically these involved any physical abnormality. As studies of psychopathological disorders intensified, however, so too did the nosological accuracy with which it was thought that physical stigmata could be identified. Some of the more common physical stigmata included facial tics, epilepsy, migraines, visual problems, impotence and eating disorders, which in turn prefigured or coincided with psychic disorders such as idiocy, insanity, eccentricity and moral delinquency (Carlson 1985: 127-28). Morel posited a critical link between degeneracy and heredity, arguing that degeneracy could be passed from parent to child. Furthermore, his concept of heredity was progressive, meaning that not only was a bad trait transmitted to offspring but also that with each passing generation the evil influence became greater.

Although *Fortunata y Jacinta* does not explicitly state that Maxi suffers from degeneracy there is sufficient evidence to support such a claim. Maxi's unusual physique, which at times seems pitiful and other times repulsive, as well as his psychological irregularities have prompted a number of critics to treat him as a case study (Randolph 1968; Allison and Ullman 1974; Larsen 1996). In the case of the physical description of Maxi, the narrator not only presents a detailed composite sketch of Maxi, but also employs medical nomenclature in order to suggest a way of interpreting the information:

> Maximiliano era raquítico, de naturaleza pobre y linfática, absolutamente privado de gracias personales. Como que había nacido de siete meses y luego me le criaron con biberón y con una cabra [...] Era de cuerpo pequeño y no bien conformado, tan endeble que parecía que se lo iba a llevar el viento, la cabeza chata, el pelo lacio y ralo [...] la cabeza de Maximiliano anunciaba que tendría calva antes de los treinta años. Su piel era lustrosa, fina, cutis de niño con transparencias de mujer desmedrada y clorótica. Tenía el hueso de la nariz hundido y chafado, como si fuera de sustancia blanda y hubiese recibido un golpe, resultando de esto no sólo la fealdad sino obstrucciones de respiración nasal, que eran sin duda la causa de que tuviera siempre la boca abierta. Su dentadura había salido con tanta desigualdad que cada pieza estaba, como si dijéramos, donde le daba la gana [...] Padecía también de corizas y las empalmaba, de modo que resultaba un coriza crónico, con la pituitaria echando fuego y destilando sin cesar.
> (Pérez Galdós 2002b: I, 449, 456)

Maxi's chronic ailments, slight build, thinning hair, misshapen face and uneven teeth are all classic signs of degeneracy.

As would be expected, Maxi's aberrant exterior corresponds to an equally dysfunctional interior as he eventually loses his mind. With respect to his mental state, the text provides details in which the contemporary jargon of psychiatry appears. This time the description comes from Maxi himself as he gives a summary of his madness to Guillermina, and the manner in which Maxi describes himself is as if he has seen a doctor and has now taken over these diagnoses of himself: "Primero tuve el delirio persecutorio; después, el delirio de grandezas [...] Padecí también furor de homicidio, y por poco mato a mi tía y a Papitos. Siguieron luego depresiones horribles, ganas de morirme, manía religiosa, ansias de anacoreta y el delirio de la abnegación y el desprendimiento" (Pérez Galdós 2002b: II, 491). The inclination to view Maxi as a specimen stems from his physical and mental descriptions, which are imbricated with the medico-psychiatric language of the day. Such passages invite the reader to interpret the signs of his maladies with only one possible conclusion: Maxi is a degenerate. By the end of the novel, however, such a diagnosis proves to be problematic.

If Maxi's physical inadequacies constitute the outward symptoms of his degeneracy and indicate a predisposition to madness, the cause most likely lies in his genealogy. As I mentioned in my discussion of the Rufete family (Chapter 2), in his work *The Pathology of the Mind* (1867) Henry Maudsley explains the hereditary component of mental illness, stating that the insane individual gets his madness "from where his parent got it–from the insane strain of the family stock: the strain which, as the old saying was, runs in the blood" (Maudsley 1979: 47). In the first chapter of Part II, entitled "Maximiliano Rubín", the narrator signals two aspects of Maxi's dubious heritage. The first involves the origin of his surname, Rubín, which an unnamed historian (within the novel) claims is a modified form of Rubén and indicates Jewish heritage. However, the narrator dismisses the historian's claim as "pura fluxión de su acatarrado cerebro" and insists that Nicolás Rubín, Maxi's father, "era cristiano viejo, y ni siquiera se le pasaba por la cabeza que sus antecesores hubieran sido fariseos con rabo o sayones narigudos de los que salen en los pasos de Semana Santa" (Pérez Galdós 2002b: I, 448). Such an exaggerated defense by the narrator is puzzling. Francisco Caudet views the narrator's denial as an example of irony, citing the name of Maxi's uncle, Mateo Zacarías, as further proof that, with respect to Maxi's Jewish ancestry, "no cabe la menor duda" (Pérez Galdós 2002b: I, n449).[12] At the very least the passage raises doubts about Maxi's lineage by suggesting the possibility of Jewish ancestry and in the process it opens the door to common prejudices and stereotypes such as the linkage between Jews and mental illness. Data collected in the early 1870s compared rates of insanity among European Catholics to European Jews. The statistics showed that rates of insanity were four times greater in the Jewish population than in the Catholic (Fishberg 1901: VI, 603), a fact attributed to the belief that centuries of inbreeding had predisposed the Jewish race to mental illness. The popularity of this theory peaked in Europe during the 1880s (Gilman 1984: 152-53), around the same time that Galdós wrote *Fortunata y Jacinta*.

The second link between Maxi's heritage and his possible degeneracy involves his mother's sexual behaviour. Sexual perversions, such as homosexuality, prostitution and promiscuity, were believed to be common causes of degeneracy (Pick 1989: 43; Gilman 1985: 78-79), and according to friends of the Rubín family, Maxi's mother was "desarreglada y escandalosa" and unfaithful to her husband (Pérez Galdós 2002b: I, 448-49). The narrator attempts to keep a neutral position with regard to the character of Maxi's mother, stating: "Podía ser calumnia, podía no serlo; pero debe decirse para que el lector vaya formando juicio" (Pérez Galdós 2002b: I, 448-49). Despite the disclaimer, this citation makes explicit the narrator's expectation that the reader will judge the circumstances surrounding Maxi's suspect pedigree and arrive at a logical conclusion.

While the information in the text concerning Maxi's physical condition and his genealogy invites the reader to view him as a degenerate, the narrator himself remains undecided. It must be admitted that despite many clear indications that Maxi suffers from physical and mental disorders, on occasion he comes across as a model of lucid thinking. This contradiction produces confusion on the part of other characters, like Fortunata who, after a conversation with Maxi, wonders: "Pero, ¿este hombre está cuerdo, o cómo está? ¿Eso que dice es razón, o los mayores disparates que en mi vida le he oído?" (Pérez Galdós 2002b: II, 463). Guillermina expresses similar doubts

---

[12] Doña Lupe's work as a usurer could also be seen as an indication of Jewish ancestry, as usury was typically viewed as a business dominated by Jews.

after talking with Maxi: "Lo último que me ha dicho es el colmo de la sabiduría y de la cordura; pero..." (Pérez Galdós 2002b: II, 493). The narrator's refusal to clarify Maxi's condition creates a subtle sense of ambiguity surrounding Maxi's status. This ambiguity indicates a mistrust of categorizations that will become even more prevalent in later works such as *Nazarín* and *Misericordia*.

The inability to be sure that Maxi is insane makes his incarceration in Leganés at the end of the novel seem somewhat harsh or at least worthy of the reader's sympathy. If he is sane, then he is being unjustly locked up. On the other hand, if he is insane, then he is a victim of circumstances beyond his control. Mike Gordon identifies Maxi as a character who is "doomed to suffer, not so much because of [his] own or society's vices, but because of [his] own essential nature" (Gordon 1977: 36). Gordon's conclusion is corroborated by the narrator's evaluation of Maxi, who he describes as "aquel joven, tan desfavorecido por la Naturaleza que física y moralmente parecía hecho de sobras" (Pérez Galdós 2002b: I, 456-57). Maxi's apparent physical and psychological degeneracy stem from hereditary factors and are therefore intractable, yet society reacts unsympathetically to his condition. Like those of the *cuarto estado* or the women in Las Micaelas, he is eventually pushed to the periphery of society, both geographically and symbolically, when his friends and family send him to the Leganés asylum. Certainly Maxi's condition warranted drastic steps–his intention of killing the female members of the Samaniego family as well as his violent reaction at being disarmed by friends shows how unstable he has become. But because Galdós was well aware of the inadequacies of Leganés and the inability of the staff there to treat mental disorders this solution can only be seen as a failure.[13] Incarcerating Maxi offers no hope for rehabilitation. It is simply society's way of disposing of someone.

BEARING FRUIT

In the opening chapter of his *Bosquejos médicos-sociales para la mujer* (1876), Ángel Pulido–a doctor, writer, politician and intellectual celebrity of nineteenth-century Madrid–describes the symptoms of a barren woman he once met as follows:

---

[13] See M. Gordon (1977) for a discussion of Galdós's familiarity with Leganés.

Padece una monomanía extraña. Cree hijos suyos cuantos niños ve. Se ha hecho necesario traerla aquí [al manicomio], porque a todos los besaba y quería llevar consigo, sufriendo horriblemente cuando se los separaba de ella. (Pulido 1876: 2-3)

This passage, taken from a chapter entitled "Árbol sin fruto", bears a striking similarity to Galdós's portrayal of Jacinta. Pulido's recourse to the image of a fruitless tree seems especially apt when applied to Jacinta, whose inability to conceive threatens to halt the growth of the Santa Cruz family tree, the very tree that occupies such a prominent place in this narrative. Moreover, his description of the barren woman desperate to the point of delusion, certainly resonates with the novel's depiction of Jacinta who, "de tanto cavilar en esto, su mente padecía alucinaciones y desvaríos" (Pérez Galdós 2002b: I, 289). Her desperation to mother children is so extreme that she suffers hysteria-like symptoms (2002b: I, 252, 255), and has recurring dreams about nursing (Pérez Galdós 2002b: I, 289). Similarly, her fixation on other people's children (Pérez Galdós 2002b: I, 250-51), her dream about the suckling man-child (Pérez Galdós 2002b: I, 290-91), her mollycoddling of Juanito (Pérez Galdós 2002b: I, 295, 309) and her sister's children (Pérez Galdós 2002b: I, 252), the imagined crying of an infant (which turns out to be some kittens) (2002b: I, 253-54), and her attempt to adopt the young Pitusín (Pérez Galdós 2002b: I, 356-76, 408) all stem from her "afán de la maternidad" (Pérez Galdós 2002b: I, 251).

In one of the final scenes of the novel Jacinta contemplates the countenance of her adopted son. Continuing with the themes of inheritance, degeneracy and physiognomic reliability, this passage is representative of the middle-class preoccupation with family lines, a preoccupation that, in Jacinta's case, leads her to construct an identity from an illusory genealogy. This evocative scene occurs after Fortunata's death and the adoption of her baby by the Santa Cruz family. Jacinta's marriage to Juanito has by now been reduced to a relationship of loveless cohabitation but she finds solace in her new son. Consumed by her role as a mother, Jacinta soon begins to fantasize that she is the baby's true birth mother, to the point that the fantasy becomes hallucinatory. She begins to imagine that she carried him in her womb and that she can still remember the pains of giving birth. All the while she dwells obsessively on the countenance of "el heredero niño", recombining his features in her mind so that he resembles both herself and an ideal being: "recomponía las facciones de éste, atribuyéndole las suyas propias, mezcladas y confundidas con las de un ser ideal, que bien podría tener la cara de Santa Cruz, pero cuyo corazón era seguramente el de Moreno" (Pérez Galdós 2002b: II, 534).

The reference to the baby as the *heredero* warrants the question, what does he stand to inherit? The obvious response is to view the epithet as a reference to the boy's new legal standing. As a member of the Santa Cruz family he inherits their name, social standing and financial wealth.[14] A claim by Segunda, Fortunata's aunt, that "el chico en la cara trae la casta" (Pérez Galdós 2002b: II, 518) invokes two meanings of the word *casta*. The first corresponds to lineage–"Familia o ascendencia de una persona"–while the second connotes the privileges of class–"Grupo de individuos de cierta clase, profesión, etc., que disfrutan privilegios especiales o se mantienen aparte y como superiores a los demás" (Moliner 1998: I, 533). Though Segunda's reference to the baby's face relates to the first definition, her other comments imply the second: "Todavía me he de ver yo cogida al brazo de don Baldomero, dando vueltas en la Castellana [...] si sabemos aprovecharnos, de esta hecha vamos para marquesas" (Pérez Galdós 2002b: II, 518). Significantly, Jacinta is not opposed to viewing the appearance of Juanito, who is, by all accounts, a handsome man, so long as the boy's character corresponds to her friend Moreno, who possessed a superior character despite a flawed body. By combining the best of both men Jacinta has invented an ideal being who fulfills her dream of physiognomic reliability.

The section of text in which Jacinta uses the term *heredero*, however, deals with physical appearance, paternity and character and thus suggests another interpretation for the appellation. In addition to the definition of *heredero* indicated above, "se aplica también al que ha heredado ciertos caracteres de sus padres" (Moliner 1998: I, 1470). It should be noted that *carácter* implies either physical or non-physical traits. The text makes clear, through the testimony of various characters, that the baby has inherited his father's

---

[14] Such is Moliner's definition of *heredero*: "se aplica, con respecto a una persona, a otra que recibe o ha de recibir sus bienes en herencia" (Moliner 1998: I, 1470).

looks, yet the theories of heredity in vogue at the time Galdós wrote *Fortunata y Jacinta*, as noted in the analysis of Maxi, maintain that physical characteristics are not the only thing passed from parent to child.[15] When Maxi first sees the infant he comments on the baby's appearance–"¡Se parece a tu enemigo!"–and warns that "si en lo moral saca la casta, peor que peor. El niño inocente no es responsable de las culpas del padre; pero hereda las malas mañas" (Pérez Galdós 2002b: II, 465). While Jacinta does not express a fear of degeneracy explicitly, her musings about the link between physical appearance and character would suggest that her desire to distance the baby from Fortunata and Juanito by erasing all physical signs that he is their offspring is motivated by this type of anxiety. After all, according to popular thought, "Beneath every face are the latent faces of ancestors, beneath every character their characters" (Maudsley 1979: 48).

Jacinta's feelings about her husband are clear. She refers to him simply as "ese falso, mala persona" (Pérez Galdós 2002b: II, 534). What is less certain is her attitude toward Fortunata. Jacinta expresses some sympathy for Fortunata on two separate occasions: when Juanito tells her about the death of Fortunata's first baby and again when she hears about Fortunata's fight with Aurora. But Jacinta shows no signs of sympathy in this passage. The only mention of Fortunata is a reference to her as "la otra" (Pérez Galdós 2002b: II, 534), an appropriate label in that it highlights Jacinta's view of Fortunata as Other.

Jacinta's personal interactions with Fortunata are very limited but cannot be overlooked. Fortunata and Jacinta come together on a handful of occasions but only on two of them does Jacinta recognize Fortunata as her husband's lover. Both of these encounters end in physical violence. The first occurs in the home of Severiana where Mauricia la Dura has been taken to die. The narrator describes the brutal passion of Fortunata as she contemplates Jacinta: "Toda la rudeza, toda la pasión fogosa de mujer del pueblo, ardiente, sincera, ineducada, hervía en su alma, y una sugestión increíble la impulsaba a mostrarse tal como realmente era, sin disimu-

---

[15] Estupiñá (Pérez Galdós 2002b: II, 457), Maxi (Pérez Galdós 2002b: II, 464), Guillermina (Pérez Galdós 2002b: II, 473-4), Segunda (Pérez Galdós 2002b: II, 518), and Fortunata (Pérez Galdós 2002b: II, 521) all confirm the baby's resemblance to Juanito.

lo hipócrita" (Pérez Galdós 2002b: II, 208). This account of Fortunata portrays her as a primitive beast rather than a civilized woman, someone who is driven by instinct rather than reason. The "ardiente" passion that burns in her soul becomes uncontrollable when she sees Jacinta enter the room:

> Verla y cegarse fue todo uno. No podía darse cuenta de lo que le pasó. Obedecía a un empuje superior a su voluntad, cuando se lanzó hacia ella con la rapidez y el salto de un perro de presa. Juntáronse, chocando en mitad del angosto pasillo. La prójima le clavó sus dedos en los brazos, y Jacinta la miró aterrada, como quien está delante de una fiera... Entonces vio una sonrisa de brutal ironía en los labios de la desconocida, y oyó una voz asesina que le dijo claramente:
> –Soy Fortunata. (Pérez Galdós 2002b: II, 208)

The passage contains a number of images associated with the theory of atavism. The comparison to animals ("un perro de presa", "una fiera") suggests a lack of humanity and the statement that she blindly obeys an instinctual power rather than her own will also expresses this link with a primordial inner beast. Commenting on the latent atavism of certain individuals, Hippolyte-Adolphe Taine describes how the bestial instincts of the degenerate take over under the right circumstances: "we can see how, from the peasant, the labourer, and the bourgeois, pacified and tamed by an old civilization, we see all of a sudden spring forth the barbarian, and still worse, the primitive animal, the grinning sanguinary, wanton baboon, who chuckles while he slays, and gambols over the ruin he has accomplished" (cited in Pick 1989: 71). Taine's comment resonates with the description of Fortunata, whose "sonrisa de brutal ironía" and "voz asesina" reveal an innate but inexplicable pleasure in her violent fury.

A second encounter between the two women results in a similar altercation. Fortunata is again portrayed as a savage in thought and action who possesses animal-like qualities. Fortunata comes to the home of Guillermina Pacheco to speak with the elderly woman about her relationship with Juanito. To Fortunata's surprise, Jacinta is hiding in the next room. Guillermina directs the following thought at Fortunata after the young woman expresses no remorse for her relationship with Juanito: "Usted no tiene sentido moral;

usted no puede tener nunca principios, porque es anterior a la civilización; usted es una salvaje y pertenece de lleno a los pueblos primitivos" (Pérez Galdós 2002b: II, 1983).[16] Moments later Jacinta confronts Fortunata who responds violently:

> Apoyando las manos en el respaldo, agachó el cuerpo y meneó las caderas como los tigres que van a dar el salto. Miróla Guillermina, sintiendo el espanto más grande que en su vida había sentido... Fortunata agachó más la cabeza [...] La ira, la pasión y la grosería del pueblo se manifestaron en ella de golpe, con explosión formidable. (2002b: II, 252)

Again the same images appear as before, namely the animal-brutality of Fortunata. In a post-Darwinian era the belief in man's superiority to animals suggests the inferiority of any person likened unto an animal. Fortunata appears as someone who is beyond the civilizing power of society, a throwback to a primitive age. But unlike Taine's suggestion that even a member of the bourgeoisie could possess dormant atavistic qualities, the passage just cited identifies Fortunata's brutality as a product of "el pueblo".

Fortunata's social status would be central to Jacinta's misgivings about her son's future. Early in the novel Jacinta refers to the atmosphere of a working-class neighbourhood as "salvajismo" (Pérez Galdós 2002b: I, 211). Her attitude is typical of her class and expresses the belief that the working class constitutes a primitive group of people. It is for this reason, Gilman explains, that in the nineteenth century society viewed inter-class marriages as being just as dangerous as miscegenation (Gilman 1985: 77). In one sense such a union would disrupt superficial divisions based on such factors as education or economic possessions. However, it was believed that these superficial divisions were symptoms of deeper, essential differences between classes that should not be bridged, and for this reason class mobility of any type was perceived as threatening. Due to the belief that the offspring of people from different social classes ran a greater risk of being degenerate, Jacinta is at pains to erase all traces of the child's true genealogy. By recreating the child's physical pedigree in her imagination, Jacinta is supposedly

---

[16] Even Juanito refers to Fortunata as "una salvaje que no sabía leer ni escribir" and mentions her "pasiones brutales" (Pérez Galdós 2002b: I, 205-06).

altering his moral dispositions. By eliminating signs of Otherness she makes him her own.

Despite contextual evidence corroborating Jacinta's misgivings about the baby's true origin, the narrator assumes a slightly mocking tone in portraying her eugenic musings and in doing so he challenges her desire for physiognomic reliability. The language used in the passage emphasizes the illusory nature of her ideas:

> A solas con él, la dama se entretenía fabricando en su atrevido pensamiento edificios de humo con torres de aire y cúpulas más frágiles aún, por ser de pura idea. Las facciones del heredero niño no eran las de la otra, eran las suyas. Y tanto podía la imaginación, que la madre putativa llegaba a embelesarse con el artificioso recuerdo de haber llevado en sus entrañas aquel precioso hijo, y a estremecerse con la suposición de los dolores sufridos al echarle al mundo. Y tras estos juegos de la fantasía traviesa, venía el discurrir sobre lo desarregladas que andan las cosas del mundo. También ella tenía su idea respecto a los vínculos establecidos por la ley, y los rompía con el pensamiento, realizando la imposible obra de volver el tiempo atrás, de mudar y trastocar las calidades de las personas, poniendo a éste el corazón de aquél, y a tal otro la cabeza del de más allá, haciendo, en fin, unas correcciones tan extravagantes a la obra total del mundo, que se reiría de ellas Dios, si las supiera, y su vicario con faldas, Guillermina Pacheco. (Pérez Galdós 2002b: II, 647)

The verb *fabricar* as well as the images of smoke, air and the phrase "pura idea" all show that her faith in physiognomic reliability exists only in her imagination and has no place in reality. Not only does the narrator repeatedly call attention to the fact that her worries and proposed solutions are merely thoughts–"pensamiento" appears three times in addition to "idea", "imaginación" and "fantasía"–but he presents them in such a way as to make them appear eccentric–"*su* atrevido pensamiento", "*su* idea", "traviesa", "extravagante"–as well as improbable–"artificioso", "frágil", "imposible". The idea that God and Guillermina, both austere and wise authority figures, would laugh at her if they knew her thoughts makes her seem even more ridiculous.

The same narrator who identifies with the Santa Cruz family in Part I of *Fortunata y Jacinta* does not, at the close of the novel, share Jacinta's bourgeois fantasy of physiognomic reliability. It is difficult to account for this change, but it may be that our narrator has become jaded against the ideology of the middle class as a result of witnessing the injustices brought about by Juanito, whose wealth and privilege lead to idle cavorting and, ultimately, tragedy. At every turn the panoptic and physiognomic practices depicted in the novel fail. Instead of producing stability and order, they breed the very maladies which they seek to contain. By making the inequalities present in society more rigid these dividing practices merely drive impoverished members of the lower class to crime, prostitution and other "deviant" practices in order to survive or to cope with reality, as in the case of Fortunata who turns to prostitution as a last resort (2002b: I, 610). Dividing practices, like those employed by Madrid's middle class, fail not because their physical structures are weak or because their implementation is inadequate, but, rather, because the ideology behind them is flawed. *Fortunata y Jacinta* exposes this fact. The order that is restored through the deaths of Mauricia and Fortunata or the enclosure of Maxi in Leganés may appear on the surface to restore order but, contrary to the principle of physiognomic reliability, the superficial order does not guarantee order within. Below the surface the disorder and tragedy remain.

CHAPTER 5

MAPPING THE BODY IN *NAZARÍN*

> Between madness and truth, the links are enigmatic.
> –Michel de Certeau

IN *Nazarín*, perhaps even more so than in any of Galdós's other novels, the text suggests a possible connection between the characters' physical appearances and their mental, moral and emotional states. Lombroso's name never appears in the text, yet the influence of his theories about genius, madness and criminality can certainly be felt, especially with respect to the characterisation of the eponymous protagonist and his two female disciples, Ándara and Beatriz. The popularity of Lombroso's theories in Spain reached a peak in 1895 (Maristany 1983: 362), and it is within this atmosphere of heightened interest in social deviance and degeneration that Galdós composed *Nazarín*.

One might suspect that the main characters from the novel– Nazarín, an unconventional priest and potential madman who abandons Madrid for a life of mendicancy, Ándara, an ex-prostitute and fugitive, and Beatriz, a hysteric turned mystic–could have come out of any number of Lombroso's many case studies. At first glance, Nazarín and his *discípulas* form a comical trinity of degenerates and Galdós's implied reader, who would have been familiar with the theories of Lombroso, would have been inclined to draw such a conclusion based on each character's physical appearance. However, these same characters possess a number of qualities that, when examined more closely, lead to uncertainty rather than clear categorisation. Galdós's use of ambiguous physical details combined with accounts of harmless and even benevolent behaviour makes it difficult to classify them as degenerates. Furthermore, the novel's underlying carnival theme suggests that all forms of categorisation are imperfect and that the concept of undecidability is actually worthy of celebration.[1]

READING WITH AN ETHNOGRAPHER'S EYE

Both Peter Bly (1991: 9-24) and Labanyi (1992-93: 227) describe Part I of *Nazarín* as a key for understanding the novel as a whole. In the first part of *Nazarín*, they argue, Galdós articulates many of the questions and problems that arise later on in the narrative, thereby offering suggestions on how a reader might approach the text. This being the case, the presentation of Nazarín and Ándara in Part I provides crucial details for carrying out an analysis of these characters.

A number of comments made by the narrator support the notion that people can be classified through visual observation, yet many of the details of Part I highlight the difficulties of putting such a theory into practice. The narrative begins when the narrator and a reporter friend arrive at a boarding house in southern Madrid with the objective of observing the tenants. When the pair first enter the establishment they avoid direct contact with the occupants and limit themselves to looking and listening to everyone they encounter. Upon seeing Nazarín for the first time the narrator uses the term *examinar* rather than the more common *ver* or *mirar*, and also reveals a desire to engage in "una observación más atenta" of the protagonist, indicating a studious and even scientific encounter as opposed to a casual meeting (Pérez Galdós 2001b: 87-88). He then sums up his experience at the boarding house in the following words:

---

[1] In her article, "Representing the Unrepresentable: Monsters, Mystics, and Feminine Men in Galdós's *Nazarín*" (1992-93), Jo Labanyi identifies strands of Lombrosian theory in the novel and also mentions the significance of Bakhtin's notion of carnivalization. Though she discusses some of the issues that will be examined here, her emphasis lies on the tenuous nature of language in the novel. My emphasis will be on the human body and its role as a site of confusion and undecidability rather than a source of reliable information as Lombroso argued. Inasmuch as my analysis reveals the body to be a well of (mis)information–an ambiguous physical text–my thesis complements Labanyi's argument that an insurmountable rift exists between words and things.

> Por cierto que la visita a la que llamaré *casa de las Amazonas* iba resultando de grande utilidad para un estudio etnográfico, por la diversidad de castas humanas que allí se reunían; los gitanos, los mieleros, las mujeronas, que sin duda venían de alguna ignorada rama jimiosa, y, por último, el árabe aquel de la hopalanda negra, eran la mayor confusión de tipos que yo había visto en mi vida. (Pérez Galdós 2001b: 89)[2]

As before, the narrator employs scientific terminology to describe his visit. The reference to a potential "estudio etnográfico" sets him up as a Lombrosian-type figure engaging in anthropological research. In mentioning the word ethnography, which is the area of anthropology "que se ocupa de la clasificación, descripción, etc., de las razas" (Moliner 1998: I, 1239), he alludes to classifying methods comparable to those used by Lombroso and also signals the importance of race–a detail which is further highlighted by the reference to Nazarín as "el árabe". Equally relevant is the reference to the "mujeronas" (which includes Ándara) as an obscure branch of simians. This detail contains clear Darwinist connotations and evokes Lombroso's notion of atavism. The narrator's scientific tone and affirmative phrases "por cierto" and "sin duda" lends credibility and authority to this classificatory bent. Given the chronological correspondence between the publication of *Nazarín* and Lombroso's popularity in Spain, Part I can easily be read as an invitation to the readers to conduct their own "estudio etnográfico" by performing similar categorising acts on the multitude of fictional figures within the narrative.

In spite of this expressed affinity for classification, Part I also contains evidence suggesting the fallibility of attempting to make categorical observations. The narrator's visit during carnival means that a number of occupants are wearing masks, makeup and other disguises. Typically reliable categories such as sex and class become indeterminable and the narrator mistakes women for men and Ándara's everyday appearance for a carnival disguise.

These and other visual ambiguities are complemented by verbal ambiguities. The narrator acknowledges his attention to word choice, such as when he discusses the name and description of the

---

[2] The word "jimio", which the narrator uses to describe Ándara and her friends, is a synonym for "mono".

boarding house (Pérez Galdós 2001b: 78-80) or when choosing adjectives to describe Chanfaina (Pérez Galdós 2001b: 79), not wanting to mislead the reader with inaccurate titles or terms. One effect of this hesitation over word choice is a reaffirmation of the narrator's role of careful and attentive scientist–one whose precision grants him more authority to speak. A consequence of this self-conscious attention to language is that the descriptions of characters stand out. However, when describing Nazarín the narrator shows little reservation in employing a series of seemingly contradictory soubriquets–"clérigo semítico", "clérigo árabe", "árabe manchego"– each of which alludes to a unique set of stereotypes and beliefs, and perhaps suggests that they are not as clearly distinguishable from one another as we might expect. Because these labels are so apparently contradictory they would seem to weaken the narrator's credibility as a precise and cautious observer and possibly destroy the reader's faith in his ability to accurately categorise Nazarín and the other characters. On the one hand the term *semítico* designates people of either Hebrew or Arabic origin, but in popular usage the term was synonymous with *Jewish* (Moliner 1998: II, 1053). This usage, which is both vague and a sweeping generalization, accentuates the narrative's blurring of categories as well as the inability to accurately or completely classify Nazarín. As Bly observes: "From the beginning to the very end of Part I, the narrator has succeeded in baffling us and preventing us from drawing any definitive conclusions about places, people's appearances or beliefs [...]" (Bly 1991: 24). This is, as we shall see, not only true of Part I but of the entire work. Clues are given, often by way of physical appearance, as to each character's mental, moral and emotional condition but they often prove to be inadequate, confusing or clearly incorrect.

AMBIGUOUS BODIES

Nazarín is an ambiguous character that embodies contradiction. His physical appearance contributes to an ongoing debate within the novel as to whether Nazarín is a crazy fool or a selfless saint. According to late-nineteenth-century degeneration theory, some aspects of Nazarín's physical makeup–especially those details that involve his suspect gender, race and religion–encourage a diagnosis of degeneracy, and more specifically of insanity.

Nazarín's gender provides the first in a series of paradoxes. When the narrator first encounters Nazarín he mistakes the priest for a woman: "en el marco de la ventana apareció una figura, que al pronto me pareció de mujer. Era un hombre. La voz, más que el rostro, nos lo declaró" (Pérez Galdós 2001b: 88). In explaining that Nazarín's true gender was revealed in his voice rather than his face, the narrator draws attention to the fact that Nazarín falls short in the most basic of gender distinctions: physical appearance. Nazarín exhibits the physical characteristics of a woman as described by Baltasar de Viguera, father of modern gynaecology in Spain, who in 1827 observes that "en [el hombre] todo su exterior representa la fuerza y la majestad: en [la mujer], la blandura y delicadeza" (cited in Jagoe 1998: 371). These very general criteria, which represent popular stereotypes as well as medical fact in the nineteenth century, correspond to the information provided in the text; Nazarín has a slight build, is physically weak and prone to illness. Nazarín's ambiguous gender is further highlighted by the references to his cassock, which resembles a dress in form yet belongs to a strictly male office.

Nazarín's perceived femininity is derived from his personality as well. His overt religiousness, for instance, is interpreted as being un-masculine by the mayor of one town who describes Nazarín's beliefs as "cosas que están bien para las mujeres, pero que no debemos creerlas los hombres" (Pérez Galdós 2001b: 294).[3] Like domesticity, religious worship came to be viewed in the nineteenth century as a feminine pursuit and as something unbecoming in men, an attitude that scholars refer to as the feminization of religion (Ford 2005, Abrams 2002). Labanyi explains that "Nazarín's qualities are those associated with the nineteenth-century feminine ideal: asexual, meek, passive, resigned to misfortune to the point of masochism" (Labanyi 1992-93: 233). This association, she argues, is illustrated by the fact that several characters refer to Nazarín as "ángel", a word closely associated with women and the "ángel del hogar" ideal so popular during the latter part of the nineteenth century in Spain (Labanyi 1992-93: 232-3).

Notwithstanding his feminine qualities, Nazarín does display

---

[3] In *Ángel Guerra* (1891) Dulcenombre makes a similar observation about religious devotion: "En una mujer todo eso es natural y hasta bonito, ¡pero en un hombre...! quita allá..." (Pérez Galdós 1967: V, 1407)

some masculine attributes. After leaving Madrid he grows a beard (Part III, Chapter 5) that, despite the absence of other physical evidence, reminds the reader that biologically Nazarín is indeed a man. Similarly, as a Catholic priest he has a profession that is limited to men. Also, among the travelling threesome of Nazarín, Ándara and Beatriz, he assumes a position of authority (Part III, Chapter 5). The sum of these masculine traits as well as his feminine qualities earns Nazarín the hybrid title of "feminine man" from Labanyi (1992-93: 232), for he defies even the most basic of classifications, that of gender.

The importance of this ambiguity becomes clearer when one considers the issues of gender involved in diagnosing madness and other forms of degeneracy. Lombroso, Gustave Le Bon and other anthropologists ascribed to women the same degenerate status as criminals, the insane, and "savage" races, arguing that their smaller skulls and frames provided evidence that they had not evolved to the same degree as men had. According to Catherine Jagoe, this image of the woman as a degenerate being sprang from the sexual prejudices of the period: "En el siglo XIX la salud tiene un género, el masculino. El varón es la pauta del cuerpo sano, desde la cual se mide al sexo femenino" (Jagoe 1998: 307). A similar trend can be found during this time with respect to mental health. Reason, the ideal of mental health, was typically associated with man who in turn was perceived as the standard of sanity. Woman, to the contrary, was understood to be less rational and more prone to madness and other psychological disorders. The gender bias with which authorities gauged physical and mental health represents more than a casual parallel. Women's supposed predisposition to mental illness tied in directly to their unique physical makeup (primarily the reproductive system) thereby linking psychological degeneracy with its physical counterpart (Moscucci 1990: 102). As a feminine man Nazarín enjoys (or suffers) the stereotypes of each sex. As a man he would be viewed as inherently rational. Conversely, his femininity suggests that he could suffer the maladies that are typically interpreted as female, including madness. As a hybrid his psychological status is unclear.

Nazarín's physical appearance also generates a series of unfavorable associations based on nineteenth-century ethnic and religious stereotypes. In Part I of the novel the narrator provides a brief physical sketch of Nazarín: "Era de mediana edad, o más bien joven prematuramente envejecido, rostro enjuto tirando a escuálido, nariz aguileña, ojos negros, trigueño color, la barba rapada, el tipo semítico más perfecto que fuera de la Morería he visto: un castizo árabe sin barbas" (Pérez Galdós 2001b: 88-89).

In addition to pointing out physical details associated with people of middle-eastern origin according to popular physiognomic discourse, the narrator also applies the ambiguous yet racially and religiously charged term *semítico* to sum up Nazarín's appearance.[4] In the majority of instances the appellatives *semítico* and *árabe* (or some derivatives of these) appear juxtaposed with *clérigo* and *manchego*, combinations that encapsulate the dual nature of Nazarín in that they represent contradictory stereotypes. The religious and cultural contrasts evoked by these terms are obvious, but there are underlying connotations that are best understood as coming out of intellectual climate of the day. In the closing decades of the nineteenth century a widespread belief existed concerning the mental instability of Jews. Despite his own Jewish heritage, Lombroso accepted the prevailing notion that Jewish populations had higher incidences of insanity. In *L'uomo delinquente* Lombroso cites Servi's *Gli Israeliti di Europa* (1872) and Verga's *Archivio di Statistica* (1880) in order to compare rates of insanity among Jews and Catholics. The statistics show the number of mentally ill individuals among Jews to be four times greater than that found among Catholics (Lombroso 1891: 136). Thus, when the text applies the combination of terms *semítico* and *clérigo* to Nazarín, a man of dubious mental health, it only serves to compound the confusion for it invokes specific allusions associated with both sides of the Catholic/Jewish binary. Following the data provided by Lombroso one would expect Nazarín to be sane for being Catholic (and a priest no less) and yet the Semitic allusion hints at psychological instability. Context also supports an ambiguous reading of the conflicting nomenclature. The narrator's reference to Nazarín as a "clérigo semítico" (Pérez Galdós 2001b: 89) is immediately preceded by the "estudio etnográfico" reference cited above. This sequence allows the hybrid epithet to stand out as its inherent ambiguity contrasts with the classificatory tone of the previous paragraph.

---

[4] "Nariz aguileña" was typically used to describe an Arabic person's nose while a Jewish person's nose was likened unto a vulture's beak (Álvarez Chillida 2002: 223). For a detailed analysis of the Jewish visage and physique as a sign of degeneracy see Gilman's *The Jew's Body* (1991).

On another occasion Nazarín struggles to ascertain whether a man he meets on one of his adventures, Don Pedro Belmonte, is good or bad, and whether he is mad or sane. The passage has an ironic tone as Nazarín asks the very questions that are typically asked of him. Like the other characters and the reader who find it difficult to categorise Nazarín, the priest cannot determine what type of man Don Pedro truly is: "¿Pero este hombre es malo o es bueno...? La cavilación en que cayó el pobre cura semítico no llevaba trazas de concluir; tan embrollado y difícil era el punto que su magín propuso dilucidar" (2001b: 230). Readers find themselves in a similar quandary as they are constantly pressured into asking similarly difficult questions about Nazarín's psychological state. By not providing definitive answers to such questions Galdós casts doubt on the whole idea of identifying people by their physical characteristics.

Nazarín's mental health, or lack thereof, is also tied to the references to the protagonist as a *manchego*. The repetition of Nazarín's geographic origin produces a telling intertextual link between Nazarín and another well-known *manchego*, Don Quijote. Like Don Quijote, Nazarín embodies the dual characteristics of the *cuerdo loco*, showing moments of lucidity, especially during conversations with others, while at other times behaving absurdly, as when he masochistically goes in search of adversity.[5] The *manchego* label not only serves as a constant reminder of Nazarín's enigmatic psychological state but it also acts as an alternative to the Jew/Arab allusions. As a region of Spain, La Mancha is centrally located and lacks the cultural and ethnic implications of other provincial areas such as Galicia, Andalucía, Valencia or Cataluña, which all boast a peripheral geographic orientation and possess an autonomous character with unique cultural values. There is the sense that La Mancha, unlike other these other regions, is purely Spanish. This notion was already being circulated by the '98 writers, and while it is difficult to say whether or not Galdós subscribed to the idea, it was at the very least useful for the purposes of his narrative. In this respect Nazarín's origin suggests that he is something of a clean slate, a

---

[5] Nazarín is also called "el clérigo andante", a name with obvious Quixotic intimations (Pérez Galdós 2001b: 171). For stylistic similarities between *Nazarín* and *Don Quijote*, see Dolgin (1990, 1989), Ruiz Ramón (1964: 174-95) and for other parallels between these two works see Bly (1991: 93-94) and Parker (1967).

Spaniard without complications. This is, of course, contradicted by the non-*castizo* designations *árabe* and *semítico* that are also applied to the priest.

Inasmuch as *árabe* and *semítico* are viewed as part of a binary relationship that is placed in opposition to *manchego* or *clérigo*, the terms can be used interchangeably and not as opposing terms themselves (as Jew and Arab would be used today). In *The Jew in the Novels of Benito Pérez Galdós* (1978) Sara Schyfter discusses the role the Jew plays in Galdós's novels: "As the unredeemed outsider who haunts the conscience of his old homeland, the Jew in Galdós is a symbol of man in search of acceptance, universal brotherhood, human compassion and love, religious transcendence and true faith" (Schyfter 1978: 117). Schyfter's point applies equally well to the Arab figure in the novel. In a historical context the Jew and the Arab both represent groups who are treated as social, racial and religious outsiders in Spain. Arab, Jew, priest and *manchego*–the quartet of designations most frequently applied to Nazarín other than his proper name–represent antagonistic ethno-religious groups yet in ascribing these disparate labels to a single individual Galdós allows Nazarín to simultaneously occupy the roles of Subject and Other. The wayward priest comes to stand for fusion and unity rather than exclusion and difference.

Female Offender?

While Nazarín is physically ambiguous, the female characters in *Nazarín* are less so. Of the figures that people the fictional world of *Nazarín*, Ándara most closely resembles the degenerate type in the form of the female offender that Lombroso describes in *La donna delinquente, la prostituta e la donna normale* (1893). In contrast to the examination of Nazarín, the textual reports of Ándara's unique physique and conduct do not suggest contradictory interpretations. Instead, they situate her unmistakably within the category of female deviance set forth by Lombroso. Nevertheless, the humor and playfulness that surround her undermine the seriousness of her possible degeneracy. The text does not portray Ándara as a fearsome criminal but as a comic character, challenging the reliability of applying Lombroso's theories concerning female criminality to her.

Lombroso sees the female criminal/prostitute as an atavistic subclass of woman who bears the physiognomy of degeneracy. Some of the characteristics that Lombroso notes in higher percentage among female criminals and prostitutes include cranial asymmetry, asymmetry of the face, virile physiognomy, crooked noses and anomalous teeth (Lombroso 1958: 76-81). He concludes with the following description of female degeneracy:

> And when youth vanishes, the jaws, the cheek-bones, hidden by adipose tissue, emerge, salient angles stand out, and the face grows virile, uglier than a man's; wrinkles deepen into the likeness of scars, and the countenance, once attractive, exhibits the full degenerate type which early grace had concealed. (Lombroso 1958: 102)

Whether or not Ándara ever possessed the "early grace" that Lombroso speaks of cannot be known. What is beyond doubt, however, is that her body as it is presented in the novel bears an uncanny likeness to the "full degenerate type" described above:

> El tiempo, que las cosas más sólidas destruye, había ido descostrando y arrancando de su rostro la capa calcárea de colorete, dejando al descubierto la piel erisipelatosa, arrugada en unas partes, en otras tumefacta. Uno de los ojos había llegado a ser mayor que el otro, y entrambos feos, aunque no tanto como la boca, de labios hemorroidales, mostrando gran parte de las rojas encías y una dentadura desigual, descabalada y con muchas piezas carcomidas. No tenía el cuerpo ninguna redondez, ni trazas de cosa magra; todo ángulos, atadijo de osamenta [...] (Pérez Galdós 2001b: 171)

The description of Ándara, which is remarkably similar to Lombroso's description of the delinquent woman, provides a sublime example of the grotesque in Galdós's work. It is at once horrible and humorous, shocking the reader with vivid details of a monstrous body and simultaneously producing laughter with the incongruities that such a sight offers. The narrator prefaces his description of Ándara by noting that she resembles a walking, talking scarecrow. Ironically, it is not Ándara's hideous countenance that leaves Nazarín shocked, but Ándara's timidity when she approaches him. Her behaviour offsets the grisly account of her physical appearance and weakens the view that she represents a dangerous, degenerate type. Immediately following the reference to her disarming shyness, the narrator again invokes the image of Lombroso's female offender by calling her "la criminal" (Pérez Galdós 2001b: 171), presumably referring to her violent altercation with another prostitute and her subsequent arson of the boarding house. This shifting emphasis between her comicality and her criminality is characteristic of the manner in which the narrative portrays her and as a result her deviant conduct appears somewhat less criminal.

Ándara's behaviour often suggests a connection with Lombroso's theory of atavism. Lombroso argued that atavistic individuals possessed "atavistic stigmata" or physical traits–large, jutting jaws, small skulls, hirsutism, canine-like teeth, dark skin–that were more similar to beasts and pre-historic humans than to modern, "civilised" humans. Lombroso saw atavism as the root of most crimes and discusses its specific connection to prostitution and female criminality in *La donna delinquente*:

> Due also to [atavism] is the virility underlying the female criminal type; for what we look for most in the female is femininity, and when we find the opposite in her we conclude as a rule that there must be some anomaly. And in order to understand the significance and the atavistic origin of this anomaly, we have only to remember that virility was one of the special features of the savage women. (Lombroso 1958: 112)

Ándara's combativeness gives her a virile quality like that identified by Lombroso in the female degenerate. A series of violent outbursts reinforces an early allusion to *las Amazonas* in the opening pages of the novel. Considering the reversal of gender roles that the term denotes, the Amazon reference is particularly appropriate. Not only were the Amazons fierce fighters, as is Ándara, but the removal of one breast to improve their archery was an overt sign of their lack of femininity.

A further example of Ándara's combative spirit comes in the novel's final pages. Nazarín suffers a fever induced hallucination and in his delirium he sees Ándara transformed into a masculine warrior woman:

> Venía Ándara, transfigurada en la más hermosa y brava mujer guerrera que es posible imaginar. Vestida de armadura resplandeciente, en la cabeza un casco como el de San Miguel, ornado

de rayos de sol por plumas, caballera en un corcel blanco [...] la terrible amazona cayó en medio de la caterva y con su espada de fuego hendía y destrozaba las masas de los hombres. Hermosísima estaba la hembra varonil en aquel combate (Pérez Galdós 2001b: 346-47).

Barry McCarthy's socio-historic study of masculinity shows that virtually all societies in all historic periods view the warrior figure as a paragon of masculine ideals (McCarthy 1994). Certainly Ándara's bellicose nature is far from feminine, but the very phrases which seem to highlight her un-feminine, atavistic aggression –phrases like "brava mujer guerrera", "terrible amazona" and "varonil"–are somewhat offset by the words "hermosa" and "hembra". It is significant that this idealized vision of Ándara is part of Nazarín's hallucination. It lends the entire scene a feeling of fantasy and spiritual symbolism. Her violent character ceases being a case of atavism and becomes something almost divine. By presenting bellicose femininity in this way, Galdós does not reject the warrior ideal, but, rather, reshapes it. He gives us an alternative where gender roles are more fluid and where seemingly incompatible spheres come together in the most remarkable way. Ándara comes across as beautiful not in spite of her manliness, but because of it.

The narrator's recourse to animal analogies also lends Ándara a violent, atavistic quality. She is compared to an ape (Pérez Galdós 2001b: 89), a lioness and a panther (Pérez Galdós 2001b: 94), and a tiger (Pérez Galdós 2001b: 287). The first reference, discussed above, compares her and her friends to a forgotten branch of primates, while the other three address her confrontational behaviour, using the appropriate image of a large, predatory cat. The tiger comparison comes at the end of the narrative when the Civil Guards and some villagers arrive to arrest her and Nazarín. When one of them insults and then kicks her spiritual leader she attacks the assailant with a potato peeler: "saltando hacia él como un tigre [....] Ciega de ira, ardiendo en sanguinario frenesí, no sabía lo que hacía" (2001b: 287-88). The imagery suggests a bloodthirsty beast controlled only by primitive instincts and is reminiscent of Lombroso's comments on atavism. Even after they tie her up she continues to roar (*rugir*) and gnaw at the ropes, furthering her likeness to a savage creature.

Ándara's manliness and animalism may indicate atavistic tendencies according to Lombrosian thought, but in the novel her savagery is almost always depicted in a humorous light. Such is the case when she misdirects her anger and spits in Ujo's face after the Civil Guards arrest her and Nazarín. Ujo declares his undying love for her despite the offence: "yo *diz* que te estimo... *Manque* me *escupites* otra vez, te lo *diz*", to which Ándara responds: "Es que yo soy así: cuando quiero decir que estimo, escupo" (Pérez Galdós 2001b: 302). Later, as she marches with the chain gang back to Madrid, she quarrels with a thief who had assaulted Nazarín the previous night:

> –Quisiera ser culebra, una culebrona muy grande y con mucho veneno, para enroscarme en ti y ahogarte y mandarte a los infiernos, grandísimo traidor, cobarde.
> –Guardias –gritó el bandido sin fiereza, más bien con plañidera entonación–, que esta señora me está *fartando*.
> –Yo no soy señora.
> –Pues esta pública... Yo no *farto* a nadie..., y ella me dice que es culebra y que *quié* abrazarse conmigo... No estamos para fiestas ni abrazos, compañera. (Pérez Galdós 2001b: 334-35)

Again Ándara is described as being part of the animal world, only this time it is not the narrator but she herself who suggests the association. What is perhaps more important to an examination of her character is the tone of the quarrel. As with her treatment of Ujo, the comical exchange between the two prisoners, including the thief's use of the malapropism *fartar* and the pejorative term *pública* in response to Ándara's claim "Yo no soy señora", gives an impression of childish fighting rather than harmful fury. These examples are typical of her character; deviance is almost always accompanied by silliness. In the grotesque figure of Ándara Galdós combines horror and humor to produce a walking, talking oxymoron, each aspect of her personality contradicting the other so that Ándara is at once funny and frightening, dangerous and harmless. Ultimately, this disparity makes her as unclassifiable as Nazarín.

Hysteria/Mysticism as Feminine Rebellion

The internal/external connection championed by Lombroso runs into difficulties in classifying the hysteric/mystic from Móstoles, Beatriz, who embodies many of the complexities of gender-based classifications. The topic of hysteria (as well as its counterpart, mysticism) is an appropriate one for the novel to address as it too was a highly debated topic in the medical discourse of the time. Indeed, the most prolific period in Lombroso's career, as well as the most popular, coincides with what Elaine Showalter calls "the golden age of hysteria" (Showalter 1985: 129). Like Lombroso's ideas about degeneracy, hysteria presented a possible link between the body and the psyche. It is precisely this presumed continuity between the physical realm and the psychical realm that has led current critics to study the similarities between hysteria and mysticism.[6] Even before the hysteria/mysticism parallel became a subject of modern scholarship authors explored the link in their literary writings, as in the case of Ana Ozores in Clarín's *La Regenta* (Labanyi 1991). Galdós depicts the hysteria/mysticism dynamic in the figure of Beatriz, whose initial hysterical fits are replaced with mystic visions. Her character thus provides a further opportunity to analyse the physical/psychological binary within the context of nineteenth-century dividing practices.

Lombroso was well aware of the preoccupation with hysteria in the closing decades of the century and he even contributed to the vast discourse on the subject, devoting an entire chapter of *La donna delinquente* to the study of "Hysterical Offenders" (Lombroso 1958: 218). Writing in 1893, the same year Freud and Breur's *Studies on Hysteria* was translated into Spanish, Lombroso states that: "In the asylums for the insane hysteria is most common, and chiefly contributes to differentiate insanity in the male from insanity in the female" (Lombroso 1958: 218). In addition to indicating how frequently the diagnosis of hysteria was made at the end of the nineteenth century, Lombroso's comment reveals the implicit gendering of the disorder. Hysteria was considered a female malady and its very etymology, from the Greek "hystera" or uterus, tied the condition to the female anatomy. While the Egyptians and Greeks believed that the condition resulted from a wandering uterus, whence its name, it eventually became an umbrella term under which physicians lumped innumerable clinical descriptions including paralysis, muscular spasms, insomnia, visual and auditory abnormalities, loss of appetite, dramatic mood swings, sexual deviance, loss of con-

---

[6] See Mazzoni (1996), Saillard (1989) and Ober (1985).

sciousness, loud outbursts and screaming, suicidal behaviour, and even seizures.[7] In short, hysteria became a medical wastebasket for all aspects of female anatomy and behaviour that caused men anxiety.

Mysticism's emphasis on altered bodily states, such as visions, ecstasy, and trances, as well as the subtext of female sexuality, provide a number of comparisons with hysteria. Like hysteria, mysticism became a topic of study for nineteenth-century physicians who considered the phenomenon "a gender-specific neurotic manifestation" (Mazzoni 1996: 17). Charcot referred to the symptoms of hysteria as "hysterical stigmata" (Charcot 1971: 160), recalling not only the designation used by Morel in his discussion of degeneracy, but also the condition of the mystic who suffers wounds similar to those of Christ. He even went so far as to map out the hysterogenic zones on his patients' bodies, in the same way that phrenologists mapped out regions of the cranium. Whether Charcot's choice of nomenclature is a case of the hystericizing of mysticism or mysticizing of hysteria is irrelevant in that he did not really distinguish between the two. Likewise, for Lombroso mysticism was simply a subcategory of hysteria. In the chapter of *La donna delinquente* devoted to hysteria Lombroso is brief yet categorical in asserting that: "Among hysterical women we also find saints, ecstatics, and fasting girls" (Lombroso 1958: 237). For Charcot, Lombroso and their contemporaries, hysteria and mysticism were in reality the same illness.

Beatriz's hysteric/mystic tendencies represent a retreat from the "objective" (male) rationality expounded by contemporary positivist scholars and lead to an avoidance of the classifications and domination of a patriarchal culture. During their first meeting, Beatriz describes some of her symptoms to Nazarín–loss of appetite, insomnia, seizures and mood swings–each of which is consistent with common hysteric symptoms. He suggests that the cure, like the illness, is essentially psychological:

> Tales trastornos son imaginarios [...] Yo le aseguro a usted que no tiene ya dentro del cuerpo ningún demonio, llamemos así a esas extrañas aberraciones de la sensibilidad que produce nues-

---

[7] For a historical overview of hysteria, see Veith's *Hysteria: The History of a Disease* (1965, especially Chapter 1) and Chapter 1, by Helen King, of *Hysteria Beyond Freud* (Gilman et al., 1993).

tro sistema nervioso. Persuádase usted de que esos fenómenos no significan lesión ni avería de ninguna entraña, y no volverá a padecerlos. (Pérez Galdós 2001b: 192)

Nazarín's comments suggest that Galdós was well informed of current trends in the study of hysteria. 1893, two years before Galdós wrote *Nazarín*, marks a turning point in medical thinking on the subject of hysteria. Until this time Charcot had been the major voice in the discourse on hysteria. In addition to the infamous seminars that he conducted during his tenure at the Salpêtrière women's hospital, Charcot was known for developing a leading theory on the cause behind the hysteric's physical symptoms, attributing them to a lesion in the brain (which he was never able to locate). After his death in 1893 physicians abandoned the search for the missing lesion or somatic basis and turned their attention to strictly psychological explanations. In this same year Freud, in collaboration with Josef Breuer, published an article titled "On the Psychical Mechanism of Hysterical Phenomena: Preliminary Communication", which was quickly translated and published in a number of European countries, the first of which was Spain.[8] Two years later Freud and Breuer published a second study, *Studies on Hysteria* (1895), that would set Freud apart as the new authority on the subject of hysteria. In these studies they definitively reverse the direction of the mind-body relation, dismissing the notion that hysteria is somatically based (i.e. Charcot's lesion), instead arguing that hysteria originates in the psyche and projects the individual's wishes, anxieties and traumas onto the body (Veith 1965: 257-74). Nazarín's observations concerning Beatriz are closer to Freud and Breuer's position than that of Charcot, as evinced by the fact that Nazarín instructs Beatriz to discard the notion that a lesion or some other somatic defect is responsible for her hysteria and instead to treat it as a psychological disorder.

According to Breuer and Freud, hysteria develops in response to an earlier trauma that has been suppressed. Eventually this suppression gives way to inexplicable physical symptoms (Breuer and Freud 1974: 53-69). Although Beatriz never discusses the issue beyond revealing her symptoms, Nazarín learns from Ándara the un-

---

[8] Published in the *Revista de Ciencias Médicas* as "Primera comunicación sobre la histeria" (1893). See Jagoe, et al. 1998: 346-47.

derlying cause of Beatriz's condition. According to Ándara, Beatriz recently suffered two miscarriages while in an abusive relationship with a man named Pinto (Pérez Galdós 2001b: 194). Pinto only appears twice in the novel (and one of those instances is a flashback), but his symbolic role and his relationship with Beatriz are paramount to the discussion of hysteria, for Pinto is a caricature of nineteenth-century hyper-masculinity: authoritarian, possessive and violent.

Beatriz's hysteria/mysticism functions as a defense mechanism, a way of dealing with the underlying cause of her condition. Her hysteric symptoms draw her away from Spain's hegemonic gender norms by excluding her from areas that are traditionally considered female domain:

> Hace tres meses perdí las ganas de comer [...] Y tras el no comer, vino el no dormir; y me pasaba las noches dando vueltas por la casa [...] Y lo peor era cuando me entraban los horrores de las cosas. No podía pasar por junto a la iglesia sin sentir que se me ponían los pelos de punta. ¿Entrar en ella? Antes morir.... (Pérez Galdós 2001b: 190-91)

Just as the hysteric's wandering womb (the anatomical essence of woman) abandons its proper place, so too does Beatriz flee from the spatial confines imposed upon her by society. Each symptom she mentions is related to a specific place or activity. Her anorexia and insomnia keep her out of the kitchen and the bed (and by extension, away from sexual intercourse) while her aversion to church precludes her from religious matters, all of which fall under the sphere of acceptable female activities and places according to the "ángel del hogar" discourse. Eventually her re-channelled hysteria, now in the form of mysticism, prompts her to abandon the quintessential female space, the home, and follow Nazarín, a figure who represents the antithesis of the existing patriarchal order. Beatriz's new course of action resembles Lombroso's description of "philanthropic hysteria". Making reference to Legrand du Saulle's *Les Hystériques* (1883), Lombroso writes that:

> There are some ladies who, though remaining in the world, take an ostentatious part in all the good works going on in their parish; they collect for the poor, work for the orphans, visit the sick, give alms, watch by the dead, ardently solicit the benevo-

lence of others, and do a great deal of really helpful work, while at the same time neglecting their husbands, children, and household affairs. (Lombroso 1891: 349)

Lombroso continues to reveal misogynistic sentiments when he explains that vanity rather than true charity is always the motive behind such acts. In the above citation he identifies the "proper" place of women as the home, under the authority of their husbands. When Beatriz refuses to abandon Nazarín and Ándara and return to Móstoles, Pinto's reaction is one of anger and confusion. He cannot tolerate anything existing outside of his control and understanding and so he threatens to kill them rather than have his perception of "proper" order upset. Pinto's exclamation, "¡Lo veo y no lo creo!" (Pérez Galdós 2001b: 336), upon finally seeing Beatriz in the company of Nazarín and Ándara could be taken literally–he cannot come to terms with these figures that refuse to be classified and controlled within the parameters of his phallocentric ideology. Beatriz's refusal to join Pinto is thus a rejection of masculine authority and the place allocated to women under such a scheme.

CARNIVAL AND THE UNDECIDABILITY OF IDENTITY

It is likely that Galdós anticipates, perhaps even encourages, the reader's inclination to make Lombrosian-like evaluations of his characters, but does so in order to expose the limitations and ambiguities that can result in attempting to make classifications based on physical data. This lack of confidence in physiognomic typing represents a clear break from the ideological undercurrents of *La desheredada*, in which degeneration theory is depicted as reliable. Compounding this sense of undecidability is the novel's carnival theme and setting. It is certainly no coincidence that *Nazarín* begins on "Un martes de Carnaval" (Pérez Galdós 2001b: 81). As Peter Goldman remarks: "The use of Carnival is indeed a stroke of genius on Galdós' part. Carnival is the great metaphor for the totally fluid reality of the urban poor in the 19th and 20th centuries" (Goldman 1974: 11, note 159). Although the carnival festivities are over by the beginning of Part II, the carnival setting in the opening chapters sets the tone for the rest of the novel. Allusions to carnival continue throughout each subsequent section of the narrative, increasing in frequency toward the end, and Ujo's presence in the final third of the novel acts as the final piece of the narrative's carnival frame. The text describes the way the residents of Ujo's village "le hacían comer mil cosas inmundas, a cambio de dinero o cigarros, y los chicos del pueblo tenían con él un Carnaval continuo" (Pérez Galdós 2001b: 270). Like the characters in La tía Chanfaina's boarding house, Ujo bears a carnivalesque physique with his compact body and "cabeza carnavalesca" (Pérez Galdós 2001b: 276). Ujo also accompanies the mayor and other townspeople when the Guardia Civil finally arrest Nazarín and his companions in a chaotic scene that the narrator relates to a carnival image: "Más parecía aquello bullanga de Carnaval que prendimiento de malhechores" (Pérez Galdós 2001b: 288). The result of the numerous references to carnival as well as the temporal setting of the initial section is in an ever-present carnival subtext from the beginning to the very end of the novel.

No figure, aside from Ujo, exemplifies the novel's spirit of Bakhtinian carnival as much as Ándara. Her misshapen body, her job as a prostitute (because it involves the lower stratum of the body), her verbal blunders and vulgar phrases, and her animal-like behaviour truly earn her the frequently used, polysemic label *tarasca* (literally "carnival dragon" but also "hussy" in popular speech). In particular, her oral attributes provide a substantial connection between Galdós's novel and Bakhtin's discussion of the grotesque body. Ándara's garrulousness distinguishes her from the other characters. When the reader first encounters Ándara, she and her companions are hurling insults at Nazarín. She later explains to Nazarín that: "Yo fui mismamente la que le insulté más y la que le dije cosas más puercas" (Pérez Galdós 2001b: 121). Her insults (not only here but throughout the novel) and her frequent use of interjections (such as "¡mal ajo!") provide examples of what Bakhtin, via English translation, calls "Billingsgate" and is a distinct feature of carnival.[9]

Ándara's excessive talking contrasts with the frequent mutism of hysterics. Following a violent altercation with a fellow prostitute, she seeks refuge in Nazarín's apartment. Despite being badly injured and on the run, she cannot stop talking and in recounting the fight she shares many unimportant details with her would-be protector. At one point during her story Nazarín interrupts to com-

---

[9] This term has been described as "market-place abuse", and appears to be a reference to the major London fish market of that name.

plain: "Cállate, repito..., y no hagas comentarios. Cuéntame el caso liso y mondo, para saber yo si debo ampararte o entregarte a la Justicia" (Pérez Galdós 2001b: 125). She unapologetically tells him that she is unable to stop: "No, señor; yo estoy hablando, si me dejan, hasta el día del *Perjuicio* final, y cuando me muera hablaré hasta un poquito después de dar la última boqueada" (Pérez Galdós 2001b: 125).

Ándara loves food almost as much as she loves to talk. Unlike her two travelling companions, Ándara is not inclined to fasting. This fact is most clearly apparent when Nazarín returns from Don Pedro Belmonte's house with a knapsack full of provisions. Significantly, the first three items of food that Ándara removes from the sack are meat products–"Lengua escarlata... y otra lengua... y jamón... ¡Jesús, cuánta cosa rica!" (Pérez Galdós 2001b: 237)–representing flesh and death and its connection to the body and life (as a source of sustenance). The presence of tongue in the bag of food provides a particularly rich image, representing the mouth and its importance in digestion–as an article of food and also as an organ for eating–and speech. That there are two tongues mentioned rather than one only serves to underline this duality. Nazarín and Beatriz forgo the snacks and decide to give them to local villagers while Ándara samples everything, "y toda la noche, aun después de dormida, estuvo relamiéndose" (2001b: 245). This comical remark by the narrator stresses her link with food and eating, both significant components of Bakhtin's theories of the carnival feast. Between incessant chatting and her voracious appetite, Ándara's mouth seems to be open more often than not. In his discussion of the grotesque body, Bakhtin explains the significance of the open mouth: "But the most important of all human features for the grotesque is the mouth. It dominates all else. The grotesque face is actually reduced to the gaping mouth; the other features are only a frame encasing this wide-open bodily abyss" (Bakhtin 1984: 317). The gaping mouth offers a point of exchange between the body and the world, between the internal and the external. It is the focal point of the carnival feast, where death (cooked flesh) leads to new life (nourishment), where waste (feces) gives way to growth (compost). The open mouth and grotesque body symbolize the "act of becoming", in which "the beginning and end of life are closely linked and intertwined" (Bakhtin 1984: 317).

Bakhtin's argument that the grotesque body is involved in the process of becoming has implications for an analysis of *Nazarín* and the topic of identity. Each of the characters examined has a grotesque body, one that is abnormal, undesirable and degenerate by traditional standards. Couched in the details of each character's physical appearance is an implied social category based on scientific, and therefore "objective", criteria. But carnival seeks to overcome these categories by blurring their boundaries:

> One might say that carnival celebrated temporary liberation from the prevailing truth and from the established order; it marked the suspension of all hierarchical rank, privileges, norms, and prohibitions. Carnival was the true feast of time, the feast of becoming, change, and renewal. It was hostile to all that was immortalized and completed. (Bakhtin 1984: 10)

The relevance of this passage is obvious enough. As a feminine man/Jew/Arab, as a prostitute and female criminal, and as a hysteric turned mystic, Nazarín, Ándara and Beatriz are truly social outsiders. Yet the carnivalesque atmosphere of the novel grants them the freedom to adopt alternate identities. Rather than viewing it as a swapping of identities, it would be more accurate to say that carnival allows an individual to be both things at once: crazy and sane in the case of Nazarín, "diabólica mujer" and "guerrero divino" in the case of Ándara. In perpetuating the carnivalization of the narrative beyond the scope of the traditional carnival festivities, Galdós creates a permanent carnival society in which identity is not static, complete or deterministic as Lombroso contends, but fluid, in progress and ambiguous. Attempts at categorisation are nullified by a sense of undecidability.

Absent from the novel's pages is the middle class in whom Galdós had expressed interest and hope in "Observaciones sobre la novela contemporánea en España". Instead, in truly carnivalesque fashion, we witness a new faith reborn in the grotesque bodies and waste of society's lowest strata. In *Nazarín* Galdós plays off the types of prejudices fostered by Lombroso's theories and does so in order to question the positivist belief in the supremacy of reason as well as the bourgeois need for classification. The fictional people that appear in *Nazarín*, as Labanyi rightly states, "constitute a gallery of freaks" (Labanyi 1992-93: 225). Nazarín, Ándara, and Beatriz (as well as La tía Chanfaina, Ujo, *el parricida* and *el ladrón sacrílego*) recall the photos and descriptions of "abnormal" persons found in Lombroso's works but one should not mistake their appearance in a so-called realist text as an indication that they are representative of contemporary Spanish society. Instead, one must see such figures as a projection of social anxieties about conventional divisions based on gender, race, and religion. Galdós situates these anxieties within conflicting contexts–the textual frame of carnival is set up against the extratextual frame of Lombroso's criminal anthropology–so as to make them stand out and to point out the limitations of dividing practices. In so doing, *Nazarín* undermines the positivist belief that truth or knowledge about the Other comes from the observation of external phenomena.

CHAPTER 6

MAPPING THE SOUL IN *MISERICORDIA*

> Una cosa sé, que habiendo yo sido ciego, ahora veo.
> —Juan 9: 25

GREEK mythology tells of a competition of creative powers among the gods in which Momus, the god of satire, was judge. In this contest Momus judged three divinely created objects: the bull, a house and man. Momus was, unsurprisingly, critical of all three creations. The bull's eyes were misplaced, he complained, causing it to lose sight of the target when it bows its head to charge. He denounced the impractical construction of the house, arguing that a lack of mobility renders it useless when its occupants travel. As for man, Momus argued that he should have been created with a window in his breast so that others could look into his soul and know his true nature and intentions (Babrius 1960: 59).

Momus's suggestion was taken up wholeheartedly by Europe's bourgeoisie in the nineteenth century as this new scopic regime attempted to render the human body legible in an effort to counter the blurring of social and physical boundaries brought about by urbanisation. Through urban reforms, physiognomic typing and gender norms, the discourse of the day promised to fulfil Momus's request.

Like Balzac and Dickens, Galdós reflected in his work the categorising impulse of his social milieu. In his early works Galdós even seemed to accept the reliability, if not necessarily the motives and goals, of such dividing practices. But, as this study has shown, Galdós grew wary of Madrid society's mapping efforts. Written in the final stage of his career, *Misericordia* is Galdós's most imaginative critique of the categorising gaze. In *Misericordia* Galdós creates one of his most memorable characters, Almudena, who, as a blind, mendicant Moor, represents the epitome of otherness that middle-class dividing practices targeted. Almudena's blindness is highly symbolic in a novel that is dominated by visual descriptions of characters and settings, to the point of being ocularcentric. Although visual language is the primary tool in Galdós's verisimilar depiction of Spanish society, the other senses can and do operate as supplements. In his last great novel Galdós invites us to "see" beyond the body to the very soul by refocusing his literary lens and leading his readers beyond the limits of the visible.

SEEING THE SOUL

The spiritual realm is highly personal, often obscure and sometimes even contradictory. As such it cannot be obviously divined by what is seen from the outside. And yet, at a time when the gaze was almighty, and in a nation where Catholicism had traditionally meant so much, it is understandable that religious devotion would be viewed as an attractive measuring stick.

Spain's spiritual landscape underwent significant changes in the nineteenth century. Despite the richness and diversity of Spain's religious history, it is often viewed through an idealized lens as a hierocratic nation, one that was divinely ordained to be Catholic. In reality Spain's religious landscape is not so straightforward. Religious difference has always existed in Spain, yet following the religious division of Europe in the sixteenth century non-catholic religions were suppressed to such an extent that the terms "Spanish" and "Catholic" became virtual synonyms.[1]

For centuries, then, the religious landscape of Spain remained theoretically homogeneous. In the nineteenth century, however, the nationalization of monastic estates, urbanism, the rise of the middle class and the spread of socialist ideas resulted in a Spain that was, in the words of Frances Lannon, "conspicuously Catholic in some

---

[1] This suppression was not limited to other religions but also extended to suspect trends within Catholicism, as can be seen in the Inquisition's mistrust of mysticism.

areas and social strata and hardly Catholic at all in others" (Lannon 1987: 10). Adrian Shubert was more specific: "Religious practice was clearly divided along class lines" (Shubert 1990: 161). By century's end the middle class made up the core of the Church's faithful while the lower classes of the urban centers were decidedly less religiously oriented (Portero Molina 1978: 192). The so-called "dechurching" of Spain's lower classes in the latter half of the nineteenth century is popularly attributed to the effects of urbanisation. William Callahan, for instance, observes that "the advance of urbanisation and industrialization created conditions that did not encourage observance among those uprooted from rural villages and small towns", resulting in a working class that was "religiously indifferent" (Callahan 2000: 248). Given the unending battle for survival, along with a growing attraction to movements like socialism, which denounced religion's suppression of or indifference toward the proletariat, it is easy to see why the lower classes had become disenchanted with the Church.

What is perhaps less obvious is why this same period witnessed a growing bond between the Church and the middle class. In his study of religious ideology in nineteenth-century Spain, José Antonio Portero Molina argues that the mutual attraction between the Church and the middle class was not merely a relationship of convenience, but one of necessity (Portero Molina 1978: 192). Having been dispossessed of its wealth and facing anticlerical sentiment in many regions, particularly in the larger urban centres where the dislocating effects of developing capitalism and the spread of liberal and positivist thinking were increasingly prominent, the Church saw a lifeline in the middle class. Not only did the middle class possess an abundance of wealth that could alleviate the Church's financial problems, but it was also becoming a political and social force to be reckoned with. Alternatively, the middle class recognized in the Church the one thing it wanted most–legitimacy. Despite a slump in popularity the Catholic Church was still the official religion of Spain and it remained steeped in tradition and authority. The Church adapted its ideology to fit the capitalist attitudes of the middle class–attitudes towards wealth and work ethic that differed from traditional Catholic views–thereby legitimizing the interests of its new bedfellow (Portero Molina 1978: 188-203). The middle class reciprocated, providing monetary support for the establishment of new religious communities (Callahan 2000: 218-19) as well as propagating Catholic ideals via discourse. It was a match made in heaven, or, rather, a match made in fear. As Callahan observes: the union between the two "emerged from a new identification of interest between a Church frightened by the secular political revolution that began in 1868 and a wealthy Catholic bourgeoisie alarmed by the prospect of social revolution" (Callahan 2000: 218). As an anxious middle class exchanged economic capital for symbolic capital, religious devotion served as yet another dividing line of Spanish society.

As I have noted, the nineteenth century was characterised by a tendency to convert every aspect of social life into a visual spectacle. So profound was this desire to see and be seen that even something as highly personal as religious devotion was used as an indicator of social status. Galdós made his opinion on the subject clear when, in his speech to the Real Academia Española, he complained about the desire of the middle class to police the minutiae of everyday life, including spiritual matters:

> La llamada clase media, que no tiene aún existencia positiva [...] absorbe y monopoliza la vida entera, sujetándola a un sin fin de reglamentos, legislando desaforadamente sobre todas las cosas, sin excluir las espirituales, del dominio exclusivo del alma. (Pérez Galdós 1972: 178)

Galdós's use of the term "legislar" seems to be metaphoric rather than literal. Galdós was a long time critic of organised religion, and his statement is a critique of the way the Church had numerous structures in place–special days, unspoken standards of dress, prescriptions on how often certain devotions should be carried out and even how they should be carried out, lists of different types of members, and the various "deberes anuales", "mensuales", "semanales", and "diarios" that members of various religious associations were expected to keep–that effectively regulated spiritual devotion. As his statement makes clear, Galdós considered the regulation of something as personal as spirituality to be an abuse of power.

A further manifestation of visualizing spiritual worth was the perceived link between hygiene and holiness. The belief that personal cleanliness reflected the spiritual purity of the individual is due in large part to the hygiene craze that had gripped Spain during the preceding decades and that targeted specific social strata. But the hygiene-holiness connection had deeper roots that formed part of the spiritual identity of Christians everywhere. According to William Andress, the "hygienic laws" found in the book of Leviticus were meant to "restore the broken relationship that exists between man and his Creator" (Andress 2000: 5). These laws emphasized personal cleanliness and equated it with holiness, leading to the popular adage that "cleanliness is next to Godliness". At the heart of this "Mosaic Health Code", as Andress calls it, is a call for segregation, the separation of the Israelites from the other cultures of the region. Thus these codes of cleanliness were as much about establishing order as they were about hygiene, which, according to Mary Douglas, are really one and the same: "As we know it, dirt is essentially disorder. [...] Eliminating it is not a negative movement, but a positive effort to organise the environment" (Douglas 1984: 2). As I outlined in Chapter 1, the squalor of lower-class neighbourhoods was viewed as both a reflection and a cause of immorality. Madrid's begging population, like those described in the opening chapters of *Misericordia*, were thus viewed as a type of physical and social disorder. They dwelt in dirty neighbourhoods, wore shabby clothes, and perhaps bathed less frequently, all of which contributed to a stereotype of spiritual inferiority.[2]

ON THE SURFACE

Misericordia presents the struggles of Benina, an elderly servant whose selfless acts of charity convert her into one of Galdós's most notable and, as a woman, unusual Christ-figures. Benina is the maid of Francisca Juárez de Zapata, the matriarch of an upper middle-class family who has fallen on extremely hard times. By clandestinely begging at a local church Benina is able to provide food for Doña Paca and her family, but Benina's part-time mendicancy draws her into the most unsavoury parts of Madrid and even lands her in prison for a short time. Her begging also introduces her to a truly unique individual by the name of Almudena, a blind Moor and fel-

---

[2] See Teresa Fuentes Peris's *Visions of Filth: Deviancy and Social Control in the Novels of Galdós*, especially pp. 132-94, for a discussion of changing attitudes toward poverty and mendicity in the nineteenth century.

low beggar whose love for Benina is based on what can only be described as spiritual vision. It is Almudena's ability to "see" Benina's inner beauty that lies at the heart of the narrative.

The novel begins with the reading of faces. "Dos caras", the novel begins, "como algunas personas, tiene la parroquia de San Sebastián" (Pérez Galdós 2000b: 7). The phrase evokes the concept of duality and is reminiscent of the physiognomic theory that an individual's inner core corresponds to their exterior appearance. Indeed, the idea is confirmed a few lines later when the narrator explains that the church's façade is an accurate reflection of a morally corrupt Madrid: "Habréis notado en ambos rostros una fealdad risueña, del más puro Madrid, en quien el carácter arquitectónico y el moral se aúnan maravillosamente" (Pérez Galdós 2000b: 7). This nod to physiognomy, here illustrated by an architectural metaphor, highlights the appearance/substance binary that Galdós explored time and time again in his novels, a theme with which his readers would be familiar. But the opening line can, and in fact should, be read differently. The novel's first words offer a caution. The idea that an individual has two faces is common as a metaphor for dishonesty and hypocrisy–two faces with different agendas–and is a warning not to be fooled by appearances. As was the case with *Nazarín*, the outer/inner binary of physiognomy is eventually discredited in *Misericordia*–not merely because the physical markers send contradictory signals, but also because these visual codes are excluded within the world of blindness that is a central theme of the novel.

When the reader encounters the first characters, a group of beggars huddled in the entrance of the church, the language used to describe them again suggests a link between a visible exterior and an individual's character. One of the mendicants, *La Burlada*, is a foul-mouthed woman whose "ojuelos sagaces, lacrimosos, gatunos, irradiaban la desconfianza y malicia" (Pérez Galdós 2000b: 16). The poignancy of this description is more forceful when one considers that eyes were considered by physiognomists to be windows to the soul and thus enjoyed a particularly prominent place in physiognomic discourse (Aguirre de Venero 1865: xii, 334).[3] The invo-

---

[3] See Mariano Aguirre de Venero's *Primer sistema del lenguaje universal, fisiognómico de los ojos* (1865) and Ronald Quirk's "Physiognomy in Pardo Bazán's Portrayal of the Human Body" (2002) for a discussion of the importance of eyes within physiognomic discourse.

cation of physiognomic discourse is even more explicit when the narrator begins making animal comparisons:

> Si vale comparar rostros de personas con rostros de animales, y si para conocer a la Burlada podríamos imaginarla como un gato que hubiera perdido el pelo en una riña, seguida de un chapuzón, digamos que era la Casiana como un caballo viejo, y perfecta su semejanza con los de la plaza de toros, cuando se tapaba con venda oblicua uno de los ojos, quedándose con el otro libre para el fisgoneo y vigilancia. (Pérez Galdós 2000b: 17)

As the previous chapters mentioned, animal comparisons like the ones in the above citation are part of a long-standing practice within the physiognomic tradition. While these comparisons are comical they are also effective for characterisation; given what little the text says about these women the analogies appear accurate. This appearance of accuracy produces an inclination on the part of the reader to conduct similar physiognomic readings of the other character descriptions.

The echoes of physiognomic discourse present in the novel's first chapters are just part of a larger emphasis on the visual that pervades the entire first half of the text. Most notably, this emphasis surfaces in the form of a narrative preference for visual description over the other senses. As a more complete picture of the church develops, the narrator observes that the nearby flowershop "recrea la vista" but fails to mention the more obvious smells that one would expect from a flowershop (Pérez Galdós 2000b: 7). Similarly, the roof and walls of the church, "con su afeite barato de ocre, sus patios floridos, [y] sus hierros mohosos" do not evoke the olfactory or tactile responses that one might expect; instead they are described simply as "un conjunto gracioso, picante, *majo*" (Pérez Galdós 2000b: 8). Galdós is providing his readers with verbal pictures to delight our eyes, but nothing more.

Misericordia is certainly not the only novel to favour visual description over the other senses. Given the very nature of the medium, literature in general has an undeniable visual quality, and realism in particular, with its emphasis on observation (as in Stendhal's famous mirror analogy), is inherently visual (Jay 1993: 110-11). But in *Misericordia* the attraction to all things visual is exaggerated. Not only does the narrator bombard the reader's sensorium with visual

imagery, but he leaves the other senses undisturbed, failing to mention smells or sounds when their presence would be most appropriate. Even the characters get caught up in this sensorial favouritism, as illustrated by a passage in which Obdulia, Doña Francisca's daughter, and Ponte, a distant relative, dream of a better life. "No puede usted imaginar cuánto me gustan las flores: me muero por ellas", declares Obdulia as they wait patiently for Benina to bring some food (Pérez Galdós 2000b: 131). Contrary to what we might expect, it is not the fragrance of the flowers that attracts the girl, but the sight of them: "Mi deseo es admirarlas en la planta. Dicen que hay tantísimas clases de rosas; yo quiero verlas" (Pérez Galdós 2000b: 132). The dialogue in question contains nine references to seeing or looking at the flowers but only once mentions a desire to smell them. For Obdulia, as well as for most of the characters in *Misericordia*, sight is the principal means of cognition while smell and the other senses are merely something extra, a supplement.

By engaging in physiognomic typing and emphasizing the visual, the narrator misleads the reader into trusting appearances. When the readers are introduced to Benina, the protagonist of the novel, they are fully prepared to make judgments about her character based on her appearance:

> Tenía la Benina voz dulce, modos hasta cierto punto finos y de buena educación, y su rostro moreno no carecía de cierta gracia interesante que, manoseada ya por la vejez, era una gracia borrosa y apenas perceptible. Más de la mitad de la dentadura conservaba. Sus ojos, grandes y oscuros, apenas tenían el ribete rojo que imponen la edad y los fríos matinales. Su nariz destilaba menos que las de sus compañeras de oficio, y sus dedos, rugosos y de abultadas coyunturas, no terminaban en uñas de cernícalo. Eran sus manos como de lavandera y aún conservaban hábitos de aseo. [...] parecía una Santa Rita de Casia que andaba por el mundo en penitencia. Faltábanle sólo el crucifijo y la llaga en la frente, si bien podía creerse que hacía las veces de ésta el lobanillo del tamaño de un garbanzo, redondo, cárdeno, situado como a media pulgada más arriba del entrecejo. (Pérez Galdós 2000b: 20-21).

In some respects the description of Benina is positive. Through the use of negative declarations–"no carecía de cierta gracia", "sus ojos apenas tenían el ribete rojo", "su nariz destilaba menos que las de sus compañeras de oficio", "sus dedos no terminaban en uñas de

cernícalo"–Benina is set apart, and above, from the other mendicants in the church. But it would be going too far to say that the description is flattering. Even the details that are described as positives ("más de la mitad de su dentadura conservaba") hardly suggest Benina is a paragon of Christian values or an individual worthy of adulation. In fact, we could say that this description borders on the grotesque. As the truth is revealed, however, the discrepancy between exterior and interior reality becomes obvious. Benina is, in the very words of Galdós, a "criada filantrópica, del más puro carácter evangélico" (Pérez Galdós 1972: 224). When this fact becomes apparent in the narrative, through her actions and through the estimation of other characters, the readers are not only prepared to accept the fallibility of physiognomic typing, they are also more sensitive to shortcomings of visual knowledge in general.

BEYOND THE SURFACE

One purpose of this narrative bias for all things visual, as I have already alluded, is that when non-visual descriptions do occur they tend to stand out. Nowhere is this sensorial juxtaposition more apparent than in the scenes involving Almudena. For Almudena smell is also a supplement, but not as something extra as in the example of Obdulia and the flowers. For Almudena smell is a supplement in the sense that it replaces or fills an emptiness. Derrida makes the following observation about supplementation:

> The supplement supplements. It adds only to replace. It intervenes or insinuates itself *in-the-place-of*; if it fills, it is as if one fills a void. If it represents and makes an image, it is by the anterior default of a presence. Compensatory [*suppléant*] and vicarious, the supplement is an adjunct, a subaltern instance which *takes-(the)-place* [*tient-lieu*]. (Derrida 1976: 145)

It is not enough for Almudena to simply develop a hypersensitive sense of smell. To supplement in the way described by Derrida, Almudena's sense of smell must be a proxy, it must result in vision.

Literature contains numerous examples of vision coming to those who are blind. Though physically devoid of sight, Teiresias alone can see the fullness of what Oedipus has done. Indeed it is only after Oedipus gouges out his own eyes that he can finally appreciate the truth. The New Testament tells of Saul, later called Paul, who temporarily loses his vision. During this period of physical darkness Paul's spiritual eyes are opened and he sees Christ (Acts 9). The cause of Almudena's blindness–swimming in a contaminated river–is certainly not as dramatic as these examples previously mentioned. But the result is. The visual void left by Almudena's blindness is filled by olfaction. Through a process of sensorial supplementation Almudena is able to "see" Benina's soul, something no one else is able to do.

On more than one occasion Almudena's nose functions as a pair of spiritual eyes. The first instance occurs when Almudena and Benina leave San Sebastián church in search of a *duro*. Benina, desperate to find enough money to buy food for Doña Francisca and herself, accompanies Almudena to his apartment in the hopes of finding something that can be sold or pawned. What follows is an example of narrative anosmia.[4] One would expect to encounter a number of unpleasant odours–after all, in a realist description, according to Roland Barthes in "The Reality Effect", "the *having-been-there* of things is sufficient reason for speaking of them" (Barthes 1982: 15)–yet no mention is made of any smells whatsoever. It is as if the narrator has reached out to plug the reader's nose. As the couple enters the building they pass through a patio "lleno de montones de basura, residuos, despojos y desperdicios de todo lo humano" (Pérez Galdós 2000b: 37). Absent is any indication of the accosting smells that would accompany such a spectacle. Inside the apartment the anosmia continues. Unlike most kitchens, that of Pedra and Almudena is seemingly devoid of aroma, despite the presence of old pots, bottles and food. And when Almudena searches through Pedra's clothing (the clothing that she is wearing as she lies passed out on the floor) there is no mention of body odour, the smell of alcohol, or any other odour one might expect from a drunken beggar. Even when Benina finds "una petaca vieja y sucia" there appears to be no scent of tobacco (Pérez Galdós 2000b: 40). In fact, not until Benina leaves and we find ourselves alone with Almudena does the narrator's grip loosen and allow us to breath freely. Only then do we experience the mystical smells that follow.

---

[4] A medical term for lack of olfaction, or a loss of the ability to smell.

The overpowering aroma of Almudena's incense is juxtaposed with the narrative anosmia leading up to this point. The reader's dormant sense of smell awakens thanks to an "humareda muy densa y un olor penetrante" that come from a newly lit bit of incense:

> Era el sahumerio de benjuí, única remembranza material de la tierra nativa que Almudena se permitía en su destierro vagabundo. El aroma especial, característico de casa mora, era su consuelo, su placer más vivo, práctica juntamente casera y religiosa, pues envuelto en aquel humo se puso a rezar cosas que ningún cristiano podía entender. (Pérez Galdós 2000b: 41)

As seen in this passage–which constantly refers to the link between the incense and Almudena's geographic, cultural and religious background–smells have high symbolic value. One point made by Dan Sperber's in *Rethinking Symbolism* is that certain smells are "symbols *par excellence*" because they are "institutionalized", as in the case of incense which is used in religious rituals, and therefore belong to what semiologists call "a cultural code" (Sperber 1975: 118).

Despite Sperber's claim, smell occupies a low place in the hierarchy of the senses. The nineteenth century witnessed a "cultural repression" of smell (Classen, et al. 1994: 3-5). Freud and other scientists, basing their ideas on Darwin's theory of evolution, argued that in adopting an upright posture vision became more important than smell in ensuring the survival of the species.[5] As a consequence of this theory, a "heightened olfactory consciousness" was believed to be a characteristic of "insufficiently evolved savages, degenerate proletariat, or else aberrations: perverts, lunatics or idiots" (Classen, et al. 1994: 4). In an age when the miasma theory of disease was still very much alive, olfaction was also closely associated with the spread of disease, "the very vehicles of contagion" in the words of William Ian Miller (2005: 342). Finally, smell suffered cultural repression because it was viewed as a threat to the established social order, which was based on clear, legible divisions: "odours cannot be readily contained, they escape and cross boundaries, blending different entities into olfactory wholes" (Classen, et al. 1994: 4). For

---

[5] See D. M. Stoddart's *The Scented Ape* (1990) for a discussion of the "decline of smell" in evolutionary terms.

all of these reasons smell is the perfect vehicle for Galdós to condemn the bourgeoisie's categorising gaze.

Almudena's prayerful trance ends prematurely when Pedra is roused from her drunken stupor by the aromatic fumes. Yet we can speculate that his trance may have led to a spiritual vision as had happened years earlier under similar circumstances. In the novel's fourteenth chapter Almudena describes being visited by two angels. They tell him to go to the slaughterhouse where he will receive a visit from King Samdai of the *baxo terra*. Following their instructions, Almudena burns incense and prays "en medio de los despojos de reses y charcos de sangre" until midnight (Pérez Galdós 2000b: 103). Again the anosmatic narrator describes no foul smells coming from the blood puddles and bovine carcasses. It may be more accurate to describe the narration as selective anosmia, because despite the absence of unpleasant odours the smell of Almudena's incense is noted. As Almudena squats in the empty slaughterhouse "aspirando los vajos olorosos del sahumerio", the curtain of blindness is drawn back from his eyes. He sees a parade of animals, insects, people and riches of every kind, and his temporary eyesight is so keen that it captures every imaginable detail of King Samdai's appearance. Just before the vision ends, the King shows Almudena a woman whom the blind Moor should find and then marry. In this fantastic passage smell has become sight, nasal has become visual and the result is a synaesthetic revelation. It is a moment that mirrors what Heidegger calls "the unconcealedness of beings" (Heidegger 1986: 262) in "The Origin of the Work of Art" (1950). In this essay Heidegger contends that the only way to discover the origin of a work of art, that is, "its essence or nature", is through a moment of revelatory "opening up" or "disconcealing" which Heidegger dubs *aletheia*, the Greek term for truth (Heidegger 1986: 262-63). But *aletheia*, this revelation of an essence, is fleeting, according to Heidegger, and so too must the curtain fall once again upon Almudena's eyes. The vision ends and he is left alone in the slaughterhouse, "no quedando más que un odor penetrante del *ilcienso*" [sic] (Pérez Galdós 2000b: 106). Only the supplement remains.

Significantly, Almudena is the only character in the novel associated with smells, and the only one who experiences visions induced by sensorial supplementation. Almudena is marginal in every imaginable way: physically (blind), socially (beggar), racially (black), ethnically (Moroccan), and religiously (Jewish). His otherness is important, in part because these very qualities give him an air of exoticism, making his visions more believable, but also because it highlights the issue of boundaries. A significant amount of scholarly criticism has been devoted to Almudena's role in the novel, particularly with reference to his religious status.[6] Marcel Crespil, for instance, observes that "el moro Almudena es un carácter cuya presentación muestra algunas inconsistencias curiosas y cuyo desarrollo revela contradicciones muy significativas en cuanto a sus creencias religiosas" (Crespil 1972: 463). Crespil goes on to comment on Almudena's ambiguous ethno-religious status: "no se parece ni a un judío, ni a un mahometano" (Crespil 1972: 464), which Crespil regards as a reflection of popular stereotypes: "La gente española, a una distancia de casi cuatro siglos de contacto directo con moros y judíos, guardaba todavía una idea errada de las formas de la creencia religiosa de los semitas, confundiéndolas por considerarlas todas falsas y paganas" (Crespil 1972: 467). Sarah Cohen, on the other hand, argues that this ambiguity is a reflection of the author rather than the reading public, a result of Galdós's "belief that all religions are basically identical" (Cohen 1973: 52). However, given Galdós's extensive treatment of dividing practices and social mapping, it seems more likely that this ambiguity was intentional.

In a revealing study about the blind Moor, Vernon Chamberlin analyses the significance of the name Almudena. After suggesting and then dismissing some obscure origins for the name Almudena, Chamberlin offers the following insight:

> One is justified in turning to the most obvious referent known to Galdós and the majority of Madrilenian readers–i.e., the "Almudena", the cathedral of the patroness of Madrid. More than any other church in Madrid, it is the traditional and official spiritual center of the city. (Chamberlin 1964: 492)

The idea is a compelling one. Not only is the Almudena cathedral the "official spiritual center of the city"–offering an ironic contrast

---

[6] For works which deal exclusively with Almudena see "Almudena in *Misericordia*" (Brooks 1980), "Almudena and the Jewish Theme in *Misericordia*" (Cohen 1973), "La fe religiosa de Almudena en *Misericordia*" (Crespil 1972), "Galdós: De Morton a Almudena" (Casalduero 1964), "The Significance of the Name Almudena in Galdós' *Misericordia*" (Chamberlin 1964), and "De Almudena y su lenguaje" (Lida 1961).

with a man who is so spiritually off-centre–but it was, according to Chamberlin, the site of the principal Moslem mosque of the city at the time of the Reconquest (Chamberlin 1964: 492). By combining these details with Almudena's Jewish heritage, Chamberlin is inclined to agree with Robert Ricard's assessment that Almudena is "a composite Semite–a personification of the three great religions which have existed on Spanish soil" (Chamberlin 1964: 492). The notion that Almudena, who embodies marginality, is in some way a spiritual amalgam is extremely attractive in light of Galdós's desire to undermine the categorising gaze. It offers a subtle blurring of boundaries that parallels the illimitable nature of smell, that marginalised sense which differs so significantly from vision and which is so closely associated with Almudena.

Almudena's epiphanic experience in the slaughterhouse brings two distinct and separate realms together. There is a barrier between all things spiritual and temporal, body and soul, divinity and mortality. However, when Almudena's scent-stimulated experience leads to a spiritual vision this barrier collapses and heaven and earth unite. This fusion is a result of the relationship between the "sensing and the sensed, a separation, and at once a union, in time, a putting of the instant out of phase, and already a retention of the separated phase" (Levinas 1981: 72). The outcome of this unification is that Almudena is able to view Benina with spiritual vision. This is why he is convinced that she is the one shown to him by King Samdai:

> La suya delante, siempre delante, enpujadita y sin dejarse ver la cara... Claro, que él veía la figura con los ojos del alma... Pues bueno: cuando conoció a Benina, una mañana que por primera vez se presentó ella en San Sebastián, llevada por Eliseo, el corazón, queriendo salirse del pecho, le dijo: "Ésta es, ésta sola, no hay otra. (Pérez Galdós 2000b: 182)

Because of this, when he later tells her that she is pretty–"tú ser *bunita*" (Pérez Galdós 2000b: 216)–we must understand that he does not refer to her appearance but to her character and her very soul. Like so many parts of this novel, this disparity between physical appearance and inner quality–a striking contrast to the physiognomic typing that some of Galdós's earlier works subscribe to–is closely related to a biblical passage:

Y Jehová respondió a Samuel: No mires a su parecer, ni a lo grande de su estatura, porque yo lo desecho; porque Jehová no mira lo que mira el hombre; pues el hombre mira lo que está delante de sus ojos, pero Jehová mira el corazón. (1 Samuel 16: 7)

While others cannot see past Benina's tattered clothing, her *lobanillo*, or her aging body, Almudena remains ignorant as to her appearance. He can, however, see beyond the surface.

OPENING OUR EYES

Vision is pre-eminent and smell is often non-existent in *Misericordia*. In addition to the episodes already mentioned, there are several other instances of narrative anosmia, such as Benina's trip to the poorest part of town. She enters a building with "corrales interiores, rajas mohosas y paredes sucias", and there is even a white mule, but there are no offensive odors that one might expect under such conditions (Pérez Galdós 2000b: 204). But perhaps even more important than those things that do not smell are those that do–like Almudena's incense. Olfactory moments such as these contrast with the long periods of odourless description in such a way that the reader cannot help but take notice.

Even though vision is clearly the most important descriptive tool, the presence and absence of the other senses can be vital to understanding the story. Through a process of sensorial supplementation smell allows Almudena to see Benina for what she really is because, rather than using his "ojos muertos", the blind beggar looks on Benina "con los ojos del alma" (Pérez Galdós 2000b: 187). According to Derrida, "One goes *from blindness to the supplement*" (Derrida 1976: 149). This is literally the case for Almudena, who depends on his supplemental sense of smell to give him synaesthetic-spiritual vision. There is no doubt as to the condition of Almudena's eyes: "Los ojos eran como llagas ya secas e insensibles, rodeados de manchas sanguinosas" (Pérez Galdós 2000b: 32). But this description refers to his physical eyes: "Pero en lo de los mundos misteriosos que se extienden encima y debajo, delante y detrás, fuera y dentro del nuestro, sus ojos veían claro" (Pérez Galdós 2000b: 103). There are only two other characters that seem able to appreciate Benina's noble character, Ponte and Juliana. Ponte only fully appreciates her after his fall from the horse and his subsequent insanity (Pérez Galdós 2000b: 315). Likewise, Juliana fails to see Benina's inner worth until the final chapter of the novel when her children fall ill. It is only then that she seeks out Benina for counsel and emotional peace of mind (Pérez Galdós 2000b: 319-22). In a way similar to Almudena, these characters must first experience a loss–of vision, sanity, health–before their spiritual eyes are opened. When Almudena burns his incense he sees things that no one else can; he sees Benina's inner beauty. Although the narrator withholds aromatic descriptions from the readers, occasionally we too are allowed to breathe in the sweet smell of Almudena's incense.

Misericordia is the culmination of a visual education, one which encourages the reader to ignore the middle-class promise of physiognomic reliability. Like this study, Galdós's novelistic trajectory is telescopic, that is, characterised by a zooming effect. Beginning with a sweeping view of the city, the texts in question call for an increased focus and narrowing of the gaze. What begins as a panoramic view of Madrid society ends as a concentrated look at the individual. From the city streets to social groups to the body of the individual, Galdós's narrative gaze becomes more and more intimate as time progresses.

By playing with the reader's expectations Galdós causes the reader to be sensitive to what he or she sees. Both *Nazarín* and *Misericordia* entice the reader into making categorising judgments about the characters based on a series of visible markers, only to disprove those judgments later on. A perceptive reader cannot help but notice this pattern, which cautions against such visual assessments. Such a lesson cuts against the grain of the prevailing discourses (and even Galdós's earlier novels), which educated readers in the art of visually based social mapping. But the message in his later works is clear: the link between exterior and interior is cultural myth. Whether or not one heeds the call, Galdós is clearly inviting his readers to open their eyes.

CONCLUSION

> The real voyage of discovery consists not of seeking new landscapes but in having new eyes.
>
> –Marcel Proust

ANY traveller knows the feeling of disorientation that comes from traversing the streets of an unknown city for the first time. Without a guide it can be daunting, even frightening. Maps allay the fears of getting lost in the urban labyrinth; they provide a sense of comfort that comes from knowing where things are and where to go. They provide knowledge that is liberating and even empowering. Reading through Foucault, it becomes clear that vision is culturally specific, and what the bourgeoisie of nineteenth-century Madrid saw (and what was a considerable source of anxiety) was disorder. Life in the city felt like being stuck in a labyrinth. More than the physical reality of living in a city with narrow winding streets, this sense of disorientation was a social phenomenon and the product of urbanisation.

While the various discursive fields that surface in the novels I have examined in this study may at first seem unrelated, they actually share a common source, the urbanisation of Madrid, and a common goal, the creation of a legible social map. In *La desheredada* I argued that this map was organised according to class difference and the notion of distinction. In *Tormento* and *La de Bringas*, gender provided the dividing lines of the social map. In *Fortunata y Jacinta* boundaries are established by family relations as well as one's genealogical background. It is at this point in Galdós sprawling opus that one detects a shift as to the legitimacy of the bourgeoisie's mapping enterprise. Whereas the first novels mentioned depict dividing practices as necessary and accurate, by the end of *Fortunata y Jacinta* such practices are depicted as subjective and unreliable.

Nazarín provides an example of this new attitude. The three main characters appear, at first glance, to fit the degenerate mould. However, the physical and moral ambiguities surrounding these characters, combined with an underlying carnival theme, reveal the categorising gaze to be flawed. This is borne out again in *Misericordia* when Almudena, a blind beggar and cultural hybrid, is the only character that can "see" the inherent goodness of the novel's heroine, Benina.

In an attempt to highlight the role of social mapping in these novels I have addressed some areas that have been somewhat overlooked in Galdós studies, with the hope that they will be looked at in more detail in the future. First, because degeneration theory figures so prominently in Galdós's novels of the 1890s critics may underestimate the importance of the subject in his earlier works. As I imply in this study, degeneration is a constant theme in Galdós's work. Lombroso's theories may not have reached Spain intact until the end of the 1880s, but variations of the theory, which originated with Morel, existed in the 1860s and by the time Galdós wrote *La desheredada* in 1881 the term "degeneration" was common currency in Spain (Labanyi 2000: 28).

The majority of the characters examined in this study are, in the eyes of the bourgeoisie, in some way abnormal or deviant and therefore worthy of the label "degenerate". But they are not all depicted as such by Galdós. Though in the early 1880s Galdós's narrators offer up views that are in line with the gender norms and theories of degeneration, the perspective offered in his novels of the 1890s is antagonistic with respect to the bourgeoisie's campaign of social mapping. By presenting characters who do not fit well into any standard category, Nazarín being a prime example, Galdós welcomes the prospect of fluid society where undecidability is permitted. By comparing and contrasting Galdós's representation of degeneration theory in the 1880s with that of the 1890s we can more fully appreciate this development.

Second, one area that is in need of serious attention by scholars of nineteenth-century literature is masculinity studies. In recent decades critics such as Foucault and Butler have convincingly argued that gender is a social construct, an identity created by discursive trends. In the field of Hispanic studies scholars like Aldaraca, Jagoe and Charnon-Deutsch have applied this theory to great effect, particularly when looking at the *ángel del hogar* ideal. But thus far we have failed to do the same with respect to masculinity. The recent body of scholarship on the subject of masculinity that has emerged from the fields of history, social science and humanities evinces the importance and timeliness of this area of research. My analysis of the male characters in *Tormento* and *La de Bringas* is but a first step. Much more needs to be done.

Finally, an exploration of the senses, as subject and narrative technique, in Galdós's work and other realist texts offers significant possibilities. Given the self-conscious emphasis placed on observation and mimesis by realist authors, it is logical that vision would figure prominently in the work of Galdós. At the same time, however, the prevalence of blind characters in his work almost feels like an invitation to focus on the other senses. In *Misericordia* smell is used to great effect by Galdós to question the categorising power of vision. Smell also provides a novel approach to intersubjective relations, in this case between Benina and Almudena. With research on the haptic in film studies proving fruitful, as in the case of Laura Marks's recent works *The Skin of the Film* (2000) and *Touch: Sensuous Theory and Multisensory Media* (2002), it may be time to examine the tactile quality of Galdós's novels.

As I have sought to demonstrate in this study, Galdós's depiction of the categorising gaze, while it may be prominent, is by no means unchanging. Identifying and examining a number of targets of the gaze–including class, gender, the family and the body–we can see an evolution in his use and depiction of vision. Galdós may find fault with the visual as his career progresses, but his later novels should not be read as a complete rejection of the gaze. Rather, this critique of vision should be seen by the reader as an invitation to alter his or her perspective, to cast off the lenses of the dominant discourses in order to see with new eyes.

BIBLIOGRAPHY

Abrams, Lynn (2002). *The Making of Modern Woman*. London, Pearson Education.
Acuña, Rosario de (1882). *El lujo en los pueblos rurales*. Madrid, Establecimiento del Montegrifo.
Adams, Michele and Scott Coltrane (2005). "Boys and Men in Families: The Domestic Production of Gender, Power, and Privilege", in Jeff Hearns, Michael Kimmel, R. W. Connell (eds.), *Handbook of Studies on Men and Masculinities*. London, Sage: 230-48.
Aguirre de Venero, Mariano (1865). *Primer sistema del lenguaje universal, fisiognómico de los ojos*. New York, John F. Trow.
Aldaraca, Bridget (1991). *El ángel del hogar: Galdós and the Ideology of Domesticity in Spain*. Chapel Hill, University of North Carolina Press.
Allison, George and Joan Ullman (1974). "Galdós as Psychiatrist in *Fortunata y Jacinta*". *Anales Galdosianos* 9: 7-36.
Álvarez Chillida, Gonzalo (2002). *El antisemitismo en España: la imagen del judío, 1812-2002*. Madrid, Marcial Pons.
Álvarez-Uría, Fernando (1979). "La cárcel o el manicomio", in Julia Varela and Fernando Álvarez-Uría (eds.), *El cura Galeote asesino del obispo de Madrid-Alcalá: proceso médico-legal*. Madrid, La Piqueta: 149-73.
Alonso y Rubio, Francisco (1863). *La mujer bajo el punto de vista filosófico, social y moral: Sus deberes en relación con la familia y la sociedad*. Madrid, Gamayo.
Andress, William (2000). "Cleanliness and Holiness: Physical and Spiritual Wholeness in the Book of Leviticus". *InFo* 3(1): 5-22.
Anon. (1836). "El visaje de Napoleón". *Semanario Pintoresco Español*. 1(9): 78-80.
Anon. (1836). "Fisonomía: La nariz". *Semanario Pintoresco Español*. 1(20): 163-65.
Anon. (1854). "Problema fisonómico". *Semanario Pintoresco Español*. (19): 152.
Anon. (1863). "Origen de ciertas especies de animales". *El Mundo Universal: La Ilustración Española y Americana*. 7(24): 192.
Anon. (1875). *La Ilustración Española y Americana*. 238.
Anon. (1879). *Porvenir de la familia obrera*. Madrid, Aurelio y Alaria.
Anon. (1884). "Crónica". *La Época*.
Anon. (1911). "Madrid". *Enciclopedia Universal Ilustrada*. Madrid, Espasa-Calpe. XXXI.
Anon. (1989). "Family". *World Book Encyclopedia*. Chicago, World Book.
Arbiol, Fr. Antonio (1867). *La familia regulada con la doctrina de la Sagrada Escritura y Santos Padres de la Iglesia Católica*. 1825. Barcelona, Heredero de Pablo Riera.

Ariès, Philippe (1962). *Centuries of Childhood: A Social History of Family Life.* New York, Alfred A. Knopf.
Aristotle (1968). "Physiognomica", in W.D. Ross (ed.), *The Works of Aristotle.* Oxford, Clarendon Press.
Armstrong, Nancy (1987). *Desire and Domestic Fiction: A Political History of the Novel.* Oxford, Oxford University Press.
Babrius, Valerius (1960). *Aesop's Fables,* translated by Denison Hull. Chicago, University of Chicago Press.
Bacon, Kathy (2007). *Negotiating Sainthood: Distinction, Cursilería and Saintliness in Spanish Novels.* Oxford, Oxbow.
Bahamonde, Ángel and Julián Toro (1978). *Burguesía, especulación y la cuestión social en el Madrid del siglo XIX.* Madrid, Siglo Veintiuno.
Bakhtin, Mikhail (1984). *Rabelais and His World.* Bloomington, IN, Indiana University Press.
Barthes, Roland (1982). "The Reality Effect", in Tzvetan Todorov (ed.), *French Literary Theory Today.* Cambridge, Cambridge University Press: 11-17.
Bartra, Roger (1994). *Wild Men in the Looking Glass: The Mythic Origins of European Otherness.* Ann Arbor, University of Michigan Press.
Bayo, Ciro (1902). *Higiene sexual del soltero.* Madrid, Rodríguez Serra.
Beauvoir, Simone de (1953). *The Second Sex.* New York, Alfred A. Knopf.
(1960). *La Santa Biblia.* Nashville, Thomas Nelson.
Blanco, Alda and Carlos Blanco Aguinaga (2001). "Introduction". *La de Bringas.* Madrid, Cátedra: 9-45.
Blanco Aguinaga, Carlos (1986). "Sobre 'El nacimiento de Fortunata'", in Germán Gullón (ed.), *Fortunata y Jacinta de Benito Pérez Galdós.* Madrid, Taurus: 153-74.
Bly, Peter (1991). *Pérez Galdós: Nazarín.* London, Grant and Cutler.
Bourdieu, Pierre (2003). *Distinction: A Social Critique of the Judgement of Taste,* translated by Richard Nice. London, Routledge.
Braun, Lucille (1970). "Galdós' Re-creation of Ernestina Manuel de Villena as Guillermina Pacheco". *Hispanic Review* 38(1): 32-55.
Breuer, Joseph and Sigmund Freud (1974). *Studies on Hysteria.* London, Penguin.
Brooks, J. L. (1980). "Almudena in *Misericordia*", in John England (ed.), *Hispanic Studies in Honour of Frank Pierce.* Sheffield, Department of Hispanic Studies, University of Sheffield.
Brown, Jonathan and John H. Elliott (2003). *A Place for a King: The Buen Retiro and the Court of Philip IV.* New Haven, Yale University Press.
Butler, Judith (1990). *Gender Trouble: Feminism and the Subversion of Identity.* London, Routledge.
Calbraith, John K. (1973). "Introduction". *The Theory of the Leisure Class.* Boston, Houghton Mifflin: v-xxv.
Callahan, William (2000). *The Catholic Church in Spain, 1875-1998.* Washington DC, The Catholic University Press.
Campos Martín, Ricardo and Rafael Huertas (2001). "The Theory of Degeneration in Spain (1886-1920)". *The Reception of Darwinism in the Iberian World: Spain, Spanish America and Brazil.* Dordrecht, The Netherlands, Kluwer Academic Publishers: 171-87.
Carlson, E. T. (1985). "Medicine and Degeneration: Theory and Praxis", in J. Edward Chamberlin and Sander L. Gilman (eds.), *Degeneration: The Dark Side of Progress.* New York, New York University Press: 121-44.
Casalduero, Joaquín (1964). "Galdós: De Morton a Almudena". *Modern Language Notes* 79: 181-87.
——— (1974). *Vida y obra de Galdós (1843-1920).* Madrid, Editorial Gredos.
Casey, James (1989). *The History of the Family.* Oxford, Blackwell.

Castro, Carlos María de (1861). *Ensanche de Madrid*. Madrid, Lit. J. Donan.
Chamberlin, Vernon (1964). "The Significance of the Name Almudena in Galdós' *Misericordia*". *Hispania* 47(3): 491-96.
—— (1987). "Juan Valera and Galdós's Characterisation of Juanito Santa Cruz". *Anales Galdosianos* 22: 22-31.
—— (2001). "New Insights Regarding the Creation and Character Delineation of Maxi Rubín and Plácido Estupiñá in *Fortunata y Jacinta*". *Anales Galdosianos* 36: 99-110.
Charcot, Jean Martin (1971). *L'hystérie*. Toulouse, Privat.
Charnon-Deutsch, Lou (1990). *Gender and Representation: Women in Spanish Realist Fiction*. Philadelphia, John Benjamins.
—— (2000). *Fictions of the Feminine in the Nineteenth-Century Spanish Press*. University Park, PA, The Pennsylvania State University Press.
Charnon-Deutsch, Lou and Jo Labanyi, Eds. (1995). *Culture and Gender in Nineteenth-Century Spain*. Oxford Hispanic Studies. Oxford, Clarendon Press.
Classen, Constance, David Howes and Anthony Synnott (1994). *Aroma: The Cultural History of Smell*. London, Routledge.
Classen, Constance (2005). "McLuhan in the Rainforest: The Sensory Worlds of Oral Cultures", in David Howes (ed.), *Empire of the Senses*. Oxford, Berg: 147-63.
Cohen, Sarah E. (1973). "Almudena and the Jewish Theme in *Misericordia*". *Anales Galdosianos* 8: 51-61.
Cohen, Stanley (1985). *Visions of Social Control: Crime, Punishment and Classification*. Cambridge, Polity Press.
Comfort, Alex (1967). *The Anxiety Makers: Some Curious Preoccupations of the Medical Profession*. London, Nelson.
Connell, R. W. (1987). *Gender and Power: Society, the Person and Sexual Politics*. London, Allen and Unwin.
—— (1995). *Masculinities*. Berkeley, University of California Press.
Considérant, Victor (1979). *Description du phalanstère et considérations sociales sur l'architectonique*. Paris, Durier.
Corbin, Alain (1985). *The Foul and the Fragrant*. Cambridge, MA, Harvard University Press.
—— (1990). *Women for Hire: Prostitution and Sexuality in France after 1850*. London, Harvard University Press.
Cosgrove, Denis (1984). *Social Formation and Symbolic Landscape*. London, Croom Helm.
Crane, Diana (2000). *Fashion and its Social Agendas: Class, Gender, and Identity in Clothing*. Chicago, University of Chicago Press.
Crespil, Marcel (1972). "La fe religiosa de Almudena en *Misericordia*". *Romance Notes* 13: 463-67.
Cruz, Jesús (2000). *Los notables de Madrid: Las bases sociales de la revolución liberal española*. Madrid, Alianza Editorial.
Cubí y Soler, Mariano (1949). *Elementos de frenología, fisonomía y magnetismo humano*. Barcelona, [n. pub.].
Culler, Jonathan (1981). *The Pursuit of Signs: Semiotics, Literature, Deconstruction*. Ithaca, Cornell University Press.
Darnton, Robert (1984). *The Great Cat Massacre and Other Episodes in French Cultural History*. New York, Basic Books.
Darwin, Charles (1991). *The Origin of Species*. Buffalo, NY, Prometheus.
Dash, Robert (1990). "El desdoblamiento de Galdós en Evaristo Feijóo y don Lope". *Actas del tercer Congreso de Estudios Galdosianos*. Las Palmas, Cabildo Insular de Gran Canaria. 2: 49-56.

Davidoff, Leonore and Catherine Hall (1987). *Family Fortunes: Men and Women of the English Middle Class, 1780-1850*. London, Hutchinson.
Della Porta, Giambattista (1586). *De humana physiognomonia*. Vico Equense, Apud Iosephum Cacchium.
Derrida, Jacques (1976). *Of Grammatology*, translated by Gayatri Spivak. Baltimore, Johns Hopkins University Press.
Díez de Baldeón, Clementina (1986). *Arquitectura y clases sociales en el Madrid del siglo XIX*. Madrid, Siglo Veintiuno.
Dolgin, Stacey L. (1989). "*Nazarín*: A Tribute to Galdós' Indebtedness to Cervantes". *Hispanófila* 33(97): 17-22.
——— (1990). "*Nazarín* and Galdós's Point of View". *South Atlantic Review* 55(1): 93-102.
Donzelot, Jacques (1979). *The Policing of Families*. New York, Pantheon.
Douglas, Mary (1984). *Purity and Danger: An Analysis of Concepts of Pollution and Taboo*. London, Ark Paperbacks.
Doyle, Arthur Conan (1960). *A Study in Scarlet. The Complete Sherlock Holmes*. New York, Doubleday.
Elliot, James (1987). *The City in Maps: Urban Mapping to 1900*. London, The British Library.
Escuder, José María (1881). *Quemas y crímenes*. Valencia, E. Pascual.
Espigado Tocino, Gloria (1995). "Cómo hacerse un hombre: la pedagogía decimonónica al servicio de la construcción sexual". *La identidad masculina en los siglos XVIII y XIX: de la ilustración al romanticismo*. Cádiz, Universidad de Cádiz: 129-150.
Félix, Joseph (1863). *Conferencia sobre la familia*. Palma, V. de Villalorega.
Fernández de Rojas, Juan (1795). *Libro de moda o ensayo de la historia de los Currutacos, Pirracos, y Madamitas del nuevo cuño*. Madrid, Fermín Villalpando.
Fernández Pérez, Paloma (1999). "La empresa familiar y el síndrome de Buddenbrook en la España contemporánea: el caso Rivière (1860-1979)". *La industrialización y el desarrollo económico de España. Homenaje al doctor Jordi Nadal*. Barcelona, Universitat de Barcelona. 2: 1398-1414.
Fishberg, Moris (1901). *The Jewish Encyclopedia*. London, Funk and Wagnalls. VI: 603-05.
Ford, Caroline (2005). *Divided Houses: Religion and Gender in Modern France*. Ithaca, Cornell University Press.
Ford, Richard (1966). *Handbook for Travellers in Spain*. London, Pythian.
Foucault, Michel (1976). *The Birth of the Clinic: An Archaeology of Medical Perception*, translated by Alan Sheridan. London, Tavistock.
——— (1980). *Power/Knowledge: Selected Inerviews and Other Writings, 1972-1977*, translated by Colin Gordon, et al. London, Longman.
——— (1982). "Afterword: The Subject and Power", in Paul Rabinow and Hubert Dreyfus (eds.), *Michel Foucault: Beyond Structuralism and Hermeneutics*. Chicago, The University of Chicago Press: 208-226.
——— (1988). *Politics, Philosophy, Culture: Interviews and Other Writings, 1977-1984*, translated by Alan Sheridan. London, Routledge.
——— (1990). *The History of Sexuality*, translated by Robert Hurley. London, Penguin.
——— (1991). *Discipline and Punish: The Birth of the Prison*, translated by Alan Sheridan. London, Penguin.
——— (2001). *Madness and Civilization: A History of Insanity in the Age of Reason*, translated by Richard Howard. London, Routledge.
Fraser, Nancy (1990). "Rethinking the Public Sphere: A Contribution to the Critique of Actually Existing Democracy". *Social Text* 25-26: 56-80.

Freud, Sigmund (1991). "Family Romances". *On Sexuality*, translated by James Strachey. Harmondsworth, Penguin. VII: 217-25.
Frost, Daniel (2005). "Public Gardens and Private Affairs in the Spanish Realist Novel". *MLN* 120(2): 314-34.
Fuentes Peris, Teresa (1996-97). "The Control of Prostitution and Filth in *Fortunata y Jacinta*: The Panoptic Strategy in the Convent of Las Micaelas". *Anales Galdosianos* 31-32: 35-52.
—— (2003). *Visions of Filth: Deviancy and Social Control in the Novels of Galdós*. Liverpool, Liverpool University Press.
Gassó y Ortiz, Blanca de (1878). "La misión de la mujer". *La Guirnalda* 7(159): 105-06.
Gilfoil, Anne W. (2006). "Disease as a Dis/Organising Principle in Nineteenth-Century Spain: Benito Pérez Galdós, Leopoldo Alas, and Emilia Pardo Bazán", in Jerry Hoeg and Kevin Larsen (eds.), *Science, Literature, and Film in the Hispanic World*. New York, Palgrave MacMillan: 129-49.
Gilman, Sander L. (1984). "Jews and Mental Illness: Medical Metaphors, Anti-Semitism and the Nineteenth Century". *Journal of the History of Behavioural Sciences* 20: 150-59.
—— (1985). "Sexology, Psychoanalysis, and Degeneration: From a Theory of Race to a Race to Theory", in J. Edward Chamberlin and Sander L. Gilman (eds.), *Degeneration: The Dark Side of Progress*. New York, Columbia University Press: 72-96.
—— (1986). *Difference and Pathology: Stereotypes of Sexuality, Race, and Madness*. Ithaca, Cornell University Press.
—— (1991). *The Jew's Body*. London, Routledge.
Gilman, Sander L., et al. (1993). *Hysteria Beyond Freud*. Berkeley, University of California Press.
Gilman, Stephen (1986). "El nacimiento de Fortunata", in Germán Gullón (ed.), *Fortunata y Jacinta de Benito Pérez Galdós*. Madrid, Taurus: 135-52.
Giné y Partagás, Juan (1872). *Curso elemental de higiene privada y pública*. Barcelona, N. Ramírez.
Goldman, Peter. "Galdós and the Aesthetics of Ambiguity: Notes on the Thematic Structure of *Nazarín*". *Anales Galdosianos* 9 (1974): 113-21.
Gómez Bravo, Gutmaro (2005). "La violencia y sus dinámicas: crimen y castigo en el siglo XIX español". *Historia Social* 51: 93-110.
Gómez Urdáñez, Gracia (2005). "The Bourgeois Family in Nineteenth-Century Spain: Private Lives, Gender Roles, and a New Socioeconomic Model". *Journal of Family History* 30: 66-85.
González, Rafael A. (1999). "La introducción y el desarrollo del higienismo en España durante el siglo XIX: precursores, continuadores y marco legal de un proyecto científico social". *Scripta Nova* 3(50).
González de Tejada, José (1854). *De la familia española: Discurso por el Lic. Don José González de Tejada en la solemne investidura de Doctor en jurisprudencia*. Madrid, Antonio Pérez Dubrull.
Gordon, Felicia (1997). "Legitimation and Irony in Tolstoy and Fontane", in Nicholas White and Naomi Segal (eds.), *Scarlet Letters: Fictions of Adultery from Antiquity to the 1990s*. London, Macmillan: 85-97.
Gordon, Mike (1977). "'Lo que le falta a un enfermo le sobra a otro': Galdós's Conception of Humanity in *La desheredada*". *Anales Galdosianos* 12: 29-37.
Graham, John (1979). *Lavater's Essays on Physiognomy: A Study in the History of Ideas*. Bern, Lang.
Haidt, Rebecca (1998). *Embodying Enlightenment: Knowing the Body in Eighteenth-Century Spanish Literature and Culture*. Basingstoke, Macmillan.

Harley, J. B. (2001). *The New Nature of Maps: Essays in the History of Cartography*. Baltimore, Johns Hopkins University Press.
Harley, J. B. and David Woodward (1987). *Cartography in Prehistoric, Ancient, and Medieval Europe and the Mediterranean*. Chicago, University of Chicago Press.
Harrowitz, Nancy A. (1994). *Antisemitism, Misogyny, and the Logic of Cultural Difference: Cesare Lombroso and Matilde Serao*. Lincoln, University of Nebraska.
Harvey, John (1995). *Men in Black*. London, Reaktion Books.
Heidegger, Martin (1986). "The Origin of the Work of Art", in Mark Taylor (ed.), *Deconstruction in Context: Literature and Philosophy*. Chicago, University of Chicago Press: 256-79.
Héran, François (1990). *Le bourgeois de Séville. Terre et parenté en Andalousie*. Paris, P. U. F.
Hoff, Ruth (2006). "Questions of Gender and Religious Foundation in *Halma*". *Bulletin of Spanish Studies* 83(8): 1059-83.
Horn, David (2003). *The Criminal Body: Lombroso and the Anatomy of Deviance*. New York, Routledge.
Iarocci, Michael (2003). "Virile Nation: Figuring History in Galdós' *Trafalgar*". *Bulletin of Spanish Studies* 80 (2): 183-202.
Irigaray, Luce (1978). "Interview 1", in Marie Hans and Gilles Lapouge (eds.), *Les femmes, la pornographie, l'éroticisme*. Paris, Seuil: 43-58.
Jagoe, Catherine (1994). *Ambiguous Angels: Gender in the Novels of Galdós*. Berkeley, University of California Press.
———, Trans. (1996). "Notes on the Translation". *That Bringas Woman*. London, Everyman.
Jagoe, Catherine, Alda Blanco and Cristina Enríquez de Salamanca (1998). *La mujer en los discursos de género: Textos y contextos en el siglo XIX*. Barcelona, Icaria Antrazyt.
Jay, Martin (1993). *Downcast Eyes: The Denigration of Vision in Twentieth-Century French Thought*. Berkeley, University of California Press.
Jones, Gareth S. (1976). *Outcast London: A Study in the Relationship of Classes in Victorian Society*. Harmondsworth, Penguin.
Juliá, Santos, David Ringrose and Cristina Segura (1995). *Madrid: historia de una capital*. Madrid, Alianza.
Klein, Melanie (1988). *"Envy and Gratitude" and Other Works, 1946-1963*. London, Virago.
Klinghoffer, Arthur (2006). *The Power of Projections: How Maps Reflect Global Politics and History*. London, Praeger.
Labanyi, Jo (1986). "City, Country and Adultery in *La Regenta*". *Bulletin of Hispanic Studies* 63(1): 53-66.
——— (1991). "Mysticism and Hysteria in *La Regenta*: The Problem of Female Identity", in Lisa Condé and Stephen Hart (eds.), *Feminist Readings on Spanish and Latin-American Literature*. Lewiston, NY, Mellen.
——— (1992-93). "Representing the Unrepresentable: Monsters, Mystics, and Feminine Men in Galdós's *Nazarín*". *Journal of Hispanic Research* 1: 225-37.
——— (2000). *Gender and Modernization in the Spanish Realist Novel*. Oxford, Oxford University Press.
Lannon, Frances (1987). *Privilege, Persecution, and Prophecy: The Catholic Church in Spain*. Oxford, Clarendon Press.
Larsen, Kevin (1996). "The Medical Background of *Fortunata y Jacinta*: The Case of Maxi's Migraines". *Ometeca* 3-4: 410-25.
Lavater, Johann Casper (1797). *Physiognomische Fragmente*. London, W. Locke.
Lavin y Olea, Pedro (1863). *Origen de la familia: principales derechos y deberes consiguientes a esta institución: Discurso leído en la Universidad Central*. Madrid, M. Rivadeneyra.

Le Brun, Charles (2000). *De la physionomie humaine et animale. Dessins de Charles Le Brun gravés pour la Chalcographie du musée Napoléon en 1806*. 1806. Paris, Musée du Louvre.
LeGates, Richard and Frederic Stout, Eds. (2000). *The City Reader*. London, Routledge.
León, Fray Luis de (1984). *Poesía*. Madrid, Cátedra.
Levinas, Emmanuel (1981). *Otherwise Than Being or Beyond Essence*. The Hague, Martinus Nijhoff.
Lida, Denah (1961). "De Almudena y su lenguaje". *Nueva Revista de Filología Hispánica* 15: 297-308.
Lombroso, Cesare (1891). *The Man of Genius*. London, Walter Scott.
Lombroso, Cesare and Guillermo Ferrero (1958). *The Female Offender*. New York, Philosophical Library.
Lombroso-Ferrero, Gina (1972). *Criminal Man, According to the Classification of Cesare Lombroso*. Montclair, NJ, Patterson Smith.
López de la Vega, José (1878). *La higiene del hogar*. Madrid, La Guirnalda.
Maristany, Luis (1983). "Lombroso y España: nuevas consideraciones". *Anales de Literatura Española* 2: 361-82.
Marks, Laura (2000). *The Skin of the Film: Intercultural Cinema, Embodiment, and the Senses*. Durham, Duke University Press.
——— (2002). *Touch: Sensuous Theory and Multisensory Media*. Minneapolis, University of Minnesota Press.
Mathews, Cristina (2003). "Making the Nuclear Family: Kinship, Homosexuality, and *La Regenta*". *Revista de Estudios Hispánicos* 37: 75-102.
Maudsley, Henry (1979). *The Pathology of Mind*. London, Macmillan.
Mazzoni, Cristina (1996). *Saint Hysteria: Neurosis, Mysticism, and Gender in European Culture*. Ithaca, Cornell University Press.
McCarthy, Barry (1994). "Warrior Values: A Socio-Historical Survey", in John Archer (ed.), *Male Violence*. London, Routledge: 105-120.
McDonogh, Gary (1986). *Good Families of Barcelona*. Princeton, Princeton University Press.
Méndez Álvaro, Francisco (1874). "De la habitación del menesteroso considerada bajo el aspecto higiénico-social". *Discursos pronunciados en la Real Academia de Medicina de Madrid*. Madrid, Sres. de Roger.
Mesonero Romanos, Ramón (1967). *Obras*. Madrid, Atlas.
Miller, William (2005). "Darwin's Disgust", in David Howes (ed.), *Empire of the Senses*. Oxford, Berg: 335-54.
Moliner, María (1998). *Diccionario de uso del español*. Madrid, Editorial Gredos.
Monlau, Pedro Felipe (1984). "Higiene industrial", in Antoni Jutglar (ed.), *Condiciones de vida y trabajo obrero en España a mediados del siglo XIX*. Barcelona, Anthropos.
——— (1998). "Higiene del matrimonio", in Catherine Jagoe, Alda Blanco, Cristina Enríquez de Salamanca (eds.), *La mujer en los discursos de género: Textos y contextos en el siglo XIX*. Barcelona, Icaria Antrazyt: 386-98.
Montaner, Josep Maria (1997). *Barcelona: A City. Its Architecture*. London, Taschen.
Morel, Bénédict (1857). *Traité des dégénérescences physiques, intellectuelles et morales de l'espèce humaine et des causes qui produisent ces variétés maladives*. Paris, J. B. Baillière.
Moscucci, Ornella (1990). *The Science of Woman: Gynaecology and Gender in England, 1800-1921*. Cambridge, Cambridge University Press.
Nuez Caballero, Sebastián de la (1990). *Biblioteca y archivo de la Casa Museo Pérez Galdós*. Gran Canaria, Ediciones del Cabildo Insular de Gran Canaria.
Núñez Florencio, Rafael (1998). *Tal como éramos: España hace un siglo*. Madrid, Espasa Calpe.

Ober, William (1985). "Margery Kempe: Hysteria and Mysticism Reconciled". *Literature and Medicine* 4: 24-40.
Otis, Laura (1999). *Membranes: Metaphors of Invasion in Nineteenth-Century Literature, Science, and Politics*. Baltimore, Johns Hopkins University Press.
(1968-82). *Oxford Latin Dictionary*. Oxford, Clarendon.
Pardo Bazán, Emilia (1973). "La nueva cuestión palpitante". *Obras completas*. Madrid, Aguilar. 3: 1157-95.
Parker, Alexander A. (1967). "*Nazarín*, or the Passion of Our Lord Jesus Christ According to Galdós". *Anales Galdosianos* 2: 83-101.
Pastor Díaz, Nicomedes and Francisco de Cárdenas, Eds. (1841-46). *Galería de españoles célebres contemporáneos*. Madrid, Sanchiz-Ignacio Boix.
Patton, Cindy (1995). "Performativity and Spatial Distinction: The End of AIDS Epidemiology", in Andrew Parker and Eve Kosofsky Sedgwick (eds.), *Performance and Performativity*. New York, Routledge.
Pérez Galdós, Benito (1923). "El Elegante". *Fisonomías sociales*. Madrid, Renacimiento.
—— (1924). *Cronicón*. Madrid, Renacimiento. VI-VII.
—— (1967). *Ángel Guerra*, in *Obras Completas*. 1891. Madrid, Aguilar. V.
—— (1972). *Ensayos de crítica literaria*. Barcelona, Ediciones Península: 115-32.
—— (2000a). *La desheredada*. 1881. Madrid, Cátedra.
—— (2000b). *Misericordia*. 1897. Madrid, Alianza Editorial.
—— (2001a). *La de Bringas*. 1884. Madrid, Cátedra.
—— (2001b). *Nazarín*. 1895. Madrid, Castalia.
—— (2002a). *Tormento*. 1884. Madrid, Alianza Editorial.
—— (2002b). *Fortunata y Jacinta*. 1886-87. Madrid, Cátedra.
Perrot, Philippe (1994). *Fashioning the Bourgeoisie: A History of Clothing in the Nineteenth Century*. Princeton, Princeton University Press.
Peterson, M. Jeanne (1989). *Family, Love, and Work in the Lives of Victorian Gentlewomen*. Bloomington, Indiana University Press.
Pi y Margall, Francisco (1869). "La misión de la mujer en la sociedad". *Conferencias dominicales sobre la educación de la mujer*. Madrid, Rivadeneyra.
Pick, Daniel (1989). *Faces of Degeneration: A European Disorder*. Cambridge, Cambridge University Press.
Portero Molina, José Antonio (1978). *Púlpito e ideología en la España del siglo XIX*. Zaragoza, Libros Pórtico.
Pulido Fernández, Ángel (1876). *Bosquejos médicos-sociales para la mujer*. Madrid, Víctor Saiz.
Quirk, Ronald (2002). "Physiognomy in Pardo Bazán's Portrayal of the Human Body". *Anales Galdosianos* 37: 125-33.
Rajchman, John (1988). "Foucault's Art of Seeing". *October* 44: 89-117.
Randolph, E. Dale (1968). "A Source for Maxi Rubín in *Fortunata y Jacinta*". *Hispania* 51(1): 49-56.
Rementería y Fica, Mariano (1850). *Nuevo manual de urbanidad, cortesanía, decoro y etiqueta, o el hombre fino*. Madrid, Norberto Llorenci.
Ribbans, Geoffrey (1990). "The Making of a Minor Character: Galdós's Plácido Estupiñá". *Symposium* 46(2): 147-57.
Ríos-Font, Wadda (2005). "El crimen de la calle de San Vicente: Crime Writing and Bourgeois Liberalism in Restoration Spain". *MLN* 120(2): 335-54.
Rivière Gómez, Aurora (1994). *"Caídas, miserables, degeneradas": Estudios sobre la prostitución en el siglo XIX*. Madrid, Horas y Horas.
Rose, Mary B. (1993). "Beyond Buddenbrooks: The Family Firm and the Management of Succession in Nineteenth-Century Britain", in Jonathan Brown and Mary B. Rose (eds.), *Entrepreneurship, Networks and Modern Business*. Manchester, Manchester University Press: 127-43.

Rotondo, Antonio (1842). *La fisonomía, ó sea El arte de conocer a sus semejantes por las formas exteriores; extractado de las mejores obras de Lavater*. Madrid: Alegoria y Charlain.
Ruiz Ramón, Francisco (1964). *Tres personajes galdosianos: ensayo de aproximación a un mundo religioso y moral*. Madrid, Revista de Occidente.
Saglia, Diego (1998). "'Oh My Mother Spain!': The Peninsular War, Family Matters, and the Practice of Romantic Nation-Writing". *ELH* 65(2): 363-93.
Saillard, S. (1989). "Ana Ozores, de la mystique à l'hystérie". *Co-Texts* 18: 65-131.
Salarich, Joaquín (1984). "Higiene del tejedor", in Antoni Jutglar (ed.), *Condiciones de vida y trabajo obrero en España a mediados del siglo XIX*. Barcelona, Anthropos.
Sánchez de Toca, Joaquín (1875). *El matrimonio*. Madrid, A. de Carlos e hijo.
Sánchez Pérez, Francisco (1990). *La liturgia del espacio: Casarabonela, un pueblo aljamiado*. Madrid, Nerea.
Santivañes y Chávarri, Arturo Gil de (1868). *Ligeros estudios sobre la sociedad y la familia*. Madrid, Imprenta Española.
Schyfter, Sara (1978). *The Jew in the Novels of Benito Pérez Galdós*. London, Tamesis.
Short, John (2001). *Representing the Republic: Mapping the United States, 1600-1900*. London, Reaktion.
Showalter, Elaine (1985). *The Female Malady: Women, Madness, and English Culture, 1830-1980*. New York, Pantheon.
Shubert, Adrian (1990). *A Social History of Modern Spain*. London, Unwin Hyman.
Sieburth, Stephanie (1994). *Inventing High and Low: Literature, Mass Culture and Uneven Modernity in Spain*. Durham, Duke University Press.
Sierra, María (1992). *La familia Ybarra, empresarios y políticos*. Sevilla, Muñoz Moya.
Simmel, Georg (1997). *Simmel on Culture: Selected Writings*. London, Sage.
Sinclair, Alison (1984). *Madrid Newspapers 1661-1870: A Computerized Handbook Based on the Work of Eugenio Hartzenbusch*. Leeds, Maney.
——— (1993). *The Deceived Husband: A Kleinian Approach to the Literature of Infidelity*. Oxford, Clarendon Press.
——— (2003). "The Regional Novel: Evolution and Consolation", in Harriet Turner and Adelaida López de Martínez (eds.), *The Cambridge Companion to the Spanish Novel: From 1600 to the Present*. Cambridge, Cambridge University Press: 49-64.
Sinnigen, John (1993). "Individual, Class and Society in *Fortunata and Jacinta*". *Galdós*. J. Labanyi (ed.). London, Longman: 116-39.
Sinués de Marco, María del Pilar (1884). *La vida real: alegrías y tristezas de una familia: estudio social*. Madrid, Hijos de García.
——— (1890). *El ángel del hogar*. 1859. Madrid, J. A. García.
Sperber, Dan (1975). *Rethinking Symbolism*. Cambridge, Cambridge University Press.
Spinks, Charlotte (2001). "A New Apartheid? Urban Spatiality, (Fear of) Crime, and Segregation in Cape Town, South Africa". *Working Paper Series* (20): 1-42.
Stepan, Nancy (1982). "The Idea of Race in Science: Great Britain, 1800-1960". London, Macmillan.
——— (1985). "Biology and Degeneration: Races and Proper Places", in J. Edward Chamberlin and Sander L. Gilman (eds.), *Degeneration: The Dark Side of Progress*. New York, Columbia University Press: 97-120.
Stoddart, David (1990). *The Scented Ape*. Cambridge, Cambridge University Press.
Sypher, Wylie (1971). *Literature and Technology: The Alien Vision*. New York, Vintage.

Tanner, Tony (1979). *Adultery in the Novel*. London, The Johns Hopkins University Press.
Tiger, Lionel (1969). *Men in Groups*. London, Nelson.
Torres Villarroel, Diego de (1796). *Sueños morales, visiones y visitas de Torres con Don Francisco de Quevedo, por Madrid*. Madrid, Joseph Doblado.
Torriente, Fernando de la and Manuel Quintana (1871). *Idea general sobre el plano de reformas Madrid futuro*. Madrid, C. Moro.
Toscano, Teresa (1993). *Retórica e ideología de la Generación de 1868 en la obra de Galdós*. Madrid, Editorial Pliegos.
Trinidad Fernández, Pedro (1982). "La reforma de las cárceles en el siglo XIX: las cárceles de Madrid". *Estudios de Historia Social* 22-23: 69-188.
────── (1991). *La defensa de la sociedad: cárcel y delincuencia en España (siglos XVII-XX)*. Madrid, Alianza.
Tsuchiya, Akiko (1993). "'Las Micaelas por fuera y por dentro': Discipline and Resistance in *Fortunata y Jacinta*", in Linda Willem (ed.), *A Sesquicentenial Tribute to Galdós, 1843-1993*. Newark, DE, Juan de la Cuesta.
Tuñón de Lara, Manuel (1973). "La burguesía y la formación del bloque de poder oligárquico de la Restauración: 1875-1902". *La question de la "bourgeoisie" dans le monde hispanique au XIXe siècle*. Bordeaux, Éditions Bière: 87-118.
Turner, Harriet (1983). "Family Ties and Tyrannies: A Reassessment of Jacinta". *Hispanic Review* 51(1): 1-22.
Twinam, Ann (1999). *Public Lives, Private Secrets: Gender, Honour, Sexuality and Illegitimacy in Colonial Spanish America*. Stanford, Stanford University Press.
Valis, Noël (2002). *The Culture of Cursilería: Bad Taste, Kitsch, and Class in Modern Spain*. Durham, Duke University Press.
Varela, Julia (1979). "Técnicas de control social en 'La Restauración'", in Julia Varela and Fernando Álvarez-Uría (eds.), *El cura Galeote asesino del obispo de Madrid-Alcalá: proceso médico-legal*. Madrid, La Piqueta: 210-36.
Varey, John E. (1967). "Francisco Bringas: 'Nuestro buen Thiers'", in Jaime Sánchez Romeralo and Norbert Poulussen (eds.), *Actas del Segundo Congreso Internacional de Hispanistas*. Nijmegen, Holland, Instituto Español de la Universidad de Nimega: 679-87.
Veblen, Thorstein (1990). *The Theory of the Leisure Class*. Chicago, Encyclopedia Britannica.
Veith, Ilza (1965). *Hysteria: The History of a Disease*. Chicago, Chicago University Press.
Villanova y Jordán, Jacobo (1834). *Aplicación de la panóptica de Jeremías Bentham, a las cárceles y casas de corrección de España*. Madrid, T. Jordan.
Waller, John (2003). "Parents and Children: Ideas of Heredity in the 19th Century". *Endeavour* 27(2): 51-56.
Wechsler, Judith (1982). *A Human Comedy: Physiognomy and Caricature in 19th Century Paris*. London, Thames and Hudson.
Weisser, Michael (1979). *Crime and Punishment in Early Modern Europe*. Hassocks, Harvester Press.
White, Nicholas (1999). *The Family in Crisis in Late Nineteenth-Century French Fiction*. Cambridge, Cambridge University Press.
Willem, Linda, Ed. (1993). *A Sesquicentennial Tribute to Galdós, 1843-1993*. Newark, DE, Juan de la Cuesta.
Winnicot, Donald (1991). *The Child, the Family and the Outside World*. London, Penguin.

INDEX

Abrams, Lynn 140
abstinence 66
Acuña, Rosario 52, 69, 70
adultery 91-95, 116, 121, 123
Aguirre de Venero, Mariano 43, 163, 163 n. 3
Alarcón, Pedro Antonio 35
Aldaraca, Bridget 49 n. 1, 69-70, 80, 106, 115 n. 4, 116, 120, 176
Allison, George 125
Alonso y Rubio, Francisco 79
Álvarez Chillida, Gonzalo 142 n. 4
Álvarez-Uría, Fernando 18
Amazons 146, 147
ambiguity 24, 56, 62, 63, 92-93, 128, 139-44, 170, 136-57, 170, 171, 175; *see also* categorisation, undecidability
Andress, William 162
ángel del hogar 77, 80-81, 86-89, 91-92, 94, 99-100, 115, 140, 152, 176
animal comparisons 41, 43, 132-33, 147, 148, 164; *see also* degeneration, physiognomy
anxiety: of the middle class 10, 15, 18, 22, 34, 38, 45-46, 48, 54-55, 56, 116, 117, 118, 161, 174
Arab: and appearance of Nazarín 139, 142, 144
Arbiol, Fr. Antonio 110 n. 1
Ariès, Philippe 116 n. 5
Aristotle 41; *see also* physiognomy
Armstrong, Nancy 76, 76 n. 1
atavism 25, 40, 64, 106, 132, 133, 138, 146, 147

Babrius, Valerius 158
Bacon, Kathy 52 n. 3
Bahamonde, Ángel 21
Bakhtin, Mikhail 154, 155-56
Barthes, Roland 167
Bartra, Roger 104-105, 104 n. 6, 106
Bayo, Ciro 66, 67
Beauvoir, Simone de 77
Bentham, Jeremy 39, 39 n. 10, 40, 121 n. 6
Blanco, Alda 80, 90
Blanco Aguinaga, Carlos 90
blindness 101-02, 159, 163, 166-67, 169, 172; *see also* vision
Bly, Peter 137, 143 n. 5
body 37, 40-41, 42, 91, 136-57
boundaries 92-93, 116, 119, 120-23, 156, 158, 168, 170, 171
Bourdieu, Pierre: and distinction 53-54, 56-57; and habitus 53, 59; and symbolic capital 53, 113, 161
Braun, Lucille 124
Breuer, Joseph 151
Brooks, J. L. 170 n. 6
Brown, Jonathan 92 n. 4
Butler, Judith 77-78, 176

Calbraith, John K. 49 n. 1
Callahan, William 160, 161
Campos Martín, Ricardo 44
Cárdenas, Francisco 113
Carlson, E. T. 61, 124, 125
carnival 137, 138, 153-57, 175
cartography 10-11, 15, 16-17, 47
Casalduero, Joaquín 12

Castro, Carlos María de 14, 15, 16, 17, 20, 20 n. 1, 23-24, 29, 33-34, 38, 47, 65
categorisation 10, 11, 28, 40, 44, 47, 54, 128, 137, 138, 141, 156, 158, 176
Catholic Church: and middle class 159-61; *see also* religion, spiritual capital
Cerdà, Ildefonso 17, 20 n. 1
Chamberlin, Vernon 124, 124 n. 11, 170-71
Charcot, Jean Martin 150, 151
Charnon-Deutsch, Lou 80, 108, 116, 176
cholera 30, 31, 33
circulation 32, 65-68
city vs country 22-25, 46, 92-93, 97-98, 102, 104-07
Classen, Constance 9, 120, 168
cleanliness 121, 161-62
clothing, *see* fashion
Cohen, Sarah 170, 170 n. 6
Cohen, Stanley 18, 122
Comfort, Alex 66
Connell, R. W. 97, 109
Considérant, Victor 19
conspicuous consumption 49, 52
contagionism 31-34; *see also* miasmatism
contamination 28-34, 39, 123-24; *see also* miasmatism and germ theory debate
Corbin, Alain 67
Cosgrove, Denis 16, 26
country, *see* city vs country
Crane, Diana 50 n. 2, 84
Crespil, Marcel 170, 170 n. 6
criminality/criminology 18, 24, 26, 34-40, 45, 64, 141, 144-48; *see also* degeneration
Cruz, Jesús 111, 113, 113 n. 3
cuarto estado 115-21, 123-24
Cubí Soler, Mariano 43
cuckoldry 102
Culler, Jonathan 89
cursilería 54-55, 59-61

dandyism 84, 85, 91, 96; *see also* fashion, masculinity
Darwinism 22-23, 25, 44, 138, 168
Davidoff, Leonore 116 n. 5
degeneration 11, 24-25, 61-62, 68, 106, 112, 124-28, 139, 144-48, 149, 175
Della Porta, Giambattista 41

Derrida, Jacques 166, 172
determinism, *see* degeneration, heredity
Díez de Baldeón, Clementina 20, 28
discourse 11, 25, 26-28, 46; and criminality 35; and gender 78-81, 107-08; and public hygiene 29-34
disorder 10, 17-19, 23, 24, 115-24, 135, 162, 174
distinction, *see* Bourdieu
Dolgin, Stacey 143 n. 5
domesticity 69-70, 80-81, 87, 98, 100; *see also ángel del hogar*, public and private spheres
Don Quijote 65, 143, 143 n. 5
Donzelot, Jacques 110
Douglas, Mary 162
Doyle, Arthur Conan 19, 35
drainage 65-67

Elliot, James 17
Elliott, John 92 n. 4
Enríquez de Salamanca, Cristina 80
ensanche 14, 15, 17, 20, 38; *see also* Carlos María de Castro
Escuder, José María 64
Espigado Tocino, Gloria 100, 101
ethnography 137-39

family 11, 61-65, 109-31; *see also* heredity
fashion 50-51, 58, 81-85, 87-88, 90; and gender 87, 90, 96; *see also* dandyism, *lujo*
Félix, Joseph 110 n. 1
femininity: and degeneracy theory 141, 144-46, 149-50, 152-53; and gender ideology 86-95, 107-08; *see also ángel del hogar*, gender, masculinity
Fernández de Rojas, Juan 85
Fernández Pérez, Paloma 111 n. 2
Fishberg, Moris 127
flow 65-68, 70
Fonssagrives, Jean Batiste 30
Ford, Caroline 140
Ford, Richard 19
Foucault, Michel 10, 16, 20, 28, 34, 37, 39, 40, 77, 118, 174, 176; and discourse 26-28
Fraser, Nancy 116 n. 5
Freud, Sigmund 74, 102, 151, 168
frontier/frontiersman 96-99; *see also* city vs country, masculinity, wild-man tradition

Frost, Daniel 89 n. 3
Fuentes Peris, Teresa 18, 29, 32-33, 66, 120, 121 n. 9, 162 n. 2

gardens 23-24, 89; *see also* parks
Gassó y Ortiz, Blanca de 79
gaze 10, 20, 39-41, 49-50, 85, 101-02, 159, 175-76
gender: ambiguity 140, 146, 147; discourse 78-81, 107-08; ideology 86-89, 107-08; identity 77-78; theory 77-78, 95
genealogy, *see* family, heredity
Gilfoil, Anne W. 18
Gilman, Sander 24, 44 n. 12, 127, 133
Giné y Partagás, Juan 31 n. 5
Gobineau, Arthur de 44
Goldman, Peter 153
Gómez Bravo, Gutmaro 35
Gómez Urdáñez, Gracia 110, 111-12, 112 n. 2, 116
González, Rafael 29
González de Tejada, José 110 n. 1
Gordon, Mike 128, 128 n. 13
Graham, John 42
grotesque 145, 155-56, 166

Haidt, Rebecca 85
Hall, Catherine 116 n. 5
Harley, J.B. 15, 16
Harrowitz, Nancy 44 n. 12
Harvey, John 85
Heidegger, Martin 169
Héran, François 113 n. 3
heredity 61, 72-73, 112, 113-14, 124-34; *see also* degeneration, family
Hoff, Ruth 12
home 89-92; and domesticity 120-21; symbol of female body 86, 120-21; *see also* public and private spheres
Horn, David 44 n. 12
Huertas, Rafael 44
hysteria 129, 148-53

insanity 62-63, 126, 127-28, 139, 141-43
Irigaray, Luce 101

Jagoe, Catherine 78-79, 80, 80-81, 94, 115, 116, 120, 141, 176
Jay, Martin 10 n. 1, 102, 164
Jew/Jewish 126-27, 139, 142, 142 n. 4, 144, 170, 171
Jones, Gareth 45

Juliá, Santos 19
Jutglar, Antoni 31 n. 4

Klein, Melanie 109
Klinghoffer, Arthur 16-17
knowledge 15, 16, 26, 40, 101-02, 157, 166, 174

Labanyi, Jo 22, 65, 80, 92, 93, 116, 137, 137 n. 1, 140, 141, 149, 156, 175
Lannon, Frances 159-60
Larsen, Kevin 125
Lavater, Johann Casper 41-43; *see also* physiognomy
Lavin y Olea, Pedro 110 n. 1
law: and criminal behaviour 18; and inheritance 72
Le Brun, Charles 41
Leganés 18, 47, 128
LeGates, Richard 21, 24
León, Fray Luis de 23, 80
Levinas, Emmanuel 171
Lida, Denah 170 n. 6
Litvak, Lily 44
Lombroso, Cesare 40-41, 43-45, 44 n. 12, 68, 136, 144-45, 146, 149, 150, 152-53, 156, 175
Lombroso-Ferrero, Gina 40
López de la Vega, José 30, 66
lower class, *see* working class
lujo 52, 68-71, 87-88, 94

map, mapping 10-11, 16-17, 42, 47-48, 174, 175; *see also* cartography
Maristany, Luis 44, 45, 136
Marks, Laura 176
marriage 98; as social contract 92-93
masculinity 82-85, 90-91, 95-108, 140-41, 146-47, 175-76
maternal 87, 128-34; *see also* femininity
Mathews, Cristina 116
Maudsley, Henry 44, 61, 64, 112, 126, 131
Mazzoni, Cristina 149 n. 6, 150
McCarthy, Barry 147
McDonogh, Gary 113 n. 3
Méndez Álvaro, Francisco 31
Mesonero Romanos, Ramón 19-20
miasmatism 29, 31, 32-34, 66; and germ theory debate 31, 32-34, 168
middle class 12, 23-24, 117, 135, 160-61, 175
Miller, William 168

Moliner, María 52, 54, 86, 96, 130, 130 n. 14, 138, 139
Monlau, Pedro Felipe 23, 30, 31, 31 n. 4, 79
Montaner, Josep 20 n. 1
Morel, Bénédict 44, 61, 112, 124-25
Moscucci, Ornella 141
mysticism 149, 150, 159 n. 1; *see also* hysteria

Nuez Caballero, Sebastián de la 30 n. 2

Ober, William 149 n. 6
odour, *see* smell
otherness 10, 13, 15, 44, 45, 55, 85, 131, 134, 157, 159, 169-70
Otis, Laura 31-33

panopticism 20, 37-40, 121 n. 9
Pardo Bazán, Emilia 45
Parent-Duchâtelet 66, 67
Parker, Alexander 143 n. 5
parasitism 67-68
parks 23-24, 89-93; *see also* gardens
Pastor Díaz, Nicomedes 113
paternity, *see* heredity
Patton, Cindy 78
Pérez Galdós, Benito: *Ángel Guerra* 12, 140; and cholera 30, 30 n. 3, 33; and crime 34; and fashion 51, 83-84, 91; *Fortunata y Jacinta* 11, 109-35, 174-75; *La de Bringas* 11, 24, 76, 86-108, 174; *La desheredada* 10, 11, 47-75, 174; *Misericordia* 12-13, 158-73, 175, 176; *Nazarín* 11-12, 136-57, 175; *Tormento* 11, 76, 86-108, 174; *Torquemada* series 75, 113
Perrot, Philippe 50-51
Peset, Mariano and José Luis 44
physiognomy 10, 11, 41-43, 50, 61, 124, 134, 163-64
Pi y Margall, Francisco 79
Pick, Daniel 44, 44 n. 12, 61, 124, 132, 127
population growth, *see* urbanisation
Portero Molina, José Antonio 160
power 15, 16-17, 27-28, 37, 39-40, 53-54, 101-02
prostitution 18, 66-71, 91, 146, 154
psychoanalysis 102, 109
public and private spheres 80, 84, 87, 89, 101, 115-16, 116 n. 5, 119-21
Pulido Fernández, Ángel 128-29

Quintana, Manuel 20, 28-29
Quirk, Ronald 163 n. 3

Rajchman, John 10, 20
Randolph, E. Dale 125
religion 98; feminization of 103, 140, 140 n. 3; *see also* Catholic Church, spiritual capital
Rementería y Fica, Mariano 82
Ribbans, Geoffrey 124, 124 n. 11
Rivière Gómez, Aurora 62, 66 n. 7, 67, 68
Ríos-Font, Wadda 35, 36, 36 n. 7, n. 9
Rose, Mary 111 n. 2
Rotondo, Antonio 43
Rousseau, Jean-Jacques 22, 92-93, 106
Ruiz Ramón, Francisco 143 n. 5

Saglia, Diego 109
Saillard, S. 149 n. 6
Salarich, Joaquín 23, 31, 31 n. 4
Sánchez de Toca, Joaquín 86
Sánchez Pérez, Francisco 121
Santivañes y Chávarri, Arturo Gil de 110 n. 1
Schyfter, Sara 144
senses 9, 165, 176; *see also* smell, vision
sewage, *see* drainage
sex 66, 88, 91-92, 99, 102, 121, 127; *see also* prostitution
Short, John 11, 15
Showalter, Elaine 149
Shubert, Adrian 21, 29, 160
Sieburth, Stephanie 49-50
Sierra, María 113 n. 3
Simmel, Georg 50 n. 2, 51, 58
Sinclair, Alison 22, 81, 102
Sinnigen, John 117
Sinués de Marco, María del Pilar 79, 80, 110 n. 1
smell 166-69, 168 n. 5, 171, 172-73, 176; *see also* supplementation
social control 10, 39
social mobility 47, 48-51, 54, 133
space: living spaces 15, 28-29, 33, 62, 115-22, 162; social spaces 55, 56; spatiality of narrative 63
Sperber, Dan 168
Spinks, Charlotte 38
spiritual capital 161; *see also* Bourdieu and symbolic capital
Stepan, Nancy 25

stigmata 40, 61, 124-25, 146, 150; *see also* degeneration
Stoddart, David 168 n. 5
Stout, Frederic 21, 24
supplementation 165, 166, 169, 172
surveillance, *see* panopticism
Sypher, Wylie 10

Taine, Hippolyte-Adolphe 132
Tanner, Tony 92-93, 98
Tiger, Lionel 97
Toro, Julián 21
Torres Villarroel, Diego de 85
Torriente, Fernando de la 20, 28-29
Trinidad Fernández, Pedro 35, 37, 38
Tsuchiya, Akiko 121, 121 n. 9
Tuñón de Lara, Manuel 113 n. 3
Turner, Harriet 114
Twinam, Ann 72, 73

Ullman, Joan 125
undecidability 24, 153-57, 175; *see also* ambiguity
urbanisation 17, 21-22, 33, 42, 46, 48-49, 160, 174

Valis, Nöel 54, 55

Varela, Julia 119
Varey, John 124 n. 10
Veblen, Thorstein 49, 49 n. 1, 84-85
Veith, Ilza 150 n. 7, 151
Villanova y Jordán, Jacobo 39, 39 n. 10
violence 131-32, 146-47; *see also* degeneracy
vision: as means of control/power 39-40, 101-02, 174; privileging of 9-10, 164-65, 166, 172-73, 176; visual culture 9-10, 49-50, 161, 174; *see also* gaze, panopticism

Waller, John 112
warrior: as model of masculinity 146-47
Wechsler, Judith 42
Weisser, Michael 36, 37
wild-man tradition 96, 102, 104-07; *see also* masculinity
Winnicot, Donald 109
woman, *see ángel del hogar*, femininity
working class 18, 20, 23, 45-46, 160; and contamination 23, 28-34, 45-46; and crime 23, 34-38; and degeneracy 25, 62, 133; and immorality 28, 118-23, 162; and migration 21

NORTH CAROLINA STUDIES IN THE ROMANCE LANGUAGES AND LITERATURES
I.S.B.N. Prefix 0-8078-

Recent Titles

SAVAGE SIGHT/CONSTRUCTED NOISE. POETIC ADAPTATIONS OF PAINTERLY TECHNIQUES IN THE FRENCH AND AMERICAN AVANT-GARDES, by David LeHardy Sweet. 2003. (No. 276). *-9281-5.*

AN EARLY BOURGEOIS LITERATURE IN GOLDEN AGE SPAIN. *LAZARILLO DE TORMES, GUZMÁN DE ALFARACHE* AND BALTASAR GRACIÁN, by Francisco J. Sánchez. 2003. (No. 277). *-9280-7.*

METAFACT: ESSAYISTIC SCIENCE IN EIGHTEENTH-CENTURY FRANCE, by Lars O. Erickson. 2004. (No. 278). *-9282-3.*

THE INVENTION OF THE EYEWITNESS. A HISTORY OF TESTIMONY IN FRANCE, by Andrea Frisch. 2004. (No. 279). *-9283-1.*

SUBJECT TO CHANGE: THE LESSONS OF LATIN AMERICAN WOMEN'S *TESTIMONIO* FOR TRUTH, FICTION, AND THEORY, by Joanna R. Bartow. 2005. (No. 280). *-9284-X.*

QUESTIONING RACINIAN TRAGEDY, by John Campbell. 2005. (No. 281). *-9285-8.*

THE POLITICS OF FARCE IN CONTEMPORARY SPANISH AMERICAN THEATRE, by Priscilla Meléndez. 2006. (No. 282). *-9286-6.*

MODERATING MASCULINITY IN EARLY MODERN CULTURE, by Todd W. Reeser. 2006. (No. 283). *-9287-4.*

PORNOBOSCODIDASCALUS LATINUS (1624). KASPAR BARTH'S NEO-LATIN TRANSLATION OF *CELESTINA*, by Enrique Fernández. 2006. (No. 284). *-9288-2.*

JACQUES ROUBAUD AND THE INVENTION OF MEMORY, by Jean-Jacques F. Poucel. 2006. (No. 285). *-9289-0.*

THE "I" OF HISTORY. SELF-FASHIONING AND NATIONAL CONSCIOUSNESS IN JULES MICHELET, by Vivian Kogan. 2006. (No. 286). *-9290-4.*

BUCOLIC METAPHORS: HISTORY, SUBJECTIVITY, AND GENDER IN THE EARLY MODERN SPANISH PASTORAL, by Rosilie Hernández-Pecoraro. 2006. (No. 287). *-9291-2.*

UNA ARMONÍA DE CAPRICHOS: EL DISCURSO DE RESPUESTA EN LA PROSA DE RUBÉN DARÍO, por Francisco Solares-Larrave. 2007. (No. 288). *-9292-0.*

READING THE *EXEMPLUM* RIGHT: FIXING THE MEANING OF *EL CONDE LUCANOR*, by Jonathan Burgoyne. 2007. (No. 289). *-9293-9.*

MONSTRUOS QUE HABLAN: EL DISCURSO DE LA MONSTRUOSIDAD EN CERVANTES, por Rogelio Miñana. 2007. (No. 290). *-9294-7.*

BAJO EL CIELO PERUANO: THE DEVOUT WORLD OF PERALTA BARNUEVO, by David F. Slade and Jerry M. Williams. 2008. (No. 291). *-9295-4.*

ESCAPE FROM THE PRISON OF LOVE: CALORIC IDENTITIES AND WRITING SUBJECTS IN FIFTEENTH-CENTURY SPAIN, by Robert Folger. 2009. (No. 292). *-9296-1.*

LOS *TRIONFI* DE PETRARCA COMENTADOS EN CATALÁN: UNA EDICIÓN DE LOS MANUSCRITOS 534 DE LA BIBLIOTECA NACIONAL DE PARÍS Y DEL ATENEU DE BARCELONA, por Roxana Recio. 2009. (No. 293). *-9297-8.*

MAPPING THE SOCIAL BODY. URBANISATION, THE GAZE, AND THE NOVELS OF GALDÓS, by Collin McKinney. 2009. (No. 294). *-9298-5.*

When ordering please cite the *ISBN Prefix* plus the last four digits for each title.

Send orders to: University of North Carolina Press
P.O. Box 2288
Chapel Hill, NC 27515-2288
U.S.A.
www.uncpress.unc.edu
FAX: 919 966-3829

www.ingramcontent.com/pod-product-compliance
Lightning Source LLC
Chambersburg PA
CBHW020738230426
43665CB00009B/480